T0038696

OUR UNFINISHED MARCH

OUR UNFINISHED MARCH

THE VIOLENT PAST AND IMPERILED FUTURE OF THE VOTE— A HISTORY, A CRISIS, A PLAN

ERIC HOLDER

WITH SAM KOPPELMAN

ONE WORLD
New York

2023 One World Trade Paperback Edition

Published in the United States by One World, an imprint of Random House, a division of Penguin Random House LLC, New York.

ONE WORLD and colophon are registered trademarks of Penguin Random House LLC.

Originally published in hardcover in the United States by One World, an imprint of Random House, a division of Penguin Random House LLC, in 2022.

ISBN 9780593445761
Ebook ISBN 9780593445754

Printed in the United States of America on acid-free paper

oneworldlit.com
randomhousebooks.com

1st Printing

To Vivian, for walking through that door;

to John, for walking over that bridge;

and to all those whose names have been lost,

but whose march is now our own

"The vote is the most powerful nonviolent change agent you have in a democratic society. You must use it because it is not guaranteed. You can lose it."

—JOHN LEWIS

"This right to vote is the basic right without which all others are meaningless."

—PRESIDENT LYNDON B. JOHNSON

CONTENTS

OUR UNFINISHED MARCH

INTRODUCTION

For most of our country's history, a man who looked like me might not have wanted to leave the north for Selma, Alabama—where the Confederate army manufactured its shot and shell, cartridges and cannons; where separate water fountains and lunch counters, public schools and public pools were anything but equal; where lynchings were not prosecuted by the government but perpetrated by it; where marches for justice and cries for freedom were answered with poll taxes and literacy tests, billy clubs and batons—but on March 7, 2015, I wouldn't have wanted to be anywhere else.

Because, on that day, the history of Selma wasn't a stain on America's past. It was a reminder that a better future is always within reach, as long as you're willing to fight for it.

After all, just fifty years had passed since the march on the Edmund Pettus Bridge, and I was coming to Selma as the first African American attorney general, alongside Barack Obama, the first African American president of the United States. We were two of the forty thousand Americans who descended on the town to honor the anniversary, tripling its population overnight.

The mood was celebratory—like a church service and a block party all in one. By seven-thirty A.M., drivers had abandoned their vehicles in the middle of the street, realizing there was too much traffic to get anywhere. But no one was complaining.

Because everyone knew we were in Selma to witness something special.

So much of our history and our mythology is about dreamers who never have a chance to harvest the fruits of their labor. Martin in Memphis. Moses on the Mount. But in Selma that day, heroes who had marched fifty years earlier—foot soldiers of the civil rights movement like Diane Nash, Amelia Boynton, and Bernard LaFayette—bore witness to a new America, an America they had built with their steps and sweat, their hands and hearts, an America where they didn't only have the right to vote, but had exercised it to elect people who looked like them to the highest offices of power in the world. And that was a big deal, even as the presence of the relatives of Eric Garner, a forty-three-year-old man whom a police officer had recently choked to death as he pleaded, "I can't breathe," stood as a testament to how much more work we had left to do.

In his remarks introducing President Obama, Congressman John Lewis declared: "If someone had told me when we were crossing this bridge that one day I would be back here introducing the first African American president, I would have said, 'You're crazy, you're out of your mind, you don't know what you're talking about.'"

And who could blame him?

Only half a century earlier, on the same bridge where he was now standing next to our first Black president, the then twenty-five-year-old suffragist had been beaten close to death. I was fourteen at the time, and I remember watching reports of the violence in Selma on my family's basement television set in Queens—discussing with my parents how Americans could allow such cruelty to take place in our country. They didn't have an answer. No one did. But they used that moment as an opportunity to tell me never to take my right to vote for granted, because in America, for people who looked like us, it wasn't guaranteed. And I remember noticing, at a young age, that my parents walked the walk. Any time there was an election, whether it was a race for president or school board, they would show up to the polls.

Those were the lessons that shaped me as a kid—and they were the ones on my mind leading up to the fiftieth anniversary of the Selma march. By that point in my tenure as attorney general, more than half a decade after I had taken my oath of office, I was ready to step down. The prior year, I'd had to speak to President Obama three times about my desire to leave the Department of Justice before he agreed to appoint a replacement. And months after he finally nominated one, Congress was still stalling on confirming her. Which is to say: I was in serious need of a vacation, a long vacation, with good books and smooth Bajan rum.

But as March 7 drew nearer, I secretly started to harbor a hope that Republicans in Congress would obstruct for just a little longer—as they reflexively did—so I could remain in office on this sacred day. Because I had a message I wanted to share, as the first Black attorney general of the United States, about how far we had come and how far we still had left to march.

So when I arrived at the historic Brown Chapel AME Church that day to deliver my remarks, I knew exactly what story I would tell about what had taken place fifty years earlier. It's a story about believing that, despite the evil in the world, good will prevail, but only if you refuse to relent. A story about resilience in the face of racism; courage in the face of cowardice; bravery in the face of brutality. A story about America.

It's a story you could open with the agony of the Middle Passage, or with the tortured writing of the Constitution, or with the violent end of Reconstruction, and in Selma, I alluded to all that. But for the purposes of this introduction, I think it makes the most sense to start with what went down in 1962—when a young man named Jimmie Lee Jackson accompanied his eighty-year-old grandfather, Cager Lee, to the town registrar's office in Marion, Alabama.

For Jimmie, growing up without a father, Cager was the defining male presence in his life—and as soon as he was old enough to drive, he chauffeured his grandfather everywhere. To town. To the store. To church. By the time Jimmie entered his twenties, he and Cager were more than family; they were friends. So when, on that day in 1962, Jimmie saw his grandfather's face sink as his attempt to register to vote was rejected, for no reason other than racism, he felt a duty to join the civil rights movement himself.

After all, he knew Cager wasn't an exception. In Marion, where Jimmie was raised, African Americans made up two of every three citizens but just one of every fifty registered voters. That meant that functionally, almost a hundred years after the ratification of the Fifteenth Amendment, Alabama still hadn't granted Black Americans the right to vote.

So Jimmie began attending meetings, joining demonstrations, and preaching about the importance of ending segregation. He was a leader in his community—becoming, at twenty-five years old, the youngest deacon in the history of his church. And in 1965, he was in the middle of the action as his hometown of Marion, less than thirty miles outside Selma, became one of the epicenters of the civil rights movement.

Marion is where hundreds of Black students—children—had recently been dragged to jail by the busload for protesting segregation in their schools. It's where police had arrested civil rights hero James Orange for trying to register young people like them to vote. And on the night of February 18, it's where the Ku Klux Klan had made plans to seek revenge on Orange by lynching him.

But civil rights leaders in Alabama, including Reverend C. T. Vivian, a man I would come to know and admire years later, were going to do everything in their power to save Orange from that fate—so they organized a protest, which Jimmie and the rest of his family members joined. At sunset, hundreds of African Americans came together in Zion United Methodist Church, prayed for the safety of Orange and the others, and sang hymns with so much conviction that the melodies caught the attention of an FBI agent spying on them from a second-story window across the street. He even wrote in his notebook: "The singing was louder than other nights."

When the service concluded, the protesters filed out of the church and began marching toward the prison where Orange was being held. But before they could make much progress, police surrounded them and demanded that they disperse.

There are no photographs of what happened next—because the officers on the scene shot out or turned off the streetlights. But what we know from those who survived that night is that law enforcement began indiscriminately beating marchers over the head with clubs, starting with the Reverend James Dobynes, who was kneeling in prayer when he was bludgeoned.

Wanting to protect his mother and sister, Jimmie brought them to a café to take cover. They waited for Cager, who was still in the church when the violence broke out, until he, too, walked through the door, bloodied and beaten. "They hauled me off and hit me and knocked me to the street and kicked me," the five-foot-tall, one-hundred-pound, eighty-two-year-old grandfather later told a reporter. "It was hard to take for an old man whose bones are dry like cane."

Jimmie tried to bring Cager to the hospital, but when they set out to leave the café, they were blocked by troopers, who began attacking the protesters taking shelter there. Jimmie's mother was among those beaten. Desperate, Jimmie ran over to help her, but before he could make it, an officer threw him against a cigarette machine and shot him from just feet away. Twice.

Wounded but not unconscious, blood spilling from his stomach, Jimmie once again tried to leave the café, but troopers followed him out and beat him over the head until he collapsed. A few days later, Jimmie was served an arrest warrant in his hospital bed by the head of the Alabama state police for causing a disruption. A few days after that, Jimmie died in the hospital. He had just turned twenty-six years old.

News of Jimmie's death spread quickly around Alabama—and echoed across the country. Thousands attended his funeral. And Dr. Martin Luther King, Jr., realized that, despite death threats, he had no choice but to come to Selma, where, as he had observed, there were more African Americans locked up in the jail than on the voter rolls. His solution? "We are going to bring a voting bill into the streets of Selma."

At Jimmie's funeral, Dr. King called him "a martyred hero of a holy crusade for freedom and human dignity," adding that the murder "says to us that we must work passionately and unrelentingly to make the American dream a reality. His death must prove that unpermitted suffering does not go unredeemed."

At the time, leaders in Selma considered a few different ways to respond to what had happened to Jimmie. One idea they tossed around was dropping his body on the steps of Governor George Wallace's mansion so the whole state would see the injustice that had been committed. But eventually, they decided instead to organize a march from Selma to Montgomery for voting rights.

The rest is history.

Literally.

On March 7, 1965, six hundred suffragists, led by John Lewis, began walking along the fifty-four-mile path to Montgomery until they were stopped by state troopers on a bridge named after Edmund Pettus, a former Alabama senator, Confederate general, and Ku Klux Klan grand wizard.

They were brutalized on that bridge, met with hostility and hatred, but with the drumbeat of their steps, they awoke the conscience of the nation.

President Lyndon B. Johnson, who earlier in the year had told Dr. King he wouldn't prioritize a voting rights bill, was swayed by the courage and sacrifice of the foot soldiers in Selma. "At times history and fate meet at a single time in a single place to shape a turning point in man's unending search for freedom," he declared in a joint address to Congress. "So it was at Lexington and Concord. So it was a century ago at Appomattox. So it was last week in Selma, Alabama."

Watching LBJ's speech, tears rolled down Dr. King's face, the first time his closest confidants had seen him cry. And within days, Congress passed the Voting Rights Act of 1965—expanding the definition of "We the People" to include African Americans once and for all.

It was a landmark piece of legislation, rightly remembered as the crown jewel of the civil rights movement. And as Ari Berman notes in *Give Us the Ballot*, his seminal book on voting rights, President Johnson's administration made sure it was enforced, sending officials all across the South to register voters—including to Marion, Alabama, where, five years after his grandson had watched him be denied the ballot, Cager Lee once again visited the registrar's office.

Only this time, Cager, like millions of others who had previously been denied, was added to the rolls. Photographers on the scene captured him holding his certificate in the air, a quiet smile on his face. His grandson was gone. But because of the march sparked by Jimmie's death, Cager Lee was finally a registered voter—and there was some justice in that.

"He had to die for something," Cager said, "and thank God it was for this."

That was the first part of the message I wanted to communicate in Selma—gratitude for all who had shepherded our nation to this point. "The fact that I stand here today," I said, "is cause for great optimism and a sign of tremendous progress." Indeed, I added, "the failure to acknowledge that is an insult to those we must always honor and hold in our hearts."

But I had another message I wanted to communicate—one that was far less hopeful but no less urgent: For the first time since 1965, America was making it harder, not easier, to vote.

From the moment President Obama took office, states began restricting voting rights—signing into law photo ID bills to combat nonexistent voter fraud and then closing the offices where you could get those forms of identification in low-income neighborhoods. After Republicans won a historic landslide victory in the 2010 midterms, taking over state legislatures and governor's mansions across the country, they boxed Black Americans out of political power through gerrymandering and introduced close to two hundred bills aimed at reducing access to the ballot across forty-one states. The motivation behind this legislation was no secret, but it was clarified by an embarrassment of a congressman named Steve King, who lamented the passing of "a time in American history when you had to be a male property owner in order to vote."

And then, in 2013, the Supreme Court gutted the Voting Rights Act, opening the floodgates for suppression. That ruling will go down as one of the most flawed, ideologically driven Supreme Court decisions in history—and it's a case to which I just so happened to be a party: *Shelby County v. Holder.*

Here's why it was so damaging: When the Voting Rights Act became law, one of its key features, Section 5, was a provision called preclearance, which allowed the Department of Justice to review voting laws enacted by states that had a quantifiable history of discriminating against Black voters, according to a coverage formula laid out in Section 4 of the act. And these provisions worked. Across the country, in the decades following the passage of the Voting Rights Act, Black Americans registered at record rates and the number of Black elected officials soared, even in the states where Jim Crow had been most endemic.

To Chief Justice John Roberts, Jr., this was an indication that the discrimination that made the Voting Rights Act necessary in the first place had been overcome—which is why, in his decision, he argued that the coverage formula was outdated; and that preclearance, as originally conceived, was no longer necessary.

Of course, he had it exactly backward. As Justice Ruth Bader Ginsburg wrote in her prescient dissent, "Throwing out preclearance when it has worked and is continuing to work to stop discriminatory changes is like throwing away your umbrella in a rainstorm because you are not getting wet."

She was vindicated—not years down the road, but hours. On the very day *Shelby* was decided, Texas moved forward with a law whose photo ID standards restricted the state's poorest residents from accessing the ballot. North Carolina followed suit with a law so discriminatory that even without Section 5 in effect, it was thrown out by a court for having targeted "African Americans with almost surgical precision." And on and on and on.

Since *Shelby,* state legislatures and local officials have closed nearly 1,700 polling places across the country. Voters have been unnecessarily and inexcusably stricken from the rolls—with purge rates 40 percent higher in states that were previously covered by Section 5. Over the past decade, a total of twenty-five states have instituted draconian anti-voting laws that clearly and intentionally have a disproportionate impact on communities of color.

Because I was so closely involved in *Shelby,* I knew right away that the court's decision would have ramifications for generations, and I realized, in that moment, that we stood on the precipice of two Americas—a fork in the road that I kept thinking about on that historic anniversary in Selma.

One path would take us to an America that realizes the dream of everyone who marched on that bridge fifty years earlier: an America defined by pluralism, where everyone's voice is heard, everyone's vote is counted, and everyone's interests are represented. An America that celebrates diversity and is united by a shared commitment to bringing about a future that's better than the past. An America where the unalienable right to life, liberty, and the pursuit of happiness isn't an ambition written on a piece of paper but a reality for all of our people in all of our communities. That is the America, the "beloved community," that John Lewis was marching toward—and it was the America I believed we ought to be marching toward as well.

But I also knew that if we did not confront these attacks on our democracy, America could go down a different path—one where the political and racial apartheid we had worked so hard to overcome in 1965 would reemerge; where suppression would once again rear its ugly head and lock millions out of the polls; where a minority party that doesn't represent the interests or desires of the people would hold on to power by rigging the system in its favor. After all, this had happened before, back when the progress of Reconstruction was vanquished by the emergence of Jim Crow and the Ku Klux Klan.

That is the choice I believed our country faced on that March day in 2015—and it's the question I believe we still need to answer today, with even more urgency and higher stakes: Which America will we be?

It's a question that was at the core of President Obama's speech that day in Selma, and I've found it useful to revisit some of his words—not as an exercise in studying the history of where we've been, but as an action plan for how we get where we need to go.

"What could be more American than what happened in this place?" he asked after telling the story of Selma. "The American instinct that led these young men and women to pick up the torch and cross this bridge, that's the same instinct that moved patriots to choose revolution over tyranny. It's the idea held by generations of citizens who believed that America is a constant work in progress; who believed that loving this country requires more than singing its praises or avoiding uncomfortable truths. It requires the occasional disruption, the willingness to speak out for what is right, to shake up the status quo. That's America.

"What a solemn debt we owe," he said. "Which leads us to ask, just how might we repay that debt?"

Just how might we repay that debt?

How we answer that question will determine which America our country will become. That is why, when I stepped down as attorney general, I decided to devote my remaining career to the issue of voting rights, founding an organization called the National Democratic Redistricting Committee focused on ending gerrymandering and ensuring we are all counted equally in our democracy. And it's why I wrote this book—because, as President Johnson once said, the right to vote is the right that protects all the others.

Think about it: No matter what issue you care about most—whether you're most passionate about combating climate change or protecting reproductive rights, reforming the criminal justice system or stopping gun violence—the path to progress, the path to the America we ought to become, runs through the ballot.

Because if you can't elect leaders who support the policies you believe in, that agenda will never be enacted.

In the years since I went down to Selma, the right to vote has only become more vulnerable. That's because, much like the racist Democrats who were against expanding the franchise after the Civil War, the Republican Party of today sees America as a nation of "us" and "them"—and its leaders fear that they are outnumbered.

In their minds, the easier it is for everyone to vote, the harder it will be for them to win. As President Trump declared when explaining his opposition to bills that would have expanded access to the ballot, "If you ever agreed to it, you'd never have a Republican elected in this country again."

I don't think he's right. American voters can be swayed, and as we saw in Virginia's gubernatorial elections in 2021, higher turnout doesn't always necessarily benefit Democrats. But that's beside the point. Because, irrespective of the facts, the Republican Party *believes* that protecting representative democracy is not in its interests, and we have already begun to see the consequences of this ideology—not only with the legislation their leaders passed after the *Shelby County* decision but also through the insurrection many of them condoned, and in some cases even aided, after Donald Trump lost the 2020 election.

On January 6, we witnessed an attempted coup that might have seemed wholly unprecedented and disruptive, but make no mistake: It was actually the culmination of an effort years in the making, one that has only accelerated in the months since.

That's why, in its aftermath, legislatures across the country, Republican elected officials, and conservative media outlets haven't been devoted to figuring out how to prevent an uprising like that from happening again. Instead, too many have been working strategically and methodically to make sure that next time, the coup can succeed.

In states like Texas and Florida, legislatures have passed laws designed to make it harder to vote—especially for Black and brown Americans. From Michigan to Georgia, Republican leaders have forced those in their party who stood up to President Trump to step away from positions of power, filling election administration roles with extremists who claim the 2020 election was stolen. And all these new laws and purges of anyone who stands in their way are only serving to delegitimize a democracy that was already growing more and more unrepresentative of the interests of the people.

The numbers are striking: Both Trump and George W. Bush, the last two Republican presidents of the United States, were initially elected to office after losing the popular vote—and together, they have appointed five of the nine justices on the Supreme Court. The skew of the Senate, which provides as much representation to Wyoming (population: 590 *thousand*) as it does to California (population: 39 *million*), has left Republicans and Democrats with the same number of seats, even though Democratic candidates have received over 40 million more votes. And gerrymandering has led to similarly warped results in the House of Representatives and in state legislatures.

All these are among the reasons why Freedom House, a nonpartisan nonprofit watchdog that ranks the health of democracies around the globe, says our standing in the world has collapsed, with the strength of our institutions ranking below those of most developed nations.

This presents us with a crisis unlike any we've faced since the signing of the Voting Rights Act: American democracy is on the brink of collapse.

This isn't the first time our democracy has been in jeopardy—and neither was Selma. Since our founding, America has repeatedly been faced with a question: Whose votes will we count?

Again and again, a powerful few have answered by attempting to exclude the many from our electoral process. But while they have found success for generations at a time, in the long run, the story of American democracy is one of grinding, halting, bloodstained persistence and expansion, even in the face of tyranny.

But we've had to work for it. Because the path to progress has never been blazed through inertia.

Thankfully, over the past decade, Americans have once again awakened to the threats we face—and continued this tradition of organizing and mobilizing by the millions. In response to suppression, they are investing in registration and taking to the polls like never before. And in states like Georgia, we have seen these efforts pay off, as the activism of modern suffragists like Stacey Abrams has made it possible for Democrats to start winning elections again in the South for the first time in generations.

Stories like these should fill us with strength. But whether we will win the fight for our democracy is still an open question—especially after a Democratic Congress and Democratic president failed to pass voting rights bills—and ultimately, the answer will come down to us, the American people. With this book, my goal is to show you how we can channel the courage of those who marched in Selma and build on their legacy in this new century.

Which brings me back to that momentous spring day in 2015. I brought my kids with me, and one of the things I remember I wanted to show them was the diversity of the people who had come down to Selma—not only the racial diversity, but the ideological diversity as well.

President Johnson's daughter Luci was there, as you might expect, but just feet away, as Ari Berman notes in *Give Us the Ballot*, was the daughter of Johnson's white supremacist foil, George Wallace. Barack Obama was there, but so was George W. Bush, who took the time to talk to my kids. It was a bipartisan display, as it should have been—because with the twenty-twenty vision of hindsight, no one can convincingly deny the virtue of what those who marched in Selma accomplished.

But the test of your character is not whether you can look back at history and say you would have been on the side of the righteous; it's whether you're willing to stand up for what's just when you're the one in a position to make a difference. And so many of the Republicans who said positive things about the Selma marchers on that anniversary day—just like those who wrote gushing statements when John Lewis passed away in 2020—refuse to make their actions consistent with their words.

That's why this isn't going to be a book of empty rhetoric.

I'm not just going to wax poetic about the virtues of democracy. Instead, I'm going to take you through what we can do—what we must do—to defend it.

In the first section of the book, I will lay out the hidden history of voting rights in America—how we expanded the franchise from white landowning men to white non-landowning men to white women and, eventually, to Black Americans, telling the tales of the people and places at the center of the battle for enfranchisement. Because if we want to protect our democracy today, we have to understand that for most of our country's history, it didn't actually exist; and only came into being over the course of a centuries-long, often violent struggle.

In part II, I will lay out where we find ourselves now—covering the threats to our democracy that emerged from backlash to the first Black president, threats that I was able to observe up close as the attorney general of the United States. What I saw, from my unique vantage point, was that this backlash wasn't a spontaneous and emotional response from dispossessed so-called deplorables, but a highly strategic, well-funded campaign by powerful interests committed to gutting our democracy. They are relentless and determined, lavishly funded and fully equipped for destructive work. And it is essential that we understand their motivations and tactics, so we can stop them before it's too late.

And finally, I will propose a plan for how we realize the promise of our system of government, with a focus on the policy changes we need to usher in if we're going to finally perfect our democracy. These include the baseline steps, from automatic registration to early voting, that we need to take to protect voters from suppression, but also fundamental transformations to the Supreme Court, the Senate, the Electoral College, and the redistricting process that I believe we need to make if we want our elected officials to be responsive to the will of the people. Some of these ideas may seem radical, especially coming from a former attorney general, but I promise they are way less out-there than the idea that we should reverse the progress we've made and once again silence the voices of millions of Americans.

Now, I want to be clear: This fight won't always be easy. It never has been. As I said in Selma:

> I have no expectation that our goals will be simple to achieve or that complex challenges will be easily overcome. I know that our road will be long, and that many obstacles will stand in our way. But I have no doubt that—if we stand together; if we walk together; if we believe as we always have in the power of our ideals and the forces of our shared community—not only our cause, but our country shall overcome.

If America's history is any indication, this progress won't come in a straight line—and there will be days when our feet hurt, when we grow weary, when we are tempted to let up. But when those moments come, when the road ahead of us seems too steep and the weight starts to feel like too much to bear, I hope you will remember the giants who came before us, who carried more on their shoulders than we could ever imagine but kept on marching, one foot after the other, no matter what stood in their way.

Just how might we repay that debt?

Well, it's simple:

By saving our democracy.

Here's how we'll do it.

NOTE

The Case for Democracy

This note shouldn't need to be in the book.

In fact, it wasn't in our original outline.

Because, for most of recent history, the basic rationale for democracy did not need to be defended. In the decades following the signing of the Voting Rights Act, the public message of both political parties was to build a political system where the largest number of people could freely and fairly participate. And it was obvious to the point of banality that even if we still had political disagreements, we all aspired to build a government that represented the interests of the greatest number of people.

That was the American myth—and though if it wasn't always true, both parties embraced the aspiration that we were the world's most democratic nation. Democracy, in other words, was the American brand. And we were proud of it.

But in recent years, Republicans have begun to question this idea—asking why we ever thought voter participation was such a good thing to begin with. In the aftermath of the 2020 election, a survey found that more than nine out of ten supporters of Donald Trump believe "voting shouldn't be easier." This is in line with the dangerous emerging theory of elected officials like Senator Mike Lee from Utah, who has written that "we're not a democracy" and argues that "rank democracy can thwart" values like "liberty, peace, and prosperity." Fox News, meanwhile, has produced salivating propaganda in support of authoritarians around the world, including Viktor Orbán of Hungary, who has destroyed the free press, characterized immigrants as "poison," and attacked the independence of the judiciary.

At one point, the network's highest-rated host, Tucker Carlson, spent a week broadcasting from Budapest—calling Hungary "a small country with a lot of lessons for the rest of us." (Poetically, Hungary later censored Carlson's interview with Orbán, removing negative mentions of President Xi Jinping, China's authoritarian leader, from the transcript.)

It's not hard to figure out why Republicans like Carlson look at dictators like Orbán with envy: They see a diversifying America, and after watching President Obama win back-to-back races powered by record turnout from the most diverse coalition in history, they believe attacking the right to vote is the only way they can stay in power.

But while the dismissals of democracy from Republican talking heads and elected officials may be rooted in cynical self-preservation, millions of their acolytes aren't in on the con. They actually believe the nonsense, which is why the vast majority of them, in poll after poll, say they want voting to be harder. And that's why it's important to respond to the bad-faith arguments against democracy with good-faith arguments in favor of it.

To that end, I am going to briefly lay out four reasons why all Americans, regardless of their political party, should be on board with the idea that more voters lead, necessarily, to a healthier democracy, and that a healthy democracy is the bedrock on which the American pursuit of life, liberty, and happiness rests.

Because that is the foundational belief upon which the argument of this book—and, really, this country—is premised.

1) Democracy is the best way to implement policies that are consistent with the desires of the people.

At its core, the role of a government is to represent the interests of the people—and the best way for the people to express those interests is at the ballot box.

Without elections, how would a government know what kinds of policies its citizens would want? How would they know when they have succeeded? How would they know when they have failed?

There is a famous quote by Winston Churchill that I'm sure you've heard: "Democracy is the worst form of Government except for all those other forms."

It's a funny line. But Churchill's rationale for believing in representative government wasn't actually process of elimination. He was a big fan of democracy, and went on to argue that the genius of this system is the belief it's predicated on—that "public opinion, expressed by all constitutional means, should shape, guide, and control the actions of [representatives]." Elected officials, he concluded, should be the people's "servants and not their masters."

Elections are the mechanism by which we measure that public opinion—so our leaders can act on it, and face the consequences from their masters if they don't.

2) Democracy is a critical mechanism for holding politicians accountable.

When democracy is working, and elected officials know they will be held accountable for their actions, it's much harder for them to ignore the needs of the people they represent.

This is why, according to a landmark paper from Nobel

Prize-winning economist Amartya Sen, "No famine has ever taken place in the history of the world in a functioning democracy." It's not because elected officials in democracies have more kindness in their hearts. It's because, in Sen's words, they "have to win elections and face public criticism," and as a result, "have strong incentive to undertake measures to avert famines and other catastrophes."

And democracy isn't only about stopping bad things from happening. It's also the leverage the people need to convince the government to enact policies they believe will improve their lives. "Don't want to pass a civil rights bill? Don't want to lower taxes? Don't want to save the planet? Okay, fine, we'll vote you out and elect someone who does."

3) Democracy is the right that protects the rest.

Every single right we have—the right to free speech, the right to free assembly, the right to free religion—depends on the right to vote.

Because without free and fair elections, we have no way of peacefully removing politicians who attempt to take our liberties away from us.

In this way, democracy is the final bulwark against tyranny.

And it's also our best defense against oppression.

After all, when a group of people—a race, a gender, a party—is shut out of the electoral process, the government can not only ignore what they want but persecute them without consequence.

Just look at Jim Crow—an institution that was only able to persist because Black Americans couldn't go to the polls and vote out of power the elected officials who enforced segregation. That's why the Voting Rights Act was the crown jewel of the civil rights movement—because, without it, there would have been no way to guarantee that Jim Crow wouldn't return.

4) Democracy is the manifestation of the idea that we are all created equal.

If you agree with the words in the Declaration of Independence—if you believe all of us are born with certain unalienable rights—then you must also believe that all of us should have a say in determining what kind of future we want to build.

Our country has never fully lived up to those words, but the first section of this book is about the heroes who have sacrificed everything to bring us closer to realizing that founding promise. And no matter what side of the aisle you are on, I hope that reading it will bring you to the conclusion that their cause was a worthy one—one we have an obligation to build on, not tear down.

Part I

LESSONS FROM THE PAST

Every chapter in this section could be a book of its own. In fact, many such books have been published. So do not expect this history to be comprehensive. Instead, read it as a playbook on what it took to expand access to the franchise in America—on the bloody feet that kept on marching, and the bloody streets they left behind, along the winding, violent road to democracy.

1

REBELLION

How White Men Won the Vote

"The past is never dead. It's not even past."
—William Faulkner

Every generation likes to say the challenges they're facing are unprecedented—but when it comes to attacks on our right to vote, the reason we need to be vigilant isn't that this threat is novel. It's that it isn't.

For most of America's history, democracy hasn't been the rule. It's been the exception.

That was true before the first shots were fired in Lexington and Concord. Back then, each of the thirteen colonies had its own rules for voting. What they had in common, though, was that their elections didn't reflect the will of the people.

There were exceptions, but for the most part, if you were Native American, you couldn't vote. If you were African American, you couldn't vote. If you were a woman, you couldn't vote. And even if you were a white man, you couldn't vote, unless you owned enough property or paid enough in taxes.

In this way, when America was founded, voting wasn't a right. It was a privilege, one our founders believed should be reserved only for citizens with white skin, both X and Y chromosomes, and enough land, cash, or bodies—yes, bodies—to their name.

Exactly how much property you needed to own varied from colony to colony. In New Hampshire, they measured property based on its value in cash: If you weren't worth 50 pounds, you were out of luck. In Virginia, whether you could vote came down to how much land you owned: If you had 100 acres, you were good. If you only had 25, they needed to be well manicured. And if you had any fewer, you'd better not show up on Election Day, lest you be told you were too broke to vote.

In some colonies, like Connecticut, property qualifications were, as Governor Oliver Wolcott wrote, "essentially nugatory," meaning they weren't enforced at all. But in most, they were binding. And in some, if you were Catholic or Jewish it didn't even matter how much property you had; unless you were Protestant, you had no business casting a ballot.

But while restrictions on the right to vote are as old as America, so too is the desire among Americans to be the masters of our own fate. That belief in the power of the people is what inspired the colonies to declare their independence from an empire. And in the centuries that have followed, generation after generation of suffragists have devoted their lives to making the dream of self-determination a reality for all.

As you read the following chapters, you will recognize, as I do every time I reflect on the history of our country, that the expansion of the franchise was anything but inevitable. It was, instead, the work of Americans from all backgrounds—rich and poor, Black and white, men and women—none of whom were perfect, some of whom you've heard of, others of whom have been forgotten, all of whom shared a conviction that they should have a say in how they were governed, even if they had to risk their lives to win it.

* * *

Thomas Wilson Dorr was one of those Americans, but he wasn't exactly the kind of guy you'd expect to become a leader in the fight for voting rights. He was a rich kid who went to Phillips Exeter Academy for high school and became a Harvard freshman at fourteen years old. A portrait of a populist he was not.

But Dorr didn't want to be the kind of aristocrat who, as one nearby newspaper satirized, "gets up leisurely, breakfasts comfortably, reads the papers regularly, dresses fashionably, lounges fastidiously, eats a tart gravely, talks insipidly, dines considerably, drinks superfluously, kills time indifferently, sups elegantly, goes to bed stupidly, and lives uselessly."

He much preferred to spend his time with people who had it worse than he did—people like Seth Luther, a self-proclaimed "journeyman carpenter" from Providence, Rhode Island, who helped convince Dorr that their home state was in need of a revolution.

For more than a century, Rhode Island had laws in place that limited the right to vote to residents who owned property valued at upward of $134. For Luther, whose father was a veteran of the Revolutionary War, this felt arbitrary, and not only that—it also felt like a slap in the face of those who risked their lives for independence from Britain. "This law is contrary to the Declaration of Independence," he declared in his 1833 "Address on the Right of Free Suffrage," adding that it was "strange that a self-evident truth should require proof." He then left those who disagreed with him with an insult fit for a rap battle: "May all Traitors, Tyrants, Tories, and Aristocrats never find anything but onions to wipe their weeping eyes."

Dorr lacked Luther's oratory gifts, but he was a more palatable messenger—and in July 1841, a decade after Luther delivered his speech, the Harvard wunderkind teamed up with the members of the Rhode Island Suffrage Association to lead a movement aimed at expanding the franchise. Together, they convened a People's Constitutional Convention, invited folks who didn't have access to the ballot from across the state to join them, and drafted a document they proposed should be the new constitution of Rhode Island. This "People's Constitution," if implemented, would have eliminated property qualifications once and for, well, not all. Despite objections from abolitionists—and despite Dorr's past membership in the American Anti-Slavery Society—the People's Constitutional Convention decided to bar African Americans from voting.

In the months that followed, the Suffrage Association barnstormed from town to town, making the case for change, and ultimately deciding to bring the People's Constitution up for a statewide vote. At the time, it was unclear whether this referendum would have any standing, but at the very least they thought it would send a loud message. And it did: On Election Day, in April 1842, 14,000 Rhode Islanders voted for the People's Constitution, while just 52 voted against it.

Later that year, under the questionable jurisdiction of this new constitution, Dorr was elected governor. But there was a problem. Rhode Island's supreme court ruled that the People's Constitution was . . . unconstitutional. And the state's general assembly, along with the four-term incumbent governor, Samuel Ward King, made it clear that if Dorr tried to take office, he would be guilty of treason. Even President John Tyler promised to send federal troops to Rhode Island to quell the rebellion.

But none of this deterred Dorr. On May 3, 1842, the Suffrage Association came together and held an inaugural parade for him. And two weeks later, under the cover of night, they stormed the state's arsenal—even though Dorr's own father and uncles were in the building. They were living the mantra of Seth Luther: "Peaceably if we can. Forcibly if we must."

The problem was that this makeshift militia wasn't exactly built for war—especially because they had to square up against not only the state of Rhode Island, but also the African Americans who decided to fight alongside the incumbent government after they were spurned by the rebels. And when it came time for Dorr's soldiers to fire their cannons, the weapons malfunctioned. That is how Dorr's rebellion ended—not with a bang but a whimper.

Dorr tried to flee the state but eventually decided to return. And when he did, the governor declared martial law, which led to the arrest of Dorr and more than a hundred members of his militia, who were bound with ropes, starved for a day, and brutalized by the state. At his hearing, Dorr was sentenced to life and hard labor, but after public outcry when he fell ill behind bars, he was released, and died a few years later at the age of forty-nine—a riches-to-rags story.

Luther, meanwhile, had a mental breakdown during his imprisonment, robbed a bank when he was released, passed away in the Vermont Asylum for the Insane soon after, and was laid to rest in an unmarked grave.

But while the government crushed the rebellion, they did write up a new constitution within months. By the end of 1842, both white and Black Rhode Islanders without land could vote. And decades later, long after he died in infamy, Thomas Dorr was recognized by the state of Rhode Island as its sixteenth governor.

When America declared our independence from Great Britain and won the Revolutionary War, our founders were in an awkward spot.

On the one hand, they wanted to build a government that, unlike Britain's, was actually representative of the people. After all, their slogan during the revolution had been "No taxation without representation," and it would've been tough to just say, "Never mind," after the war was over. On the other hand, the framers needed to receive sign-off on the Constitution from colonies where the promise of the Declaration of Independence didn't even remotely resemble reality, as evidenced by the millions of people they enslaved. And many of the founders themselves didn't actually believe in the equality of the polity.

So at the Constitutional Convention in 1787, they saved their debate on voting rights for the end. By that point in the convention, everyone was exhausted from months of negotiations. George Washington didn't even bother showing up that day. He went fishing instead.

And when you look back on the minutes of that meeting, it's hard to blame him. Things got messy.

Back then, none of the framers had even considered granting the right to vote to women, African Americans, or Native Americans—so their debate, like the one Rhode Island would have half a century later, boiled down to whether white men who didn't own land should be able to participate in elections. At the time, most leaders believed the answer to that question was no. Their reasoning was voiced at the convention by Gouverneur Morris, the Founding Father who—because hypocrisy is as American as corn dogs, apple pie, and the McRib—is best known for deciding to start the Constitution with the words "We the People."

First, Morris explained, he was afraid that if you "give the votes to people who have no property, they will sell them to the rich who will be able to buy them." This was a common fear at the time, one that can be traced back to a judge in England named William Blackstone, who wrote that the justification for property qualifications was to "exclude such persons as are in so mean a situation that they are esteemed to have no will of their own."

"If these persons had votes," he wrote in *Commentaries on the Laws of England,* "they would be tempted to dispose of them under some undue influence."

In the eighteenth century, this fear was exacerbated by the fact that the secret ballot still hadn't become the norm. Instead, as historian Jill Lepore writes in her essential *New Yorker* essay "Rock, Paper, Scissors: *How We Used to Vote,*" "Americans used to vote with their voices—*viva voce*—or with their hands or with their feet. Yea or nay. Raise your hand. All in favor of Jones, stand on this side of the town common; if you support Smith, line up over there." This made it much easier to buy votes—because if your boss asked you to support Smith on Monday, he could see whether you lined up on the right side of the room on Tuesday.

Of course, this wasn't the only reason leaders like Gouverneur Morris opposed allowing those who didn't own property to vote. They also believed the poor didn't have the requisite judgment to help decide elections. "Children do not vote," Morris explained, comparing those without property to those without fully developed brains. "Why? Because they want prudence, because they have no will of their own." He continued: "The ignorant and the dependent can be as little trusted with the public interest."

John Dickinson, a delegate from Pennsylvania, agreed. Landowners, he argued, were "the best guardians of liberty," and added that "the restriction of the right to them" was a "necessary defense against the dangerous influence of those multitudes without property and without principle." Elbridge Gerry, the

Founding Father for whom gerrymandering was named (much more on that later), said the quiet part out loud. "Democracy," he exclaimed, is "the worst of all political evils"—an opinion that might sound radical, but actually put him in the company of James Madison, who wrote in Federalist No. 10 that democratic elections are decided through "vicious arts" by "men of factious tempers, of local prejudices, or of sinister designs," and John Adams, who wrote that if the propertyless were allowed to vote, "an immediate revolution would ensue."

That's right: The Founding Fathers believed poor people shouldn't be enfranchised both because they would be too beholden to the wealthy *and* because they might end up leading a revolution against the wealthy. It never made sense. But cognitive dissonance came easily to the generation of Americans who signed a document at work that read "all men are created equal" and then went home to plantations full of men and women they enslaved.

So, those were the two public reasons the framers believed only those with property should vote—but there was a third reason, too, one they did not bring up at the convention. And it was this: They knew that if they expanded access to the ballot to any additional group, others would clamor to be next. As Adams wrote in a private letter to a friend:

> The same reasoning which will induce you to admit all men, who have no property, to vote, with those who have . . . will prove that you ought to admit women and children; for, generally speaking, women and children have as good judgment, and as independent minds, as those men who are wholly destitute of property; these last being to all intents and purposes as much dependent upon others, who will please to feed, clothe, and employ

> them, as women are upon their husbands, or children on their parents.
>
> There will be no end of it. New claims will arise; women will demand the vote; lads from twelve to twenty-one will think their rights not enough attended to; and every man who has not a farthing will demand an equal voice with any other, in all acts of state. It tends to confound and destroy all distinctions and prostrate all ranks to one common level.

This fear was widespread among our founders, but there were some who nonetheless believed in expanding the franchise. Edward Rutledge, from South Carolina, argued that "restraining the right of suffrage . . . would create division among the people and make enemies of all who should be excluded." And George Mason, one of the three delegates to the convention who ultimately refused to sign the Constitution, had a strong conviction that "every man having evidence of attachment to, and permanent common interest with the society ought to share in all its rights and privileges." To him, the idea that you needed to own land to have a voice wasn't only wrong. It was patently ridiculous.

That's how Benjamin Franklin saw it, too. At the convention, his arguments were more restrained, full of muted, milquetoast reasoning like, "The sons of a substantial farmer, not being themselves freeholders, would not be pleased at being disenfranchised." But in other settings, he was far more direct in his rebuke of property requirements, laying out the case against them through an analogy that came to be known simply as Franklin's Jackass:

> Today a man owns a jackass worth fifty dollars and he is entitled to vote; but before the next election the jackass

> dies. The man in the meantime has become more experienced, his knowledge of the principles of government, and his acquaintance with mankind, are more extensive, and he is therefore better qualified to make a proper selection of rulers—but the jackass is dead and the man cannot vote. Now gentlemen, pray inform me, in whom is the right of suffrage? In the man or in the jackass?

It was a characteristically compelling argument—one that would be cited in the decades that followed, including by Rhode Island's Seth Luther in his "Address on the Right of Free Suffrage." But at the Constitutional Convention, after hours of debate, the founders decided to dodge the issue of voting rights altogether, leaving discretion to the states. Somehow, even with all the big personalities in the room, it was actually Oliver Ellsworth, one of the forgotten founders, whose logic won out: "The states," he said, "are the best judges of the circumstances and temper of their own people," and most ended up choosing only to allow white men with land to vote.

This meant that for all intents and purposes, at its founding, America was not a democracy. To put a number on it: When George Washington first ran for president, only one in sixteen Americans was eligible to vote. Six percent. And those who qualified didn't even cast ballots for president directly. They voted, instead, on which representatives their state should send to the Electoral College—representatives who, back then, could choose to vote for whoever they liked. Races for the Senate were even less democratic, decided not by the people but by state legislatures. And the elections themselves were corrupt in innumerable ways.

As Chilton Williamson recounts in *American Suffrage: From Property to Democracy:*

> Poll officials everywhere were variously accused of admitting illegal voters to the polls, denying qualified persons the right to vote, suppressing legal votes in the count, stuffing ballot boxes, winking at intimidation of electors, opening and closing the polls capriciously, and dropping legal votes to the floor which were later burned with the genuine debris of electoral activities.

Voter fraud may largely be a myth today, but in the early days of our democracy, it was very real. In his exhaustive survey of American elections in the eighteenth and nineteenth centuries, Williamson found tale after tale of chicanery. In Philadelphia, for a few years, elections came down to which campaign controlled the staircase at the polling station, since they could physically block their opponents from casting ballots. In Trenton, New Jersey, the result of one particularly close election was ultimately decided by a sheriff—who closed the polls early even though he knew dozens of voters were still trying to cast their ballots, because he thought doing so would help his preferred candidate. And in towns across the country, candidates would get around property requirements by buying a plot of land right before Election Day and listing their supporters as its owners, an idea you can imagine them thinking was so crazy that it just might work. (Sometimes, it did.)

Then there was the problem of distance. In many places, voters had to travel Odyssean lengths to make their voices heard. In South Carolina, for instance, there were citizens who lived more than 150 miles from the nearest polling location. Mind you, the car would not be invented for more than a century, so if you wanted to commute to the polls, you had to do so by a mode of transportation with a horsepower of one.

Things became a bit less chaotic—and corruptible—with the

proliferation of the secret ballot in the 1890s, but even then, votes were easy to suppress. As Lepore writes: "You had to bring your own ballot, a scrap of paper. You had to (a) remember and (b) know how to spell the name of every candidate and office. If 'John Jones' was standing for election, and you wrote 'Jon Jones,' your vote could be thrown out." What's worse: Those without money were the "least likely to know how to write," which meant the secret ballot amounted to a literacy test.

Votes were easy to buy, too. "Shrewd partisans began bringing prewritten ballots to the polls, and handing them out with a coin or two," Lepore writes. "Doling out cash—the money came to be called 'soap'—wasn't illegal; it was getting out the vote."

Over time, however, elections became more orderly—and more inclusive. Starting with Vermont in 1791, eventually every new state admitted to the union adopted a constitution that allowed those without property to vote, which inspired the states that had been the original thirteen colonies to do the same. In 1792, Delaware eliminated its property requirement. A decade later, Maryland followed suit. When Andrew Jackson ran his populist campaign in 1828, the vast majority of white men had been granted access to the ballot. And by the end of the 1860s, after the rebellion in Rhode Island, property requirements were entirely a relic of the past.

So what changed?

As Alexander Keyssar argues in *The Right to Vote,* the definitive book on the history of voting rights in America, there were three main reasons the United States opened up its elections.

First and foremost, our elected officials were worried about national security. During the War of 1812, it was hard to find soldiers willing to fight for our country—and since those without property didn't have a say in electing the government that would be sending them to war, who could blame them for refusing to enlist? Even among those who did join militias, there was widespread discontent with a democracy that could send them to die but did not allow them to vote. After all, in some units, more than seven in every ten soldiers were disenfranchised.

In states across the country—from New York to Alabama, Massachusetts to Illinois—this injustice was invoked at constitutional conventions. In Virginia, the landless lamented a government that "in the hour of danger" drew "no invidious distinctions between the sons of Virginia," even though, "in times of peace," it "ignominiously" blocked their access to "the polls." Ultimately, these arguments proved persuasive.

Of course, as Keyssar points out, many of those who made them were hypocrites themselves, unwilling or unable to see why the reasoning they provided for their own enfranchisement should apply to African Americans as well. The Virginia delegation, for instance, which self-righteously declared that property requirements created "an odious distinction between members of the same community," wrote that "for obvious reasons, by almost universal consent, women and children, aliens and slaves are excluded." *For obvious reasons,* huh?

In fact, the desire to preserve slavery was actually itself an impetus for states in the South to come around to the idea of granting poor whites the right to vote on the grounds of "security." As one delegate to Virginia's delegation argued, "All slaveholding states are fast approaching a crisis truly alarming, a time when freemen will be needed, when every man must be at his post." What he meant was that, when African Americans rebelled against slavery, "every free white human being" would need to "unite" to stop them.

That argument won out—and, as Keyssar lays out, it was one of the reasons the South joined the North in expanding the franchise.

The second reason was money. The United States is a big country. And in the decades after the Revolution, European settlers had still not occupied most of it, so states had to compete with one another for new settlers (and the tax dollars that came with them). One of the ways they won these settlers over was by offering them the right to vote, regardless of whether they owned property. Because, even back then, people all around the world recognized the value of the franchise. As a delegate in Illinois asked, "Should we not hold out to the world the greatest inducement for men to come amongst us, to till our prairies, to work in our mines, and to develop the vast and inexhaustible resources of our state?"

This argument gained popularity across the United States, and it led to a cycle of enfranchisement: Once one state offered an incentive for prospective residents to inhabit it, other states felt pressure to follow suit.

A similar feedback loop drove the third reason for the abolition of property requirements: politics. Beginning in the 1820s, states started to hold popular elections—and often there would be a divergence in the qualifications to vote in statewide elections and federal ones. In North Carolina, for instance, you had to own property if you wanted a say in U.S. Senate races, but didn't need a dollar to your name to vote for governor. This meant that for the first time in the history of the United States, there was an incentive for gubernatorial candidates to campaign on expanding access to the ballot to other elections, which was exactly what North Carolina's David Reid decided to do when he ran for governor in 1850.

According to Keyssar, at the beginning of the race, no one

thought Reid had a shot, but he promised that if he won, he would pass a constitutional amendment allowing all fifty thousand free white men in North Carolina who didn't own property to participate in Senate races. And it worked. Because people really wanted the right to vote.

On Election Day, Reid turned out an unprecedented number of voters, and as governor, he followed through on his promise to expand access to the franchise for Senate elections. Enfranchisement, in other words, begat enfranchisement.

Stories like this took place around the country—and eventually, political parties realized they had no choice but to fall in line. Because otherwise, their opponents would sweep election after election. That's why, after Reid's victory, the Whigs, who had previously said his proposals would lead to "a system of communism unjust and Jacobinical," joined his effort to amend the state's constitution.

Over the following decades, national turnout nearly tripled, from 27 percent of white men in the 1820s to 78 percent in the 1840s—and across the country, support for property requirements started to be seen as illogical, unless, as one delegate to the Virginia convention quipped, "there be something in the ownership of land, that by enchantment or magic, converts frail erring man into an infallible and impeccable being." (The shade!)

This marked the beginning of a new era of American democracy, one where access to the ballot was no longer viewed as a privilege. Suddenly, voting was a right—as long as you were male and white.

It was an era birthed by Americans without land who made the very short logical leap from the nation's founding creed to their right to vote and did whatever it took to get it. In Rhode Island, that meant cosplaying democracy, writing their own constitution, electing their own governor, and storming the state capitol—wielding the power of rebellion. Out west, it meant strangers agreeing to move to a strange land, but only if they were promised a say in how it was run, wielding the power of their tax dollars. In the South, it meant threatening to refuse to wear the country's uniform in wars abroad or quell slave rebellions at home unless they were granted the vote, wielding the power to inflict fear on the powerful.

Eventually, the privileged simply deemed it more costly to continue to deny landless white men the vote than to grant it to them—though they had no intention of expanding access to the franchise any further. But as John Adams had anticipated, this equilibrium was unsustainable. Once white men felt entitled to the right to vote, so too did the African Americans, women, and other disenfranchised Americans who knew they were no less deserving of a voice in their democracy. But that didn't mean they would get one. Because, as Frederick Douglass recognized, in America, "Power concedes nothing without a demand."

How the next generation of Americans demanded the right to vote, and what we can learn from them, is the subject of chapters to come.

And if you're not down with the cause, well, in Luther's words, I hope you never find anything but onions to wipe your weeping eyes.

2

A MOMENT IN THE SUN

How Black Men Won the Vote—and White Men Stole It

On May 10, 1865, thirty-two years after the American Anti-Slavery Society was founded, its members packed the Church of the Puritans in New York.

It had been quite a month. Four weeks earlier, the Confederate general Robert E. Lee had surrendered at Appomattox Court House, marking the beginning of the end of the Civil War. Six days after that, during a performance at Ford's Theatre, a stage actor named John Wilkes Booth assassinated Abraham Lincoln, the president of the United States. Now thousands of abolitionists who had been on the front lines of this fight—who had barnstormed the country delivering lectures on the evils of slavery; who had stood strong in the face of mob violence; who had mourned the loss of their compatriots to a house divided against itself—were faced with a question: Where do we go from here?

In some ways, they had already exceeded their loftiest expectations. In a matter of decades, they had awakened the conscience of a nation—and helped usher in the end of the most evil chapter in the history of the United States. With this progress in mind, William Lloyd Garrison, the American Anti-Slavery Society's founder, brought forward a resolution to dissolve the organization entirely. "Rejoicing with joy unspeakable that the year of jubilee has come, so that further anti-slavery agitation is uncalled for," he wrote, "we close the operation and the existence of this society."

He continued: "My vocation as an Abolitionist, thank God, is ended."

No one denied that Garrison had earned his rest: For a quarter of a century, he had done as much as anyone to lead the movement. But his partner in this fight, Frederick Douglass, saw things differently. Unlike Garrison, Douglass had actually lived through the horrors of slavery—separated from his mother, beaten by his overseer, barred from learning how to read—yet he did not believe the days following the Civil War were a moment to celebrate how far America had come. He believed it was a moment to recognize how much further we still had to go.

"Slavery is not abolished," he explained, "until the black man has the ballot."

African Americans, Douglass had argued in a speech earlier that year, had been treated as citizens whenever "this nation was in trouble." They had been forced to fight in the Revolutionary War, they had taken up arms during the War of 1812, and they had just played a key role in quelling the now defeated Great Rebellion. Every time America had needed their help, as we would see over and over again in the future, African Americans had answered the call, raising the question: "Shall we be citizens in war, and aliens in peace? Would that be just?" For Douglass, the answer was an unequivocal no.

"Here where universal suffrage is the rule, where that is the fundamental idea of the Government," he said, "to rule us out is to make us an exception, to brand us with the stigma of inferiority, and to invite to our heads the missiles of those about us."

That is why, at the convention in New York, he argued that slavery would never truly be abolished until Black Americans had the vote. And, at the end of the day, his fellow members agreed, rejecting Garrison's resolution to disband the Anti-Slavery Society and instead adopting a new motto:

"No Reconstruction Without Negro Suffrage."

If you're from my generation, basically everything you were taught about Reconstruction was wrong.

And that was intentional.

I bet you, like me, were told that it didn't work; that the North was too slow to welcome the South back to the Union; that Republicans advocating for universal suffrage were radical; that the African Americans who were elected after the Civil War were incompetent—to the extent that they were mentioned at all. And that's because, for half a century, members of the press and historians were committed to promulgating that narrative.

These Lost Cause propagandists called African American legislatures "monkey houses." They lied about whether African Americans in Congress could read and claimed—falsely—that they didn't pay their taxes. In some cases, the names of Black officials weren't even included in public records, because, as one Democrat wrote, "it would be absurd to record the lives of men who were but yesterday our slaves." In D. W. Griffith's *The Birth of a Nation,* one of the early twentieth century's highest-grossing films, Black elected officials during Reconstruction were portrayed as alcoholics who drank on the floor of Congress. It was nothing short of a coordinated attempt to erase the period in American history when our country saw the beginnings of a multiracial democracy—when, as W.E.B. Du Bois wrote, "The slave went free; stood a brief moment in the sun; then moved back again toward slavery."

But in recent decades, a new generation of historians, building on the work of Du Bois's groundbreaking *Black Reconstruction,* and led by Eric Foner, my former professor at Columbia, have looked back on Reconstruction and discovered a fundamentally different story—the true one—a story at once more brutal and more hopeful than the one most of us were taught growing up.

The years following the Civil War were indeed full of bloodshed—defined, in no small part, by the rise of white supremacists, the growth of the Ku Klux Klan, and the macabre massacres these racists perpetrated. But these years also opened America's eyes to the possibility of making the vision of a multiracial democracy a reality. And in so many ways, Reconstruction was a success.

In just over a decade following the end of the Civil War, close to two thousand African Americans held elected office—serving in city halls, governor's mansions, and even Congress. There were Black mayors, Black sheriffs, Black senators. And they used that power to make a difference, persisting in the face of death threats to advocate for workers, reform the criminal justice system, and most important, increase access to education.

As Du Bois wrote, "The first great mass movement for public education at the expense of the state, in the South, came from Negroes." It paid off: Within years, public school enrollment among Black Americans skyrocketed from 91,000 to 572,000, as illiteracy was cut almost in half. And poor whites benefited from this expansion to the social safety net as well.

Through reforms like these, Black Americans proved that the outcome of the Civil War wasn't meaningful only because it brought an end to the institution of slavery. It was also meaningful because it helped America realize its promise as a democracy—and demonstrated that government can be a force for positive change when it reflects the will of all the people.

Of course, the story of Reconstruction doesn't have a happy ending. Eventually, the rebirth of American democracy was aborted, as lynchings in the South and abandonment by the North allowed white supremacy to once again rule the land. But this doesn't mean that what happened in America in the years following the Civil War didn't matter. To the contrary—it couldn't be more important.

That's because Reconstruction, perhaps more than any period in the history of America, is proof that the moral arc of the universe isn't truly predestined to bend in any one direction. Our country moves forward and backward. We grant rights and then take them away. If you don't hold on to the progress you've made—if you don't remain vigilant in defending it—it will be reversed. That is the lesson of Reconstruction. And as we are faced with a new wave of attacks on our democracy, the only question is whether we will repeat the mistakes of our past or learn from them.

When Douglass, Garrison, and the rest of the American Anti-Slavery Society met at the Church of the Puritans, our country was in a liminal moment—the brief period between the end of the Civil War and the expansion of suffrage to Black Americans. It was a precarious time. Because it wasn't clear whether those who had earned their freedom would also earn the vote.

After all, before the war, even in the North, African Americans had only been allowed to cast ballots in a total of five states. And across the country, initiatives aimed at expanding the franchise were rejected over and over again, including in states led by Republicans like Minnesota, Wisconsin, and Connecticut—back when the Republican Party was the party of voting rights.

Even after the war, in the eyes of President Andrew Johnson, Republicans who supported expanding access to the ballot represented a "radical and fanatical element" of Americans. And unlike President Lincoln, who had believed in Black suffrage—though he supported it only for "the very intelligent" and "those who serve our cause as soldiers"—Johnson had no intention of making it easier for any Black Americans to vote. He wanted a "white man's government." Plain and simple.

And he had violence on his side. When Black Americans in New Orleans organized a convention in favor of suffrage in 1866, thirty-four of the attendees and their supporters were murdered. And over the following twenty-four months, according to Yale professor David Blight, a full 10 percent of folks who went to similar conventions across the country were assaulted.

Despite these threats, there were people in positions of power who believed Black Americans had earned the right to vote through their service during the Civil War. This included Union general William Tecumseh Sherman, who promised that "when the fight is over the hand that drops the musket cannot be denied the ballot." And Republicans in Congress, led by abolitionists like Charles Sumner and Wendell Phillips, were dead set on finding a way to follow through on this commitment.

The first step in this process was ratifying the Fourteenth Amendment, which enshrined the term "right to vote" in our nation's founding document—even if that right wasn't yet a reality—and established "equal protection of the laws" for all Americans, ensuring no state could "deprive any person of life, liberty, or property, without due process." In a country where slavery had persisted for centuries, in a document that condoned this original sin, this was a monumental breakthrough.

The problem, though, as Keyssar writes in *The Right to Vote,* was that nowhere in the amendment did the Constitution mandate that states expand access to suffrage, which was why Wendell Phillips called it "a fatal and total surrender."

This is where the Reconstruction Act of 1867 came into the picture. Designed to set the terms for how Confederate states could regain entrance to the union, the law required that they enfranchise Black Americans. It also mandated that they allow the federal government to deploy troops to their region—and that they ratify the Fourteenth Amendment. This didn't come without backlash. Alabama, for instance, signed a petition saying Black voters would "bring, to the great injury of themselves as well as of us and our children, blight, crime, ruin and barbarism on this fair land." Over time, though, and through the intervention of the federal government, even in the deepest, bleakest, most discriminatory corners of the Confederacy, Black Americans gained access to the ballot—and over a period of two years, the percentage of Black men in the South eligible to register to vote rose from less than 1 percent to more than 80 percent.

This set the stage for what Eric Foner calls "The Second Founding" in his landmark work of the same name, as thousands of Black voters flocked to the polls, ran for office, and changed the face of American democracy. In South Carolina, for instance, more than three hundred Black Americans ended up serving in government during Reconstruction. They included heroes of the Civil War like Robert Smalls, a former enslaved person who went undercover and stole a Confederate ship, before sparking a movement to integrate public transportation in Pennsylvania as a free man and eventually becoming a congressman.

The election of officials like Smalls—as well as Hiram Revels and Blanche Bruce, the first two African American Senators—was powered by the tens of thousands of Black Americans who were registered to vote by the Freedmen's Bureau, a department of the federal government established by President Lincoln to aid former slaves in their transition to freedom; and by grassroots organizations like the Union Leagues, which devoted themselves to building Black political power.

For the millions of Americans who had been freed, declining to exercise this right they had fought so hard to obtain wasn't an option. As a reporter on the ground in Alabama on Election Day 1868 wrote, "In defiance of fatigue, hardship, hunger, and threats of employers," as well as a "pitiless storm," Black voter after Black voter waited in line barefoot so they could make their voices heard. They embodied the idea John Lewis would capture a century later, when he was known to say, "Democracy is not a state. It is an act."

But as the participation of Black Americans in elections increased, so too did the brutality they endured. Beginning in 1869, the Ku Klux Klan—a terrorist organization founded in large part by middle-class Confederate veterans—began murdering Black Americans en masse. Their goal, as Emanuel Fortune, a former enslaved person who became a member of the Florida Constitutional Convention, explained, was to "kill out the leading men of the Republican party." On block after block, in town after town, they would assassinate Black Americans who dared to participate in democracy, from North Carolina, where they killed thirty Black political leaders, to Mississippi, where they mutilated and murdered Jack Dupree, a Republican organizer, in front of his wife and children for being "known as a man who would speak his mind," to South Carolina, where they killed minister Benjamin Randolph for the "crime" of campaigning, even though his right to do so was protected by the Constitution of the United States.

Adding to the horror, after most killings like these, the perpetrators would be exonerated in court—or never tried—and wouldn't have to serve even a night behind bars, in no small part because many of the attacks took place with the tacit approval, or in some cases willing participation, of law enforcement.

This is the democracy Ulysses S. Grant inherited in 1869 when he took the oath of office after around half a million Black Americans helped elect him president of the United States—a democracy where Black Americans had the right to vote according to the law, but, in so many places, could not exercise it without putting their lives on the line. Against this backdrop, President Grant had two priorities: One, a Fifteenth Amendment, which would build on the Thirteenth and Fourteenth by expanding Black suffrage to every state in the union; and two, an Enforcement Act aimed at cracking down on the Ku Klux Klan, so its members could be prosecuted by the federal government.

How, exactly, the Fifteenth Amendment would guarantee the right to vote remained to be seen—and, as Alexander Keyssar describes in *The Right to Vote,* there was no shortage of drafts.

The first was produced by Representative George Boutwell of Massachusetts. It was written to be narrow, with the goal, simply, of making sure no one could be denied access to the ballot "by reason of race, color, or previous condition of slavery." There were more radical drafts, too, including one by Samuel Shellabarger of Ohio that, as Keyssar explains, would have also barred "property, tax, nativity, and literacy requirements."

Unfortunately, more representatives ended up siding with Boutwell—afraid that broader language would lead to the enfranchisement of too many Americans, from Chinese workers in the West to European immigrants in the North. That's because, regardless of what the Fourteenth Amendment said, America still didn't actually view the vote as a universal right.

They viewed it as a privilege, one Congress hadn't even considered bestowing on women.

The Senate's debate on the Fifteenth Amendment followed a similar script. Like Boutwell in the House, Senator William Morris Stewart of Nevada believed that passing an amendment was essential but he didn't want it to be too sweeping. On the other side was Henry Wilson, an ardent abolitionist from Massachusetts who believed Congress had a duty to give "to all citizens equal rights, and then protect everybody in the United States in the exercise of those rights." That meant enfranchising not only Black Americans but also immigrants—and making sure states couldn't enact literacy tests.

He made a persuasive case, but it was eventually rejected—not only by racist senators like James Doolittle from Wisconsin, who claimed African Americans were "incompetent to vote," and James Bayard, Jr., from Delaware, who called Black Americans "an inferior" and "more animal" race, but also by mainstream institutions like *The New York Times.* "The country is not prepared," wrote their editorial board.

Nonetheless, the language Wilson had put together made its way through the Senate, leaving the task of reconciling the House and Senate versions of the amendment up to a committee of members from both chambers. And in the end, on February 26, 1869, the moderates—if you can call people who didn't believe in universal suffrage "moderates"—won out, with the final language hewing closely to Boutwell's draft. It read:

> Section I: The right of citizens of the United States to vote shall not be denied or abridged by the United States or by any State on account of race, color, or previous condition of servitude.

Section II: The Congress shall have power to enforce this article by appropriate legislation.

For so-called Radical Republicans, who were actually the reasonable ones, this was an outrage—with Wilson calling the draft "lame and halting," fearing that it would do nothing to stop former Confederate states from implementing literacy tests, poll taxes, and other forms of voter suppression. But across the country, the ratification of the Fifteenth Amendment was met with jubilation. Frederick Douglass declared that Black Americans had finally been "placed upon an equal footing with all other men." Wendell Phillips called the amendment "the grandest and most Christian act ever contemplated or accomplished by any nation." William Lloyd Garrison said that "nothing in all of history" could compare to "the wonderful, quiet, sudden transformation of four million human beings from the auction-block to the ballot-box."

Building on this progress, through the Enforcement Acts, Congress set out to make sure the Fifteenth Amendment would be put into practice across the country—without interference from the Ku Klux Klan. One of the biggest advocates of these laws was Robert Brown Elliott, a Black American elected to Congress from South Carolina. On the floor of the House, he lambasted the "pitiless and cowardly persecution" of his people. "It is the custom of democratic journals to stigmatize the Negroes of the South as being barbarous," he explained. "But gentlemen, tell me, who is the barbarian here?" His argument won out—and between 1870 and 1871, Congress passed three Enforcement Acts aimed at ridding America of the scourge of the Ku Klux Klan.

For the first few years, this legislation was successful, as thousands of members of the Klan were prosecuted. And for a moment, American democracy seemed like it was going to continue to expand, as seven hundred thousand Black Americans registered to vote in the years following the ratification of the Fifteenth Amendment. But as more time passed after the Civil War, the federal government's will to continue the hard work of Reconstruction eroded.

For one thing, there was an economic crisis to worry about, as the Panic of 1873 led to devastation across the country—and seeded a lack of faith in the Republican Party. Reconstruction was also hampered by a series of conservative, reactionary, reckless Supreme Court decisions that, as one dissenting justice wrote, reduced the Fourteenth Amendment to a "vain and idle enactment." In *U.S. v. Cruikshank,* the court went as far as to reverse the convictions of Ku Klux Klan members who had led an Easter Day massacre of Black Americans fighting for their voting rights in Louisiana, rendering the Enforcement Acts null and void. With these decisions, the court determined that only states, not the federal government, could prosecute members of the Ku Klux Klan for murder—states, mind you, that had led an insurrection in defense of slavery less than a decade earlier. Perhaps it's no surprise, then, that there were fewer than 10 percent as many prosecutions under the Enforcement Acts at the end of the decade than there were at the beginning.

From this moment forward, as a Republican newspaper wrote, the Fourteenth and Fifteenth Amendments had become "dead letters," and the federal government was left to implement a "let-alone policy," refusing to hold former Confederate states accountable for violations of voting rights. This led to the reintroduction of an American apartheid, as white Democrats regained complete control of their legislatures and waged destruction and violence against those trying to exercise their hard-won right to participate in our democracy.

As Adelbert Ames, a senator from Mississippi—a state where Republican leaders had been murdered, voters' lives had been threatened, and ballot boxes in Black neighborhoods had been destroyed—lamented: "A revolution has taken place—by force of arms—and a race are disenfranchised—they are to be returned to a condition of serfdom."

We were on the verge, Ames said, of "an era of second slavery." And while he wasn't precisely right—slavery as a *de jure* institution never came back, even as, in the words of historian Douglas Blackmon, "slavery by another name" surely returned—he was correct that the period of Reconstruction, the decade during which America had tried, in fits and starts, to expand the tent of its democracy, was over.

With the presidential election of 1876, it became official. Before taking office, Republican Rutherford B. Hayes, who had a lead in the Electoral College, faced a rebellion in Congress not unlike the one led by Republicans following Donald Trump's defeat in the 2020 election. Only this time it was Democrats who refused to certify the victor—and perhaps because unlike Trump, their candidate, Samuel Tilden, had actually won the popular vote, their protest proved more successful, leaving the country without a president-elect two days before the inauguration was set to take place.

With time running out and the integrity of America's elections at stake, Hayes agreed to a compromise: In exchange for the Southern electoral votes he needed to secure a majority, he would pull the remaining U.S. troops out of the former Confederacy—conceding that the federal government would no longer even try to protect the Fourteenth and Fifteenth Amendments. And the South wasted no time taking advantage of this opportunity.

Within months, Georgia implemented a poll tax—and during the next election, only 10,000 of the state's 369,511 eligible Black voters were able to register. "We are in a majority here," one Black man said, "but you may vote till your eyes drop out or your tongue drops out, and you can't count your colored man in out of them boxes; there's a hole gets in the bottom of the boxes some way and lets out our votes." Similar laws were enacted in Tennessee and Virginia, where a representative at their constitutional convention admitted that "the great underlying principle" of the Democratic Party was "the elimination of the negro from the politics of this state."

The goal, according to another delegate, was "to discriminate to the very extremity of permissible action under the limitations of the Federal Constitution, with a view to the elimination of every negro voter who can be gotten rid of, legally, without materially impairing the numerical strength of the white electorate."

Take a moment to think about the significance of this: As is the case today, even in the era following Reconstruction—even in the capital of the Confederacy—voter suppression was implemented surgically, enacted not with explicit bans on voting by African Americans that would have violated the Fifteenth Amendment but with laws that took advantage of its ambiguities, the same ambiguities Republicans like Samuel Shellabarger and Henry Wilson had warned about when it was being debated on the floor of Congress.

And in 1890, Mississippi wrote the playbook for how to block African Americans from voting almost entirely. Through a "dizzying array of poll taxes, literacy tests, understanding clauses, newfangled voter registration rules," as Carol Anderson writes in *One Person, No Vote,* Mississippi managed to rebuild a democracy not much different from the one it had before the Civil War—a democracy in which registrars could force Black

Americans to correctly answer unanswerable questions like "How many bubbles are there in a bar of soap?" before allowing them to vote while asking their white counterparts no such questions. (These were called literacy tests, even though these kinds of interrogations didn't, of course, only test literacy, which itself would have been discriminatory, since so many Black Americans had been banned from learning how to read during slavery.)

As Anderson explains, all these policies, like the voter suppression laws of today, were "dressed up in the genteel garb of bringing integrity to the voting booth," even though they were designed to be racially discriminatory. "This feigned legal innocence," she writes, "was legislative evil genius."

The numbers spoke for themselves: After the Mississippi plan was implemented, of the 147,000 Black Americans who should have been eligible to vote in the state, only 9,000 were registered. In Louisiana, where similar policies had been enacted, the numbers were even starker, with under 1 percent of eligible Black voters registered.

The same held true across the former Confederacy, including in South Carolina, where suddenly, elected officials like Robert Brown Elliott, the congressman who had spoken so eloquently in favor of the Enforcement Acts, no longer stood a chance at winning elections. And the Black power that had been built in the state over the prior decade was vanquished. Indeed, across the South, with only a few exceptions, Black Americans were shut out of elected office for close to one hundred years—until the Voting Rights Act of 1965 was signed into law.

For this reason, as the turn of the nineteenth century approached, the hope that had animated abolitionists like William Lloyd Garrison and Frederick Douglass at the American Anti-Slavery Society, and the belief that the Fifteenth Amendment would bring about equality under the law, felt like a distant memory. And over the decades that followed, with the proliferation of segregation and the rebirth of the Ku Klux Klan, the multiracial democracy that had been promised at the dawn of Reconstruction—and had had a moment in the sun in the diverse legislatures of states like South Carolina—once again grew further and further out of reach, erased from the history books as though it had never even happened.

But it did happen. And that matters. It matters that there was a time in American history when Black Americans were represented in governments across the nation—and used that power to make a difference for their communities. It matters because of the schools they funded, because of the reforms they implemented, and because of the legacy they left behind, a legacy whispered about by future generations of Black Americans, who were told by their elders that people who looked like them had once stood in the halls of power; and that they, too, could one day occupy the highest offices in the land.

And it matters that this period of American history when anything felt possible was extinguished—not by any one bad actor but by the failure of an entire nation to follow through on its promise to build a system of government where all our voices would be heard and all our votes would be counted. It matters because it's a reminder that our democracy is precious and that its condition is precarious—perfected one decade, poisoned the next, if you're not paying attention.

It's easy, more than a century after Reconstruction, to see all this as ancient history—and as the first African American attorney general of the United States, you won't find me denying that our democracy has made progress that was once unimaginable; to do so would dishonor the memory, sacrifice, and courage of those who came before me and made my success possible.

But I am also a Black man in America, whose grandmother was born in 1870, so the recency of all this, the trauma passed down through the generations, lives inside me, too. Indeed, it lives in the psyches and hearts of all Black Americans.

And that matters as well. Because the only way we're going to save our democracy is if we recognize its fragility—and if we remember how quickly the gains we have made can be taken from us before our very eyes.

3

RESISTANCE AND REALPOLITIK

How Women Won the Vote

At the end of the nineteenth century, decades after organizing the convention at Seneca Falls, Susan B. Anthony, Matilda Joslyn Gage, and Elizabeth Cady Stanton set out to write a history of women's suffrage—but before they put pen to paper, they came down with a punishing case of writer's block.

"We stood appalled before the mass of material, growing higher and higher with every mail," they wrote, "and the thought of all the reading involved made us feel as if our life's work lay before us."

Same.

As Anthony, Gage, and Stanton understood, the story of women's rights in America cannot fit into one volume, let alone one chapter. It spans centuries, with ups and downs, steps forward and back. Which is to say: There was no way for me to write about the women's suffrage movement comprehensively in this book—because you can't fit hundreds of years of American history into a few thousand words.

But in thinking about what to include, I decided to focus on the tactics that led to progress: tax boycotts and hunger strikes, backstabbing and movement building. Because the purpose of this book isn't to teach you about the past. It's to give you a sense of what it will take to change minds, and laws, in the present—and build a more democratic future.

The story of women voting in the United States may very well have started with a typo—or whatever typos were called before the invention of the typewriter.

The year was 1776. It was summer. And the delegates to New Jersey's constitutional convention didn't have time to be deliberative. They had a Revolutionary War to fight. So they drafted the document in a matter of days—and, for the most part, they did what they set out to do: establish a government of, by, and for the men of their state.

The governor, they wrote, would be a "he," as would assembly members, county sheriffs, and coroners. But in Section IV, New Jersey's constitution made clear in no uncertain terms "that all inhabitants of this Colony, of full age," who met property and residency requirements, "*they* . . . shall be entitled to vote."

Not "he."

They.

This meant that whether intentionally or not, women had been granted the right to vote in New Jersey. And for decades, they exercised it. In fact, historians have found the names of 163 women from the state who showed up to the polls to make their voices heard—often arriving in groups for protection. And eventually, in 1797, New Jersey embraced its unisex electorate, replacing the word "they" in the Constitution with "he or she." There were African Americans who voted in New Jersey, too, recognizing that they represented a subset of "all inhabitants."

In the first decades of our country's history, the Garden State was an example of what a more inclusive democracy could look like—one suffragists would cite as proof that women could play a role in government. But the legacy of women casting ballots in America actually goes back even further. As Sally Roesch Wagner details in *The Women's Suffrage Movement*, her invaluable tome of firsthand accounts, Native American women long played a role in deciding how their governments were run. And in the colony of Massachusetts, women had been voting since the 1650s.

After the signing of the Declaration of Independence, however, America began restricting suffrage to men, based on the concern that if women had access to the ballot, they wouldn't be subservient—or, as one legislator from New York put it, "If we give women the vote, our wives will soon be absorbed in caucuses instead of in housekeeping."

In 1777, New York consecrated that sentiment into law, passing a bill that banned women from voting. A few years later, Massachusetts and New Hampshire followed suit. Before long, women were shut out of our democracy altogether.

In fact, women weren't forced to only be nonvoters. In some ways, they were treated as noncitizens. (And most Black women *were* noncitizens.) What did this look like? If a woman was raped by her husband, she generally had no way to file for divorce, let alone bring criminal charges against him. If she was beaten, she would be told she deserved it. If she somehow managed to bring her case to a court, she would be forced to make her argument to a jury full of men, since women weren't allowed to serve. "In the eyes of the law," Elizabeth Cady Stanton would later write, women were "civilly dead."

But they refused to be silent. As Abigail Adams wrote in a letter to her husband, "We will not hold ourselves bound to obey laws in which we have no voice or representation." And in that spirit, women across the country spent the first decades of American history speaking out and standing up for the causes they were passionate about, despite the risks they faced by doing so.

In fact, even though they didn't have the vote, women became leaders in the fight against slavery, founding more than 130 female anti-slavery societies in the 1830s alone. This movement included everyone from Sojourner Truth, who had escaped from the man who enslaved her with her infant daughter in tow—and sued him for custody of her older child, becoming one of the first Black women in the history of the United States to win a court case against a white man—to Sarah and Angelina Grimké, the daughters of slave owners, who ran off the South Carolina plantation on which they were raised to tell stories of the horrors they had seen their parents perpetrate.

In 1838, Angelina Grimké became the first woman in America to speak before a legislative body, bringing twenty thousand anti-slavery petitions along with her to the Massachusetts capitol—and blowing the roof off the place. In fact, the defenders of slavery in the legislature said they were worried she would bring down the whole building. Which is why, instead of letting her speak again the following day as planned, they proposed forming "a committee to be appointed to examine the foundation of the State House of Massachusetts, to see whether it will bear another lecture from Miss Grimké."

Bam!

With her speech, Grimké not only made a persuasive case against slavery but proved that women belonged in the halls of power, even if they didn't have the right to vote or serve in elected office.

Abolitionism is also what led to the political awakenings of Lucretia Mott and Elizabeth Cady Stanton, who met in 1840 at the World Anti-Slavery Convention in London, where neither was allowed on the floor due to their gender. This was one of the experiences that inspired them to organize the first convention for women's rights. It would be in their hometown of Seneca Falls, New York, they decided, and they would invite as many people as they could.

That process started with an advertisement in the *Seneca County Courier*, inviting readers to "a Convention to discuss the social, civil, and religious condition and rights of women," which was also published in *The North Star*, the paper started by Frederick Douglass, who ended up being one of three hundred attendees.

At the end of the convention, after days of discussions, the organizers drafted a Declaration of Sentiments, based on the Declaration of Independence, laying out the grievances they faced and the forms of justice they demanded. It began with familiar words—"We hold these truths to be self-evident; that all men . . ."—but went on to include two new ones that were revolutionary: ". . . *and women* are created equal."

The first draft of the document didn't mention voting—but when Elizabeth Cady Stanton went home after the first night of the convention, she felt she had no choice but to include it. "The history of mankind is a history of repeated injuries and usurpations on the part of man toward woman," she wrote. "Having deprived her of this first right of a citizen, the elective franchise, thereby leaving her without representation in the halls of legislation, he has oppressed her on all sides."

Many of the conference attendees were hesitant to advocate for the vote directly, but after a speech from Frederick Douglass standing with Stanton, one hundred attendees ended up signing her draft, which concluded with a rousing call to action: Seneca Falls, the signatories promised, would be the first of many conventions, which would continue to convene until the "final triumph of the Right and the True."

They called their shot.

In 1850, the first-ever national Woman's Rights Convention took place in Worcester, Massachusetts, bringing together a much bigger crowd—one that, unlike Seneca Falls, included women of color. Sojourner Truth delivered remarks, calling on the audience not to ignore the plight of "the two million slave women at the South, the most grossly wronged and foully outraged of all women.

"In every effort for an improvement in our civilization," she continued, "we will bear in our heart of hearts the memory of the trampled womanhood of the plantation, and omit no effort to raise it to a share in the rights we claim for ourselves."

Coming out of the convention, women's rights began to enter mainstream discourse across the country—which also led to backlash. "Woman would have done much more for the advancement of the sex by staying home tending to their babies, instructing their children, and assisting their husbands," read an editorial in the *National Intelligencer*. When a petition signed by 5,931 men and women was sent to the New York state legislature advocating for the "just and equal rights of women," the elected officials responded: "They desire to unsex every female in the land, and to set the whole community ablaze with unhallowed fire." It was their "duty," they said, "to our constituents and to God," to keep women out of American democracy. In California, legislators objected to suffrage on the basis that letting women vote would constitute an attack on "the integrity of the family" that "denies and repudiates the obligations of motherhood."

And for a while, these arguments won out. In the decade following the first National Convention, women made massive strides organizing their movement, but as the country's attention turned to the Civil War, their momentum came to a halt. And even after the war, when suffragists tried to bring attention to their lack of rights, they were met with resistance. "One question at a time," said Wendell Phillips, one of America's most prominent abolitionists. "This hour belongs to the negro."

Many of the white women leading the suffrage movement, meanwhile, became resentful of the progress African Americans had begun to make. As Susan B. Anthony said to Frederick Douglass in a closed-door meeting, "I will cut off this right arm of mine before I will ever work or demand the ballot for the negro and not the woman." In this way, the Civil War marked a turning point for the women's suffrage movement. Many of its founders, who had been abolitionists, ended up building a movement that in some ways and at some times embraced white supremacy.

This is the context in which Frances Ellen Watkins Harper stood up at the National Woman's Rights Convention of 1866, the first after the Civil War, and declared: "You white women speak here of rights. I speak of wrongs." Harper, who, like Reconstruction-era lawmaker Robert Smalls in Pennsylvania, had been known at the time for refusing to give up her seat in a trolley car—close to a century before Rosa Parks did the same on a bus in Montgomery, Alabama—was tired of being told Black women were impeding the progress of white women. "We are all bound up together in one great bundle of humanity, and society cannot trample on the weakest and feeblest of its members without receiving the curse in its own soul," she said, before closing with a dagger: "I tell you that if there is any class of people who need to be lifted out of their airy nothings and selfishness, it is the white women of America."

The divide between the white women and women of color at the forefront of this movement only became more pronounced in the following years—as the ratification of the Fourteenth and Fifteenth Amendments radicalized the white suffragists even further in the direction of racism. Elizabeth Cady Stanton, for instance, criticized the expansion of the franchise to Black Americans by deploying a litany of slurs. "Think of Patrick and Sambo and Hans and Yung Tung," she said, referring to well-known racist caricatures of the era, "who cannot read the Declaration of Independence or Webster's spelling book, making laws for Lucretia Mott," the famous white activist. Suffragist Anna Howard Shaw, meanwhile, complained that the men who passed the Fifteenth Amendment had "made former slaves the political masters of their former mistresses."

Stanton became so infuriated about the Fifteenth Amendment that she teamed up with Anthony to found an organization, the National Woman Suffrage Association (NWSA), whose goal was, in part, to pass a new amendment barring Americans who hadn't received an education from voting—a stance cruel on its own terms, but especially so when you remember that during slavery, and in some cases after emancipation, African Americans could have been killed for so much as trying to learn how to read.

Lucy Stone, a prominent feminist who had been part of the movement since Seneca Falls, objected to this approach. To her, it didn't make sense for the women's suffrage movement to antagonize the abolitionists who shared the goal of bringing American democracy closer to realizing its promise. So she broke off from the others and started the American Woman

Suffrage Association (AWSA), an organization she hoped would be more "widely representative."

Together, the NWSA and AWSA were committed to expanding the franchise to women—though they took different approaches: Whereas the NWSA advocated for a federal women's suffrage amendment, the AWSA was dedicated to expanding the franchise state by state. But for all their differences, the two organizations shared a willingness to take direct action to achieve their goals.

One of the most prominent ways suffragists fought for the right to vote was, well, by voting, even before doing so was legal. In the 1860s, women stormed the polls across the country, from Topeka, Kansas, to Vineland, New Jersey, and in the 1870s, they picked up the pace. In South Carolina, Charlotte Rollin, who helped lead the state's AWSA chapter, brought a group of African American women to the polls to vote—declaring that she saw "suffrage not as a favor, not as a privilege, but as a right based on the grounds that we are human beings." In Michigan, Sojourner Truth attempted to vote, too.

This was an effective form of resistance, because it demonstrated to the country that whether women could handle the responsibility of voting shouldn't be a question. After all, they were already doing it—and it's not like households were spontaneously combusting.

Meanwhile, across the country, women were embracing a second form of resistance—one Lucy Stone had pioneered in the 1850s, inspired by America's Founding Fathers: refusing to pay taxes. "It is the duty of women to resist taxation as long as she is not represented," Stone said. "It may involve the loss of friends as it surely will the loss of property. But let them all go; friends, house, garden spot, and all. The principle at issue requires the sacrifice. Resist, let the case be tried in the courts; be your own lawyers; base your case on the admitted self-evident truth, that taxation and representation are inseparable." In 1858, that is exactly what she did, writing to her town's tax collector: "Mr. Mandeville: Enclosed I return my tax bill, without paying it."

With Stone as an inspiration, in 1873, exactly a century after angry colonists dumped 342 chests of tea in Boston Harbor, women across America went on a tax strike—because, as suffragist Clemence Lozier put it, they were "suffering precisely the same wrong" as their ancestors: "taxation without representation."

An unlikely pair of sisters, Abby Smith, 76, and Julia Smith, 81, took up this call. Unlike Elizabeth Cady Stanton and Susan B. Anthony, they continued to be tried-and-true abolitionists after the Civil War, but now they were looking for a new injustice to fight—and when they inherited the most valuable land in Glastonbury, Connecticut, it became obvious what they should do.

Already the Smith sisters were the biggest taxpayers in town, but year after year, the government kept increasing their bill, even as appraisers refused to do the same to estates owned by men. Abby believed this was a double standard and argued that women were being "ruled over by the other half."

She was fed up, and so was her sister, so instead of paying the more expensive tax bill, they decided not to pay at all, even though that meant the town's officials could begin seizing their property. Soon, according to the Smiths, they were down to two cows (whom they named Taxey and Votey), but to them, it was worth it just to make the point. And their sacrifices didn't go unnoticed. *The Republican*, a local newspaper, wrote that "Abby Smith and her sister as truly stand for the American principle as did the citizens who ripped open the tea chests in Boston Harbor, or the farmers who leveled their muskets at Concord."

Within a year, groups of women across the country, from New York to California, joined the Smiths in declining to pay taxes. Susan A. King, one of the wealthiest women in America, was among them—and she convinced her rich friends to come together and refuse to pay taxes on what today would be equivalent to hundreds of millions of dollars. It was a loud statement, with serious financial implications, one those in power could not ignore.

These protests shook the nation, but the fight for suffrage continued to progress slowly—at least in terms of legislation. Sure, women had won the right to vote in territories like Wyoming and Utah, but in the 1870s, fourteen states rejected efforts to expand the franchise. As the authors of *History of Woman Suffrage* wrote, twenty-five years after Seneca Falls, they had been defeated "at the polls, in the courts, in the national celebration, and in securing a plank in the platforms of the Republican and Democratic Parties."

And today, as we once again watch attempt after attempt to defend the franchise fail in our country, it's worth thinking about how tempting it must have been for many of the women at the forefront of this movement a century ago to become hopeless. After all, in most states, women not only still couldn't vote but lacked many other basic rights as well.

But the suffragists knew, as we should, that in America, the way you make progress is not unlike the way Ernest Hemingway described the process of going bankrupt: "Gradually, then suddenly." And so they persisted, holding on to their faith that if they kept pushing, the dam would break.

In that spirit, a quarter century after Seneca Falls, the movement's leaders invited its supporters to gather at the Apollo Hall in Williamsburg with an invitation full of resiliency: "Let our twenty-fifth anniversary be one of power," it read. "Our reform is everywhere advancing, let us redouble our energies and our courage."

Redoubling took different forms for different women. For some, it meant staying the course—continuing to fight for women's suffrage state by state. For others, it meant starting the Woman's Christian Temperance Union, deploying female political power toward the cause of prohibition. For more radical suffragists, like Matilda Joslyn Gage, it meant calling for upheaval, recognizing that the women of 1876 had "greater cause for discontent, rebellion, and revolution than the men of 1776" because "our masters, instead of dwelling in a foreign land, are our husbands, our fathers, our brothers, and our sons."

Belva Lockwood, the first woman to practice law before the Supreme Court, agreed. A lawyer who had distinguished herself by winning hard case after hard case—helping women divorce abusive husbands, advocating for equal pay, and legitimizing, in the eyes of the law, marriages between enslaved Americans—Lockwood believed "the only way for women to get their rights is to take them." What did that mean? "If necessary," she said, "let there be a domestic insurrection. Let young women refuse to marry, and married women refuse to sew on buttons, cook, and rock the cradle until their liege-lords acknowledge the rights they are entitled to." Doing her part, Lockwood ran for president.

That same revolutionary energy was present in New York Harbor, where women gathered on October 28, 1886, to protest the completion of the Statue of Liberty, a landmark they said "points afresh to the cruelty of woman's present position, since it is proposed to represent Freedom as a majestic female form in a state where not one woman is free."

Months later, women put enough pressure on Congress that a women's suffrage amendment was brought to the floor for the first time. Introduced by Senator Henry Blair of New Hampshire, it was voted down, with close to twice as many nays as yeas, but nonetheless, there was a feeling among the movement's leaders that change was on the way.

As Frederick Douglass predicted at the first International Council of Women in 1888, which brought together suffrage activists from around the world: "When a great truth once gets abroad in the world, no power on earth can imprison it, or prescribe its limits, or suppress it. It is bound to go on till it becomes the thought of the world. Such a truth is woman's right to equal liberty with man."

He was right—but the women leading the movement also knew that ideas don't win out on their own. You have to persuade people to believe in them.

The NWSA and AWSA soon merged, becoming the National American Woman Suffrage Association (NAWSA), and the new organization began holding events around the country, fighting for both state-by-state expansions to suffrage and a federal amendment guaranteeing the right—making their case to anyone who would listen to them. Unfortunately, that included Southern Democrats, who the white suffragists believed could be won over not by appealing to their sense of justice but by tapping into their bigotry.

The argument, which was first laid out by Henry Blackwell, Lucy Stone's husband, centered around the idea that expanding the franchise to white women was the best way to dilute the influence of Black voters who had been enfranchised by the Fifteenth Amendment. It was an attempt to link the fight for suffrage to efforts across the South by former supporters of the Confederacy aimed at reversing the gains African Americans had made in political power in the years following the Civil War. There were more white women than Black Americans, Blackwell wrote in a letter to Southern legislators, so he suggested giving those women the vote to ensure that "the political supremacy of your white race will remain unchanged."

In 1893, this sentiment became an official NAWSA resolution, which read:

> We call attention to the significant facts that in every State there are more women who can read and write than the whole number of illiterate male voters; more white women who can read and write than all negro voters; more white women who can read and write than all foreign voters; so that the enfranchisement of such women would settle the vexed question of rule by illiteracy, whether of home-grown or foreign-born production.

As part of this pivot to appeal to men who remained bitter about the outcome of the Civil War, NAWSA decided to move its convention to the Jim Crow South, disinviting Frederick Douglass and abandoning its abolitionist roots once and for all. The days of the Seneca Falls Convention organizers offering their homes as stops on the Underground Railroad felt like ancient history. Now many of those same women had decided the most expedient route to the vote ran through racism—and so, they embraced it.

Thankfully, new organizations stepped up to serve as a voice for Black women. Matilda Joslyn Gage started the Woman's National Liberal Union, an organization made up of working-class activists. And African American leaders in the suffrage movement, including Harriet Tubman, Ida B. Wells, and Mary Church Terrell, teamed up to launch the National Association of Colored Women's Clubs.

In this way, the suffrage movement became a multifront war, with white and Black women making different arguments for enfranchisement. And in the years that followed, their cause actually began to see real progress, as Colorado and Idaho became the first states to expand access to the ballot. Reflecting on this sea change on her eightieth birthday, Elizabeth Cady Stanton celebrated the fact that "women need no longer knit or weave, make butter or cheese," but called on the next generation of leaders to pick up where she was leaving off.

Carrie Chapman Catt, who would be the next head of NAWSA, was in the audience that day—and she was committed to turning what was still, in many ways, a fledgling organization into a juggernaut. She started raising money, used it to open offices in every state, and funded grassroots campaigns powered by armies of volunteers around the country. And while another attempt at a women's suffrage amendment failed in Congress in 1900, it did not stall the movement's momentum.

At the turn of the century, women had earned the right to vote across the West Coast, with Washington State joining Utah, Wyoming, Colorado, and Idaho in expanding access to the ballot. Next came California, where Maria de Lopez became the first woman to lead a bilingual campaign for the vote—distributing pamphlets and delivering speeches in Spanish, helping the proposition to enfranchise women pass with just over 50 percent of the vote. The following year, Arizona, Kansas, and Oregon joined the converted. And on the heels of these victories, in 1913, half a century before the March on

Washington, women set out to organize the biggest suffrage parade in the history of the United States. And they decided to host it in the nation's capital.

The woman in charge was Alice Paul, who, at twenty-eight years old, had recently returned from a stint working with suffragists in England, where she had been imprisoned for her activism three times. Her years abroad had convinced Paul there was no better way to bring about change than protest—so she decided to organize one that brought suffragists from across the country to Washington, D.C.

It was set to take place Monday, March 3, the day before Woodrow Wilson would be inaugurated as president of the United States. But the police were not down with letting that happen. "It's totally unsuitable for women to be marching down Pennsylvania Avenue," they wrote, declining Paul's application for a permit. But if Paul learned anything in England, it was that when you're fighting for your rights, you don't take no for an answer. So in the hours leading up to March 3, thousands of women descended on the nation's capital, even as they knew they would be met with resistance.

The attendees included Black suffragists, from Ida B. Wells to Mary Church Terrell, many of whom had been a part of Delta Sigma Theta, a sorority one of its members, Bertha Pitts Campbell, described as being "more oriented to service than to socialize." The problem was that a number of the white suffragists who had organized the event didn't want women of color anywhere near the parade. "The participation of negroes," Alice Paul had anticipated, "would have a most disastrous effect," because, she feared, their presence would make it harder to convince President Wilson, whose racism was no secret, to support a suffrage amendment.

In the end, Paul and the rest of the organizers decided to segregate the parade, with white women in the front and Black women bringing up the rear, separated by the Quaker men marching in the middle. This was not a concession that Ida B. Wells was willing to make—fearing that if she didn't "take a stand now in this great democratic parade," the cause of "colored women" would be lost. When the parade began, Wells appeared to be missing entirely.

The rest of the women, meanwhile, endured vitriol—and violence. As Campbell later recalled, describing the crowd of more than two hundred thousand spectators, "Some cheered, however, many jeered and tried to disrupt the marchers by throwing things, spitting on, beating and slapping the women, and trying to pull the women off the floats." That night, more than two hundred women who attended had to go to the hospital with injuries.

One of the spectators, however, didn't have violent intentions. Instead, she arrived at the protest planning to wait for precisely the right moment to join the marchers. And when the Illinois delegation of white women was approaching her spot in the crowd, that's exactly what she did, teaming up with two of her fellow suffragists to hold her state's banner above their heads.

That woman was—you guessed it—Ida B. Wells.

The next day, a photo of Wells wearing a big hat and a wide smile—not in the back of the crowd, but at the very front—ended up in the *Chicago Tribune*, a message to future generations that no matter what story the white suffragists from Seneca Falls tried to tell, there is no denying that Black women, women like Wells, Terrell, and Campbell, played as critical a role in shaping this movement as anyone else.

By all accounts, the parade was a success—but for Alice Paul, it was only the beginning. Over the next few years, starting with her first picket on January 10, 1917, she practically made the White House gate her residence, confronting Woodrow Wilson with a banner that read: MR. PRESIDENT, WHAT WILL YOU DO FOR WOMAN SUFFRAGE?

For a while, Wilson dodged the question, providing suffragists with pablum about the importance of equality without backing any of it up with action. So they kept protesting. And when the United States entered World War I in April 1917, suffragists protested that, too, because they didn't think America had any standing to fight for democracy abroad while denying women the right to vote at home. This eventually led to the Night of Terror on November 10, during which thirty-three suffragists, including Paul, were arrested.

In prison, Paul and her fellow organizers went on a hunger strike, refusing to eat even when they were punished with solitary confinement. "They tied us down with bonds around our legs, chests, and necks," Paul later recalled, "then the doctors and wardens held us down and forced a tube five or six feet long, about the size of a finger, through the nostrils to the stomach." The pain was unimaginable, but Paul endured it, even though she "never went through the experience without weeping," and in the end, her resilience was rewarded. About two weeks after they were arrested, the women were released—and their act of heroism led to support for suffrage around the country, including that of an unlikely ally.

On January 9, 1918, almost a year to the day after Paul first started picketing the White House, President Wilson announced his support for a suffrage amendment—which, for the first time, looked like it had a chance of being ratified.

There were a few reasons why that was the case. For one, women had begun to vote in states across the country, including in Montana, where Jeannette Rankin became the first woman to hold federal office. Congress had also recently ratified several amendments—including the eighteenth, which implemented a federal ban on drinking alcohol—weakening the salience of the arguments surrounding states' rights that had long been used to block a women's suffrage amendment. And organizations representing tens of millions of Americans had come out and publicly endorsed the cause of enfranchising women.

With these tailwinds at their backs, women's suffrage advocates from around the country came together to form a lobbying arm called the Congressional Committee, with the sole purpose of bringing the amendment over the finish line. Starting in 1916, the organization was led by Maud Wood Park, a close friend of Carrie Chapman Catt, who made it her mission to learn everything about the legislative branch—about how bills become laws and nays become yeas. Park would sit in the galleries of Congress for hours, studying every member she had to persuade and writing up a guidebook for how to lobby representatives.

Before long, her tactics paid off when on May 21, 1919, three months after being introduced, the amendment passed the House of Representatives by a vote of 304–90, a vote that easily could have been 302–90 but for the fact that Park's pressure had convinced one member of Congress to take a break from organizing his wife's funeral to make his voice heard and another had delayed resetting his broken shoulder until the final vote was tallied, even though the suffragists ended up with 42 votes to spare.

A couple of weeks later, the amendment was brought to the floor of the Senate, where, as has happened with so many of the voting reforms we have tried to pass in recent years, it was met with a filibuster. "When victory was within our grasp, I completely lost the self-control with which I had sat through previous debates," Park later conceded, confessing that she let out "murmurs of angry impatience" during lectures on why women's suffrage should not become the law of the land. Fortunately, the filibuster was far easier to overcome back then (for reasons I'll get into later), and on June 4, 1919, when the amendment came to a vote, it passed 56–25.

But unlike with laws, you cannot ratify an amendment solely with support from both houses of Congress and the president. You also need approval from more than three out of every four states in the union. The first few came easily, with Wisconsin, Illinois, and Michigan signing off in a matter of days. Before long, thirty-five states had declared their approval. This meant the suffragists only needed to convince one more—but they were running out of options.

Only one remained: Tennessee, the final frontier.

"Nearly every day of the Tennessee ratification campaign there was a scenario for a motion picture if anyone had had time to write it," reflected suffragist Harriet Taylor Upton.

She was right: The story of the battle for women's suffrage in the Volunteer State is nothing short of captivating, and if you want to learn about all the characters involved—about the mother who said she would "rather see my daughter in a coffin than at the polls," the father who hopped off the back of a train headed to visit his sick baby so he could vote in favor of the amendment, and everyone in between—you should read *The Woman's Hour* by Elaine Weiss. But for the purposes of this book, with everything we are living through today, what is important to know is that in Nashville, the suffragists deployed every tactic, pulled every lever, and took nothing for granted. As Upton recalled, "No group of women ever worked harder than did the Tennessee women.

"They feared nothing," she wrote, "they left no stone unturned, they were resourceful beyond anything I have ever known." They knocked on doors. They organized marches. They went from legislator to legislator, making their case, even as they knew the outcome was uncertain. Sure, it had passed the state senate 25–4, but in preliminary vote after preliminary vote in the House, the tally was 48–48, a result that would leave the future of the amendment in flux, as likely to die as it was to live. But on the morning of August 18, 1920, the suffragists in Tennessee woke up knowing they had devoted everything to this fight.

Harry Burn, on the other hand, emerged from his bed with less certainty than ever. The twenty-four-year-old legislator had indicated that he would vote against the amendment, but his mother had written him a note telling him to "be a good boy" and "vote for suffrage," and Burns had been raised to always listen to his mother. As he sat on the floor of the House, the letter tucked in his jacket pocket, he had no idea what to do.

He had sat through days of speeches from opponents of the amendment, like Speaker Seth Walker, who had declared, "We want this to remain a white man's country." And Burn knew that most of his constituents didn't support the amendment. That was why he had pinned a red rose, the symbol of its opponents, to his lapel.

But when it came time to vote, Burn let out one word, under his breath: "Aye."

For a minute, those in the gallery didn't realize what had taken place; they had written Burn off as a nay and weren't sure they'd heard him correctly. But as Elaine Weiss describes, by the time the clerk began calling out representatives whose last names started with the letter *C*, "a low murmur bubbled up in the galleries and swelled to fill the chamber." It was pandemonium. Suffragists in the crowd cheered so loudly that the vote had to be suspended for minutes, because no one would be able to hear it otherwise. And when the final count was in and the amendment was ratified by a vote of 49–47, the chamber filled with tears and cheers, dancing and screaming, the floor bouncing and the walls shaking in much the same way they must have in Massachusetts close to a century earlier when Angelina Grimké became the first woman to address a state legislature and damn near brought down the house.

The final text of the amendment was only two sentences, but all thirty-nine words in them had been earned with the blood and sweat of thousands of women from towns across the country, who had worked together—diligently, strategically, relentlessly—to bring about the kind of change that had once seemed impossible. It read:

> The right of citizens of the United States to vote shall not be denied or abridged by the United States or by any State on account of sex. Congress shall have power to enforce this article by appropriate legislation.

As news of the amendment's ratification reached the rest of the country, Carrie Chapman Catt wrote a letter to the women who had made it possible, a letter no less resonant today than it was when it was written. "The vote is the emblem of your equality, women of America, the guarantee of your liberty," she wrote, continuing:

> That vote of yours has cost millions of dollars and the lives of thousands of women. Women have suffered agony of soul which you can never comprehend, that you and your daughters might inherit political freedom. That vote has

> been costly. Prize it! The vote is a power, a weapon of offense and defense, a prayer. Use it intelligently, conscientiously, prayerfully. Progress is calling to you to make no pause. Act!

Her letter spoke of a dream fulfilled—and in so many ways, for so many people, that is what the Nineteenth Amendment had been. In the years that followed its ratification, millions of women registered to vote, shaping the policies that governed the nation. But as white women across the country marched forward, women of color were left behind—by the same Jim Crow laws, the same poll taxes and literacy tests, that had blocked Black men from accessing the ballot after Reconstruction. This wasn't by accident—it was by design, the product of a suffrage movement led by white women, who chose the expediency of supremacy over the inclusivity of justice.

In this way, the ratification of the Nineteenth Amendment was the end not of the movement for women's suffrage but of the movement for white women's suffrage. It was the conclusion of one chapter and the beginning of another—a chapter in which Black men and women would work hand in hand, step by step, day by day, at lunch counters in Woolworth's and on freedom rides in Anniston, from a church in Birmingham to a bridge in Selma, to lead a revolution that would forever change America, a revolution for civil rights, built on the shoulders of trailblazers like Frances Harper and Ida B. Wells, who, despite all the vitriol they endured, including from their fellow women, never wavered in their belief that they deserved a voice in our democracy.

4

REVOLUTION

*How Black Americans Won the Vote—
and Made America a Democracy*

There is no such thing as a happy day at Arlington National Cemetery.

But in 2013, on a Wednesday in June, walking six feet above the bodies of those who had made the ultimate sacrifice for our nation—soldiers who had served every commander in chief from Lincoln through Obama; freed Black men who had worn the uniform of a country that had kept them in captivity; wives and husbands, daughters and sons of the fallen—I found myself feeling hopeful.

I was in Arlington, as I would be in Selma two years later, to mark a significant anniversary. Half a century earlier, Medgar Evers, a patriot who returned from the beaches of Normandy to lead the battle for civil rights in Mississippi, had been assassinated—and we had come together at the site of his burial to celebrate all the ways the seeds planted by his generation had flowered, even after the storms they had weathered.

But while I felt the progress we had made, as I stood atop the rolling hills of Arlington, that hallowed ground where four hundred thousand Americans with four hundred thousand unique stories are buried under four hundred thousand identical white marble headstones, I didn't want to think about how far our country had come or where we were headed next. I wanted to live in the past, to sit with it, to remember it—not as a parable reinforcing the mythos of a country marching perpetually, inevitably, unstoppably toward perfection, but as a kaleidoscope of victories and defeats, steps forward and backward, progress won and then snatched away.

Unlike our founding, unlike Reconstruction, unlike the women's suffrage movement, I didn't study the civil rights movement in a history book. I watched it unfold on the screen of my family's basement television in Queens, New York. So at Arlington National Cemetery, I wanted to remember what it actually felt like to live through that June day in 1963 when, before tragedy struck, the embers of the civil rights movement—the freedom rides and freedom songs, the sit-ins and speeches that had kept the candle of hope burning—exploded into an inferno.

That is the story I will tell in this chapter. It won't be a linear one, and I won't spend much time on the hopeful ending that I cover in the introduction, when history and fate met at a single time in a single place in Selma, Alabama. I will focus, instead, on what happened beforehand, on the tragedies that made the triumph of the Voting Rights Act possible.

I don't know what emotions Medgar Evers felt in the moments before he was shot—when, just after midnight, he parked his car in the driveway, pulled a carton of JIM CROW MUST GO T-shirts out of his trunk, and started walking toward the front door of the home in which his wife and children were waiting up for him—but I would like to think he was proud. Because if he had turned on the news earlier that day, he would have seen that after the years he had spent speaking out for justice, the South was finally being forced to listen.

That morning, two African American students—James Hood, whose hat I remember thinking was a curious bit of style, and Vivian Malone, whose beauty I remember thinking was, well, I don't think I had the words for it as a twelve-year-old—arrived at the University of Alabama with hope in their hearts and determination in their minds. They weren't there to make a statement. They were there to receive the education they deserved. But in Tuscaloosa, in 1963, if you were Black, that was the same thing.

That's because, even though close to a decade had passed since the Supreme Court ruled that separate institutions were inherently unequal in *Brown v. Board of Education,* the University of Alabama still hadn't welcomed a single Black student into its halls. And the state had no intention of integrating its schools anytime soon. In fact, when James and Vivian showed up, accompanied by Nicholas Katzenbach, the deputy attorney general of the United States, they were blocked from accessing the door by Governor George Wallace himself.

If Medgar, like me, had watched this take place on his television, I imagine he wouldn't have been surprised by any of it. He had met the same hostility as James and Vivian when he tried to integrate the University of Mississippi School of Law—whose administrators told him, a decorated World War II veteran, that even though he had risked his life defending our democracy overseas, he did not have the right to learn about the laws that governed it when he came back home.

But what might have surprised Medgar was what happened next—when President John F. Kennedy federalized the Alabama National Guard and left Governor Wallace with no choice but to step aside and clear the path for the students to walk through the front door and make history.

Even as a twelve-year-old in the North, for whom the segregation of the South had always seemed like it was taking place a world away, watching James and Vivian break this barrier unleashed emotions I didn't know I had: Anger about all who had been denied this opportunity. Relief that the sacrifices of the civil rights movement were beginning to pay off. Fear about what kind of retribution lay ahead. And if I was feeling all that, I cannot even conceive of the variegated emotional responses being triggered by the limbic system of Medgar Evers, a man without whom this progress might have remained but a dream.

It was an emotional day for President Kennedy, too, who decided he should speak to the country—celebrating the courage of the students at the University of Alabama and committing the federal government to bringing an end to segregation. There was just one problem: He didn't have a speech. And his chief speechwriter, Ted Sorensen, didn't have time to finish drafting one. So with millions of Americans hanging on his every word, President Kennedy delivered a national address full of improvisation, an address in which some lines had been prewritten and others had come straight from the heart.

"One hundred years of delay have passed since President Lincoln freed the slaves, yet their heirs, their grandsons, are not fully free," he said. "And this nation, for all its hopes and all its boasts, will not be fully free until all its citizens are free."

Schools, he said, ought to be integrated—just as restaurants and theaters and stores should be—laying out the policies that would, after his assassination, become the Civil Rights Act of 1964. But he didn't stop there, because he knew African Americans would only be treated as equal in their communities if they had a voice in electing the leaders in charge of them. So before concluding the speech, he laid out a vision that would later become the Voting Rights Act of 1965: "It ought to be possible," he said, "for American citizens of any color to register to vote in a free election without interference or fear of reprisal."

We don't know if Medgar Evers had a chance to watch President Kennedy's speech—but if he did, that line would have been especially meaningful to him. Because Medgar always believed that the right to vote was among the most important civil rights. And it was this right that had inspired him to join the fight for civil rights in the first place as a twenty-one-year-old. "We're interested in making this country better for people, for all of us, and we feel that only through voting," he explained, "are we going to be able to do this."

In 1946, hoping to block the reelection of Theodore Bilbo—a racist senator who believed Black Americans should be sent to Africa—Medgar and his brother, Charles, registered to vote at city hall in Decatur, Mississippi. But when they and other registered Black voters arrived at the polls on Election Day, they were confronted by white supremacists who threatened their lives. "You niggers are going to wind up getting yourselves and everyone around you killed," they were told, and knowing what that actually meant—knowing they could have ended up on the list of Black men from across the centuries who were murdered for daring to participate in democracy—Medgar and Charles, like so many African Americans in the South, went back home without casting their ballots.

So if you were Medgar Evers, and only two decades after that Election Day you watched the events in Tuscaloosa followed by the president of the United States promising to bring about universal suffrage, I bet you would have found some satisfaction in the fact that the protesting and picketing you did to make our democracy more inclusive had brought about change.

I certainly was moved, even though in New York, the vote had been secure for generations.

But unlike me, Medgar had lived in Mississippi his whole life, and as a result, he would have known that the president's words were just words, and it would take a whole lot more than that to bring democracy—real, legitimate, multiracial democracy—to the South.

After all, as Kennedy alluded to in his speech, President Lincoln had delivered the Emancipation Proclamation a full century earlier—and yet in states like Mississippi, the American apartheid formed after Reconstruction was as strong as ever, calcified and codified in the form of Jim Crow. And even with the Fourteenth and Fifteenth Amendments in place, the Supreme Court had refused to stop literacy tests and poll taxes from going into effect, ruling in the 1898 case *Williams v. Mississippi* that these laws "do not on their face discriminate between the races," even though their racially disparate impacts could not be denied.

And it wasn't only Mississippi.

In fact, as Ari Berman, author of the seminal *Give Us the Ballot,* writes in an article for *Mother Jones*: "By 1907 every Southern state had changed its constitution to disenfranchise Black voters." And despite what the Supreme Court had said about intent, these laws proved to be extremely effective at blocking African Americans from participating in our democracy. To quote Berman:

> The number of Black registered voters in Mississippi fell from 130,483 in 1876 to 1,264 by 1900; in Louisiana from roughly 130,000 in 1896 to 1,342 in 1904; in Alabama's Black Belt counties from 79,311 in 1900 to 1,081 in 1901. By the early 1900s, only 7 percent of Black residents

were registered to vote in seven Southern states, according to data compiled by the historian Morgan Kousser, and Black turnout fell from 61 percent of the voting-age population in 1880 to just 2 percent in 1912.

This is because, while the laws themselves may not have mentioned race, for the most part, they were only enforced on Black Americans—while whites were protected by grandfather clauses, which guaranteed the right to vote to anyone whose ancestors had been registered, regardless of whether they had passed a literacy test or paid a poll tax.

And as historian C. Vann Woodward, who wrote *The Strange Career of Jim Crow* in 1955, explained: "If the Negroes did learn to read, or acquire sufficient property, and remember to pay the poll tax and to keep the receipt on file, they could even then be tripped by the final hurdle devised for them—the white primary."

The "white primary" is exactly what it sounds like: Starting in 1896, in states like Texas, Democrats began explicitly barring African Americans from voting in their primaries, a practice the Supreme Court upheld in the 1935 case *Grovey v. Townsend* on the basis that political parties—which ran the primaries—were private institutions. This meant that even if an African American managed to register to vote, he'd only be able to do so when the general election came around, when he'd be forced to choose between candidates he had had no say in nominating.

This complex web of laws and policies established a democracy of, by, and for white people—and only white people—in the South. But the truth was, the laws weren't even the most important tool for maintaining white electoral hegemony. Because Jim Crow was never policed just by laws written out on paper. It was enforced with broken bones and crushed skulls, with rope wrapped around trees and knots tied around necks, with bodies displayed in town squares or made to disappear at the bottom of rivers.

Medgar understood this, which was why, even as he listened to the president of the United States talking about the need to expand access to the franchise, he would also have been aware—consciously, explicitly, relentlessly aware—that at any moment he could be murdered for the work he had done to expand the franchise in Mississippi. Not only because a Molotov cocktail had been thrown into his home earlier in the year; not only because a car had tried to run him over earlier in the week; not only because he and his wife, Myrlie, were so worried about an assassin barging into their house that they had their kids practice hiding in the bathtub; but also because Medgar had spent much of his adult life investigating the lynchings of Black men in Mississippi. And what that experience taught him was that if you were white, you could kill an African American man in broad daylight and face no consequences, even if there was no doubt that you had committed the crime or that the victim had done nothing to earn that fate.

That became clear to Medgar when he was thirty years old—and began looking into the case of a fourteen-year-old boy with a stutter who came down to the Mississippi Delta from Chicago during his summer break after seventh grade, only to return in a casket. The boy's name was Emmett Till. And the story of how he died changed Medgar, and America, forever.

Just days after Emmett's arrival in Mississippi in 1955, white supremacists tore him out of his bed in the middle of the night, mangled his body, ripped his eye out of its socket, tied a seventy-five-pound cotton gin fan to his back with barbed wire, shot him in the head, and threw him into the Tallahatchie River, where his body was left to rot for days, like human flotsam, all because

Emmett had allegedly flirted with a white woman at a grocery store, an accusation she later retracted.

In the weeks following Emmett's death, his mother, Mamie, was devastated, but she refused to be debilitated. "The world," she decided, should "see what they did to my boy." So she held an open-casket funeral, where photographers captured images of the fourteen-year-old's body that helped birth the civil rights movement. But even with the eyes of the country on Mississippi, Emmett's killers were eventually exonerated by a jury of twelve white men that deliberated for just sixty-seven minutes, including a soda break, before deciding to acquit. The verdict outraged Medgar, who had worked hard to identify witnesses for the case. And over the following years, he continued investigating the murders of Black men in Mississippi, including many who had been killed for no reason other than trying to exercise their right to vote.

This history was on Medgar's mind during that week in June 1963, which was why he delivered a speech in Jackson on the possibility of his own assassination. "Freedom has never been free," he declared. "I love my children and I love my wife with all my heart, and I would die, and die gladly, if that would make a better life for them."

Days later, Medgar was shot by a member of the Ku Klux Klan outside his own home—where Myrlie had been talking to their children, who were up past their bedtime, kept awake by the kind of pride that comes from watching the president of the United States deliver a speech made possible by the courage of your daddy.

"I opened the door," Myrlie remembered years later, "and there was Medgar at the steps, face down in blood." The children screamed, "Daddy, get up!" as their neighbors flooded the driveway, lifted Medgar into Myrlie's station wagon, and rushed him to the nearby University Hospital, where they were told he couldn't be treated on account of the color of his skin. But when the hospital realized that this Black man was Medgar Evers, they changed their minds, allowing him to break one last barrier in his final moments, becoming the first African American the hospital had ever treated.

"But," Myrlie recalled, "it was too late." Within an hour, at the age of thirty-seven, Medgar Evers was declared dead—and the following week, his body was laid to rest beside his fellow veterans in Arlington, Virginia.

For three decades, his killer walked free—after two all-white juries failed to put him behind bars—but Myrlie, who went on to become the national chairwoman of the NAACP, refused to stop campaigning for a retrial, until, finally, in 1994, she got one, and the white supremacist who murdered her husband was sent to prison for life.

Standing next to Myrlie fifty years after her husband's death, only feet from the resting place of his casket, I could not stop thinking about the last day of his life—because within those twenty-four hours, you could find the entire story of America, a nation where liberation so often leads to assassination, where broken barriers so often lead to pierced arteries, where hope and fear, love and hate, beauty and brutality dance together, swaying back and forth to the alternating beats of pain and promise.

So it was on June 11, 1963, a twenty-four-hour period marked by tragedy that put our country on the path to the triumph of the Voting Rights Act.

That day was on the mind of Dr. Martin Luther King, Jr., when, during his "I Have a Dream" speech at the March on Washington, he declared that "We cannot be satisfied as long as a Negro in Mississippi cannot vote." It was on the mind of Lyndon B. Johnson when, later that year, in his first address to a joint session of Congress, he exclaimed that "no memorial oration or eulogy could more eloquently honor President Kennedy's memory than the earliest possible passage of the civil rights bill for which he fought so long." And it was on the mind of Bob Moses, one of Medgar Evers's fellow organizers in Mississippi, when he decided the civil rights movement in his state should coalesce around a single priority: securing the right to vote.

"The Mississippi monolith," Moses wrote, "has successfully survived the Freedom Rides and the assassination of Medgar Evers, without substantive change." Therefore, he argued, "The only attack worth making is an attack aimed at the overthrow of the existing political structure of the state."

This mindset inspired leaders in Mississippi, including Fannie Lou Hamer, to organize the Mississippi Freedom Vote in 1963—a mock gubernatorial election they hoped would prove that if afforded the opportunity to vote, Black residents would turn out in droves. And they did, casting eighty thousand ballots across the state.

Building on this momentum, civil rights leaders in Mississippi conceived an idea that would change the course of history. The following year, they decided, they would welcome students from around the country to the Magnolia State, where they would travel from home to home, in town after town, organizing and registering Black voters. They would call the effort "Freedom Summer." And their goal was to wake up the country to the fact that in the South, even with all the progress we had made, voting was still not a guaranteed right if you were Black, but rather still a privilege fiercely—often, violently—protected by white supremacists.

Over the course of the summer, about one thousand students came down to Mississippi to register voters—and two of them would never return: Andrew Goodman, a Jewish twenty-year-old from the Upper West Side of Manhattan; and Michael Schwerner, a twenty-one-year-old graduate student training to become a social worker.

When they arrived in Mississippi, the young men met James Chaney, a local organizer who had been a member of the civil rights movement since the age of fifteen, back when his decision to wear an NAACP badge to class led to a school suspension. Together, Andrew, Michael, and James crisscrossed the state of Mississippi registering voters—until, on June 21, 1964, they disappeared. Earlier that day, they had decided to head to the town of Longdale, a Klan stronghold, an undertaking they knew was risky, which was why, before they left, Schwerner told his fellow organizers to "start trying to locate us" if they were not back at a reasonable hour, a request he hoped they would never have to follow.

Shortly after pulling into town, the three men were arrested by Longdale police, held captive in cells for hours, and eventually released, only to be abducted as they drove back home. For forty-four days, which I remember feeling excruciatingly long as we waited for information, their bodies went undiscovered, with racist Mississippi senator James Eastland calling their disappearance a "publicity stunt." But after an investigation led by the FBI—and overseen by President Johnson himself—it became clear that the students had met the same fate as Emmett and Medgar and the rest of the freedom fighters who had been murdered in Mississippi, killed as punishment for the crime of trying to make it easier for African Americans to vote.

Left to rest in an earthen dam, Chaney had been beaten, castrated, and shot three times before his death. Schwerner had received a bullet wound in the heart. Goodman had been buried alive, his body discovered with clay in his lungs and on his fists, a fighter until the end.

These were far from the first killings in Mississippi, but they caught the nation's attention in a way previous murders never had—and the reason wasn't a mystery. As Rita Schwerner, Michael's wife, explained in an interview: "It is only because my husband and Andrew Goodman were white that the national alarm has been sounded." Her analysis may have been blunt, but its accuracy was never in doubt: At the very site where Chaney, Schwerner, and Goodman were found, investigators discovered eight other bodies nobody had ever even cared enough to look for until white men were laid to rest next to them.

This double standard was wrong—a death should be seen as a death, a murder should be seen as a murder, a lynching should be seen as a lynching, regardless of what the victim looks like—but it also presented the organizers of the civil rights movement with an opportunity. Suddenly, the country was paying attention to the South, which meant this was the perfect moment to begin building support for expanding access to suffrage.

That was why, a few months later, when Dr. Martin Luther King, Jr., entered the Oval Office in the week he won the Nobel Peace Prize, he did so with a simple demand of President Johnson: Pass a voting rights bill. This had long been one of Dr. King's top priorities: "Our most urgent request," he had declared in a 1957 speech at the Lincoln Memorial, "is to give us the right to vote." And now, seven years later, he was done waiting for that request to be granted. Because he knew the progress the civil rights movement had made could be ripped away at any moment if African Americans couldn't defend it at the ballot box.

In theory, President Johnson was on the same page. In fact, earlier in the year, he had yelled at his deputy attorney general

Nicholas Katzenbach, "I want you to write me the goddamnest toughest voting rights act that you can devise." But he also knew the odds of passing such a bill were low, especially after he had used so much political capital on the Civil Rights Act, and he didn't want the rest of his agenda—including the Great Society initiatives he claimed would lift millions of Black Americans out of poverty—to be stalled by a filibuster.

"I'm going to do it eventually," the president promised Dr. King, "but I can't get voting rights through in this session of Congress."

Perhaps Dr. King shouldn't have been surprised by President Johnson's hesitancy. This was, after all, a man who previously had been known to move with the political winds—opposing anti-lynching legislation one decade, shepherding the Civil Rights Act through Congress the next. But Dr. King believed the president when Johnson said he would bring a voting rights act to the floor of Congress as soon as it could pass. Which was why, on his way out of the White House, Dr. King quipped: "I think we've got to find a way to get this president some power."

Within weeks, in January 1965, at Brown Chapel in Selma, where I would deliver remarks fifty years later, Dr. King marked "the beginning of a determined, organized, mobilized campaign to get the right to vote."

The problem, of course, was that such a campaign was against the law in Selma, where a judge named James Hare, Jr., had issued an injunction banning groups of more than two people from even talking about civil rights—and a sheriff named Jim Clark had directed his officers to enforce that injunction with cattle prods and clubs, tear gas and fists. Soon after his arrival, Dr. King was imprisoned, alongside hundreds of his fellow organizers. "When the king of Norway participated in awarding the Nobel Peace Prize to me," King wrote in a letter from his cell, "he surely did not think that in less than sixty days I would be in jail."

With King behind bars, Malcolm X decided to pay a visit to Selma. "I think that the people in this part of the world would do well to listen to Dr. Martin Luther King and give him what he's asking for and give it to him fast," he threatened, "before some other factions come along and try to do it another way." This was a different message from the one civil rights organizations in Alabama, including the Southern Christian Leadership Conference (SCLC) and the Student Nonviolent Coordinating Committee (SNCC), had been promoting, but it was a valuable counterbalance: It demonstrated that Black Americans would make their voices heard no matter what—if not with ballots, as Malcolm X was known to say, then with bullets. "What he's asking for is right. It's the ballot," Malcolm continued. "And if he can't get it the way he's trying to get it, then it's going to be gotten, one way or the other."

Shortly after Dr. King was released from prison, Malcolm X was assassinated—and soon after that, Jimmie Lee Jackson joined him as a martyr of the civil rights movement, inspiring leaders on the ground, from Diane Nash and James Bevel to Amelia Boynton and John Lewis, to organize a march for voting rights from Selma to Montgomery.

We all know what happened next. Brutality on a bridge, beamed onto television sets across the country, including the one in my basement, shocked America out of complacency. Months after Dr. King and President Johnson's meeting in the Oval Office, the heroes in Selma had fulfilled the civil rights leader's promise of getting the president some power—power he wielded to rally the country around a bill that would protect voting rights.

And on August 6, 1965—with giants of the civil rights movement like Rosa Parks, John Lewis, and Dr. King looking on—President Johnson signed the Voting Rights Act of 1965 into law, fulfilling the promise of American democracy once and for all.

Vivian Malone was there, too, looking elegant as ever in white gloves. Just two years after the Stand in the Schoolhouse Door, she had already graduated from the University of Alabama—and was on her way to taking over the Voter Education Project from John Lewis. (I, meanwhile, came to learn that great beauty and determination ran in the women of the Malone family when I met and married Vivian's younger sister, Sharon.)

In the years following the passage of the Voting Rights Act, millions of Black Americans across the South registered to vote and began electing public servants who looked like them for the first time since Reconstruction. One of these officials was Charles Evers, Medgar's brother, who became a mayor in Mississippi only a couple decades after his life was threatened for even trying to vote.

And over the following years, we bore witness to what started to look like a rebirth of American democracy. Voting was no longer seen as a privilege. At long last, it had been recognized as a right, and a century after President Lincoln delivered the Gettysburg Address, we finally had a government of, by, and for the people—or, at least, more of the people than ever before. That wasn't a victory for Black Americans. It was a victory for all Americans. And it's worth taking a moment to consider how it was won.

The civil rights movement, like the founding of America, was a revolution—a battle whose foot soldiers broke laws they believed were unjust. To sanitize this would be to dishonor the courage of those who sat behind counters where they weren't welcome, who spoke up when they were told to be silent, who peacefully withstood violence from the state in the fight for their freedom.

But make no mistake: This was not a revolution of people who didn't believe in America. It was a revolution of patriots who loved America, who honored the words of the Declaration of Independence more than their oppressors ever did, who were clear-eyed about the ways their country had failed them but refused to give up on its promise. And there was no one who captured this spirit more than Medgar Evers—a man who defended our democracy against the Nazis overseas and then devoted his every waking hour to perfecting it when he got back home.

Despite all the evidence in front of him—despite the hatred, the violence, the discrimination he endured—Medgar never abandoned his belief in the idea of an America where all of us were equal. And that was why, in the face of death threats, he carried that carton full of JIM CROW MUST GO T-shirts up the driveway to his home. It was an act of hope, a demonstration of his belief that when your cause is righteous, you do not stop fighting until your final breath.

The next morning, when a nation that went to sleep to President Kennedy's speech woke up to news of Medgar's assassination, I can imagine there were people who believed Evers's pursuit of justice had been quixotic—and who could blame them? A civil rights hero—a war hero—had been murdered, only hours after the president of the United States had called his cause "a moral issue . . . as old as the scriptures . . . as clear as the Constitution." Could a country so cruel, so capricious, so contradictory ever be redeemed?

The jury was out. It still is. But all these decades later, what's clear is that Medgar Evers wasn't wrong to hold out hope. He was right, even if he never saw those seeds flower.

After all, if he hadn't kept up the fight, those boys very well might never have come down to Mississippi to register voters; and if it hadn't been for those boys, Martin Luther King, Jr., might never have ended up in Selma; and if Martin Luther King, Jr., hadn't ended up in Selma, well, that's the kind of counterfactual it's not even worth contemplating—but let's just say I don't think that twelve-year-old in Queens watching it all take place on his TV set would have been standing in Arlington National Cemetery fifty years later, reflecting on the events of June 11, 1963, as the first African American attorney general of the United States.

Part II

THE CRISIS OF THE PRESENT

5

BACKLASH TO A BLACK PRESIDENT

The Obama Years

When I watched Lyndon B. Johnson sign the Voting Rights Act as a fourteen-year-old, I didn't think I would be at his presidential library forty-six years later delivering a speech on threats to the right to vote as the eighty-second attorney general of the United States. To be honest, even when I was sworn in, I didn't think protecting the franchise would be at the top of my agenda.

Because access to the ballot had been steadily expanding since that day in 1965 when, with the stroke of a pen—or, rather, seventy-five pens, which President Johnson later gave out as souvenirs—the crown jewel of the civil rights movement became law.

Within hours of the Voting Rights Act's passage, the federal government sent officials to the South to make sure African Americans could register to vote—and notably, white Americans registered at record rates, too, liberated from the bureaucracy of a system designed to make it hard to vote. So did Native Americans, who even after finally being granted the right to vote in all fifty states in 1962 were subject to many of the same forms of suppression as Black Americans until the Voting Rights Act became law.

The following year, in 1966, the Supreme Court upheld the constitutionality of the VRA under the Fifteenth Amendment, calling it a "legitimate response" to the "insidious and pervasive evil" of Jim Crow. It was an 8–1 decision.

And after that, the ripples of progress that had swept the country during the civil rights movement came together to form a tidal wave of enfranchisement. In 1971, the voting age across the country was lowered from twenty-one to eighteen, as Vietnam forced America to recognize it was unfair to ask soldiers to go to war if they didn't have a say in electing the politicians who sent them there. In 1984, the Voting Accessibility for the Elderly and Handicapped Act expanded access to polling places for Americans with disabilities. The next year, as Alexander Keyssar notes, the Congressional Quarterly's *Guide to U.S. Elections* effectively declared that the right to vote was safe: "By the two hundredth anniversary of the nation," it read, "the only remaining restrictions on the franchise prevented voting by the insane, convicted felons, and otherwise eligible voters who were unable to meet short residence requirements."

America had come a long way since the days when only rich white men could vote—and at the dawn of President Obama's presidency, voting rights had received decades of bipartisan support. In the years since President Johnson signed the Voting Rights Act, it had been reauthorized, as LeBron James might put it, by not one, not two, not three, but four presidents, including Ronald Reagan and Richard Nixon, two men not exactly known for their commitment to civil rights. And as recently as 2006, when the law was up for debate during the presidency of George W. Bush, after sitting through weeks of hearings and being presented with thousands of pages of evidence, Congress voted to reauthorize the Voting Rights Act for another quarter century.

It wasn't even close: In the House of Representatives, the bill passed by a vote of 390–33. In the Senate? The outcome was unanimous, with 98 senators, including everyone from Hillary Rodham Clinton to one Addison Mitchell McConnell III, voting in favor of the bill and a grand total of zero voting against it.

To be sure, around the country, there had been some efforts by Republicans to sow distrust in elections—fomenting fear of voter fraud, even though in America, citizens are more likely to be struck by lightning than to show up at a polling place and vote under someone else's name. (This isn't hyperbole. It's a fact. According to a Brennan Center for Justice investigation that analyzed a billion votes, there's a 1 in 1,222,000 chance of being struck by lightning compared to a 1 in 32,258,064 chance of committing in-person voter fraud.) But even as Republican legislatures in states like Georgia and Indiana passed unnecessary photo ID laws to combat this imaginary crisis, for the most part, nobody challenged the core tenets of the Voting Rights Act.

That is, until 2008, when a record number of Americans showed up to the polls and made a man named Barack Hussein Obama the first Black president of the United States.

When I started campaigning for Barack in Iowa, trying to convince one white voter at a time to give him a shot, I wasn't sure America was ready. So when the country proved me wrong—when we did end up elevating that "skinny kid with a funny name" to the highest office in the land—I allowed myself, for a moment, to feel hope. No, I never believed in the idea that America had entered a post-racial era. That much was clear to any Black parent like me, who still sometimes worried when our kids left home that they might never return. But I did believe our country was on a path to a future better than anything we had seen in the past; a future where we defined ourselves by what united us, not by what divided us; a future in which our aspirations were higher and the temperature of our politics was lower.

Hah.

By the time I stood behind the podium at the LBJ Presidential Library at the end of 2011, a couple of years into Barack Obama's presidency, I had a sense of just how wrong I had been. From the moment the first Black president took office, the Republican Party had one mission and one mission only, famously distilled by Senator McConnell: "The single most important thing we want to achieve," he declared, "is for President Obama to be a one-term president." At the local, state, and federal level, this meant Republicans would do whatever they needed to tarnish the president's reputation—and get in the way of his agenda. Gone were the days of Republican presidential candidate John McCain calling Barack Obama a "decent family man." This was Fox News's party now. And with the help of its megaphone, Republicans painted the president as a radical Muslim socialist. (Naturally, they labeled me his even more out-there sidekick.)

The worst part was that, at least at first, it worked.

After a brief honeymoon period, some voters quickly turned against President Obama, who not only had to fend off these attacks on his character during his first years in office, but had to do so while bringing our country out of the recession he had inherited, the worst since the Great Depression; stopping an oil spill at a rig he did not drill or sanction; rescuing an auto industry whose bad decisions he did not make; and beginning to bring an end to a war on terror he never thought was a wise idea in the first place. After two years, when the 2010 midterms came around, the president received a "shellacking," as he called it in a press conference the following day, with Republicans coming to power at almost all levels of government across the country.

The scale of the landslide is hard to fathom. In the Senate, Republicans won six new seats. In the House, they gained sixty-three. They also dominated in the states, taking control of six governor's mansions and twenty legislatures, and winning nearly seven hundred state seats in total. Not seven. Not seventy. Seven hundred. It was the most dominant midterm performance since the Democratic wave after Republican president Richard Nixon resigned. And Republicans didn't only have a plan to win power. They had a plan to use it. As Karl Rove, former chief strategist to George W. Bush, reportedly said at the time, "People call us a vast right-wing conspiracy, but we're really a half-assed right-wing conspiracy. Now it's time to get serious."

What did this mean? First and foremost, it meant continuing to attack President Obama relentlessly in the press, but now that Republicans had legislative control of so many states, they were no longer all talk. In fact, they had a very specific agenda that they would pursue with precision, and it was this: rigging our democracy in their favor.

Strategically, you can understand where they were coming from. President Obama's election had scared them—as it should have. The most diverse electorate in history had turned out in unprecedented numbers to send an African American senator to the White House; and they knew the country would only become less white in the years ahead. This presented an existential crisis for a Republican Party whose beliefs increasingly no longer aligned with those of the majority of Americans: Sure, they could sweep a midterm here and there, but when the country turned out, when the people voted in substantial numbers, they would lose. And so their leaders came to the same conclusion as the Democrats had during Reconstruction—the only way to avoid obsolescence, they decided, was to change the rules of the game, making it harder for their opponents to vote and harder for them to win or wield power when they did.

In the aftermath of the midterms, this led Republicans to mount a two-pronged attack on our democracy. The first was on our elections themselves—introducing, as I mentioned at the beginning of this book, close to two hundred bills across forty-one states that would have made it harder to vote. Like the Jim Crow laws passed after the Civil War, nowhere in this legislation did it say the goal was to limit access to the franchise. But there was no doubt that this would be the outcome.

How else do you explain the law in Alabama that required you to show a driver's license to vote—while the same legislators who passed it tried to shut down DMV offices across the state, starting with those in predominantly African American neighborhoods? Or the law in Texas that decided student IDs, disproportionately held by Democrats, weren't enough proof of your identity to allow you to vote—but concealed-carry permits, disproportionately held by Republicans, were? Or the laws in Ohio and Florida that reduced the number of early voting days from 35 to 11 and 14 to 8, respectively—and made sure to ban early voting on Sundays, when Black churches were known to hold "souls to the polls" events?

As John Lewis, who was then a thirteenth-term congressman, said on the House floor at the time, the country was in the midst of a "deliberate and systematic attempt to prevent millions of elderly voters, young voters, students, minority and low-income voters from exercising their constitutional right to engage in the democratic process."

When I delivered my address at the LBJ Presidential Library,

I shared this quote from Congressman Lewis, whom I had come to call my friend—even though I was never quite able to see him as anything less than my hero. And I talked about what we owed to his generation, to the civil rights leaders who had "set our country on a course toward remarkable, once unimaginable, progress." They had "opened new doors of opportunity," I explained, doors that were at risk of being slammed shut, and we were now faced with the question of which direction our country would turn next: "What kind of nation—and what kind of people—do we want to be?

"For me, and for our nation's Department of Justice," I argued, "the answers are clear," promising to build election systems that were "more, not less, accessible to the citizens of this country." With this North Star in mind, I instructed the Civil Rights Division of the DOJ to put its weight behind exercising its power under Section 5 of the Voting Rights Act to fight back against suppression.

Section 5 outlined the process known as "preclearance," through which the DOJ was granted the right to approve or deny laws affecting access to the ballot passed by jurisdictions with a history of discriminating against minorities. And during the Obama presidency, enforcing it was an all-hands-on-deck effort.

Not only did we have lawyers studying precedents and filing briefs, we also had statisticians on board who crunched the numbers and modeled the bills that were passing in the states to determine if they would, in fact, disproportionately impact communities of color. Sometimes, even after withering examination, we were unable to find proof of discrimination—and would, therefore, allow legislation in covered areas to be enacted. But when bills like the ones making their way through state legislatures in the aftermath of the 2010 midterms passed—bills designed to strip Black and brown Americans of their right to vote—we took them to court.

And more often than not, we stopped those laws from going into effect, because the data couldn't have been more clear. The photo ID law in Texas, for instance, would have disenfranchised more than six hundred thousand people across the state, the majority of whom would have been Black or Latino, so we used preclearance to stop it from going into effect.

The day after our case against it was heard in court, I spoke to the NAACP in Houston—and laid out why the Department of Justice, after a "careful, thorough, and independent" review, believed the bill "would be harmful to minority voters." Under the proposed law, I explained, "many of those without IDs would have to travel great distances to get them—and some would struggle to pay for the documents they might need to obtain them."

At this point in the address, I was heated, pissed off, outraged that an organization like the NAACP was still having to fight for something as basic as voting rights. Ordinarily, one of the most frustrating parts of being attorney general is that you are constrained in what you can say, but at that moment, I wasn't just speaking as the AG. I was speaking as a Black man to a Black audience in a repressive state, and I wasn't about to watch my words. So I improvised a line that was not in my prepared remarks, a line I knew would spark controversy: "We call those poll taxes."

Let's just say the press people on my team didn't buy me a drink that night. But here's the thing: I wasn't wrong. As Ari Berman lays out in *Give Us the Ballot*, under the bill, the only way to get a photo ID in Texas would have been to provide documentation proving your identity—of which the cheapest form to obtain was a birth certificate. "A poll tax in Alabama in the 1960s cost roughly ten dollars, adjusted for inflation," Berman explains, "while the birth certificate needed to obtain an allegedly free voter ID in Texas cost twice as much." Take a second to process the significance of this: More than half a century after the Voting Rights Act, there was a price on the right to vote—$22, to be exact, a number about three times higher than the state's minimum wage.

"In our efforts to protect voting rights and to prevent voting fraud, we will be vigilant and strong," I concluded. "But let me be clear: We will not allow political pretexts to disenfranchise American citizens of their most precious right."

In the end, the district court sided with us, citing three reasons: "1) A substantial subgroup of Texas voters, many of whom are African American or Hispanic, lack photo ID; 2) the burdens associated with obtaining ID will weigh most heavily on the poor; and 3) racial minorities in Texas are disproportionately likely to live in poverty." In other words, they, like me, saw the bill as a poll tax, writing: "A law that forces poorer citizens to choose between their wages and their franchise unquestionably denies or abridges their right to vote."

Through Section 5, we found similar success fighting voter suppression across the country. As Berman writes, on the eve of the 2012 election, "courts had blocked ten major voting restrictions, including voter ID laws . . . limits on voter registration drives . . . cutbacks to early voting . . . partisan voter purges . . . hurdles to student voting . . . and the disqualification of provisional ballots." It was a resounding demonstration of the continued relevance of the Voting Rights Act.

And on Election Day 2012—with Osama bin Laden dead, General Motors alive, the economy on the mend, and healthcare access expanded for tens of millions of citizens—the American people once again turned out in record numbers to send President Obama back to the White House for a second term.

President Obama's victory in the 2012 election made me optimistic about where our country was headed—but what happened downballot that cycle demonstrated the success of the second prong of the Republican Party's attack on democracy, one that was even more insidious, because it wasn't implemented with laws passed on the floors of legislatures, but with maps designed in private, in hotel rooms and law offices, where opportunistic operatives, cagey cartographers, and sketchy statisticians plotted the best ways to draw Democrats out of democracy. What they did wasn't new. It's called gerrymandering. And it's been around longer than the Bill of Rights.

Here's how it works: At a basic level, gerrymandering inverts the way democracy is supposed to function. Rather than voters picking their politicians, with gerrymandering, politicians pick their voters—drawing lines around districts in a way that makes it more likely for one candidate, or one party, to win over another.

This is done in one of two ways: Legislators either "pack" their opponents into one district—knowing that doing so will limit their ability to win in other districts—while distributing their own voters as efficiently as possible. (For example, a party would want their opponents to win seats 90 percent to 10 percent, while they won their seats 60 to 40, because that would mean they "wasted" fewer votes.) Or they "crack" a district in half—splitting their opponent's voting bloc in a particular area between two districts. (For example, Republicans might want to draw a line that split a college campus in half so the students, who tend to vote Democrat, wouldn't have enough representation in either of the two districts to meaningfully impact the outcome—as you'll read more about in chapter 9, "Saving Congress.")

The first time a map was gerrymandered was in 1789 when Patrick Henry, of "Give me liberty or give me death!" fame, then an influential member of the Virginia House of Delegates, redrew the lines of the district where his enemy James Madison lived so Madison would have to run against the more popular James Monroe, but the practice didn't receive a name until a few decades later.

The year was 1812. The governor of Massachusetts was a guy whose parents had named him Elbridge, which may have explained his vindictiveness, but as far as history is concerned, his last name is what was important: Gerry. Elbridge Gerry hated the Federalist Party. Like, he *really* hated the Federalist party. As Erick Trickey wrote for *Smithsonian Magazine:* "Gerry replaced Federalists in state government jobs . . . got his attorney general to prosecute Federalist newspaper editors for libel . . . and seized control of the Federalist-dominated Harvard College board."

But Gerry didn't stop there. He also wanted to make sure the Federalists would never win an election again. So he signed into law a map that flew in the face of precedent. Unlike past districting in Massachusetts, which had been drawn in line with county borders, these districts were designed with one goal and one goal only: blocking Federalists from power. The map was so strange that critics at the time said it was full of "carvings and manglings." And it formed a shape that didn't look like a district as much as it looked like a reptile—specifically, a salamander. And thus the portmanteau "gerrymander" was born.

Two hundred years have passed since then—and the way we draw districts is basically just as insidious. Every ten years, after the census, there is a process called reapportionment, through which the number of seats each state is allotted in the House of Representatives increases or decreases depending on whether its population has grown or shrunk as a percentage of the national population. At the same time, states have a chance to change where the boundaries of their districts are drawn. In a few, this process is governed by nonpartisan commissions, but in most, it's run by state legislatures, just as was the case in Elbridge Gerry's Massachusetts. And while there are some constraints on how the redistricting process works—you can't, for instance, create two districts with radically different populations, because that would be an overt violation of the "one person, one vote" guidepost—there is still a tremendous amount of room for treachery.

Both political parties have long understood this—and embraced gerrymandering when they were in control of state governments. But in 2010, a census year, Democrats were caught asleep at the wheel while Republicans decided that instead of devoting all their attention to what was happening in Congress, they would drive a seismic investment into the local races whose victors would run redistricting processes across the country. The goal of this effort, as REDMAP, the Republican initiative piloting it, wrote on their website, was to "shape the political landscape for 10 years."

The story of how, exactly, Republicans won so many of these elections, while Democrats barely even fought back, is told in exhaustive, scintillating, nauseating detail in David Daley's riveting book *Ratf**ked.* But the way it worked was actually simple. REDMAP would target a state like Ohio, where Democrats held a narrow majority in the statehouse, and attack incumbents with unprecedented sums of money—in some cases, more than a million dollars per race in support of candidates whose entire spend would normally be way less than that. Out of the six Ohio races in which REDMAP was involved, they won five, enough to flip control of redistricting. And the organization found similar success across the country, including in crucial swing states like Pennsylvania, Florida, and Wisconsin.

Republican operatives had long had their eyes set on these races, but their effort was supercharged by the 2010 Supreme Court ruling in *Citizens United v. FEC,* which allowed corporations and dark money groups, including those funded by the billionaire Koch brothers, to devote as much money to the cause as they wanted. It was an investment in local elections on a scale that had never been seen before—more than $30 million from REDMAP alone—but it was also a bargain, because for the price of a few federal Senate races, Republicans won hundreds of state seats and set themselves up to dictate our politics for a decade.

As Vann Newkirk notes in *The Atlantic,* Republicans also "outspent Democrats by over $300 million in that year's gubernatorial races," providing them with control of governor's mansions—in part so they could make sure that the maps drawn by their legislatures wouldn't be vetoed.

At the Department of Justice, we harnessed Section 5 to fight back against redistricting, too—and we had some victories. For instance, we were able to overturn a map in East Feliciana Parish, Louisiana, that had been drafted by a cartographer who had met exclusively with white officeholders before drawing lines in a district where close to one of every two residents was African American. And we successfully fought back against maps in Texas that would have diluted the political power of Latino voters, even though their growing population was the reason the Lone Star State was apportioned more districts after the census in the first place.

But for the most part, in the aftermath of the 2010 midterms, the maps drawn by gerrymanderers were upheld. And in 2012, their redistricting paid off.

On the whole, as Daley observes, more Democrats than Republicans voted in that election, which is why President Obama won handily—332–206 in the Electoral College, 65 million to 60 million in the popular vote—and why the GOP went down in two of every three Senate races. It's also why Democrats won more than 1.4 million more votes for the House of Representatives than the Republicans did. Which, you'd think, would have given them the majority.

But it didn't.

Because of redistricting, Republicans held on to the House by a thirty-three-seat margin.

How does this actually work? Look, for instance, at a state like Pennsylvania, which President Obama won by similar margins in 2008 and 2012. As Daley writes: "In 2008, that led to the election of 12 Democratic congressmen. In 2012, it generated 5." What changed? Well, the maps did, which enabled Republicans to double the number of seats they won even as they received around the same number of votes.

In Michigan, Daley continues, the exact same story played out: "Obama carried the state, [Democrat] Gary Peters won election to the Senate by 20 points—and Republicans captured 9 of the 14 House seats."

Coming out of the 2012 election, I was clear-eyed about what these threats meant for the future of our democracy. But what I didn't know, what I didn't quite believe, despite all the evidence before me, was that the central provisions of the Voting Rights Act itself—the bill President Kennedy had paved the path for on the night of Medgar Evers's assassination and President Johnson had signed into law two years later, standing next to my future sister-in-law Vivian while kids like me around the country watched with hope in our hearts—could be thrown out altogether.

As soon as the opening arguments were over, everyone in the Department of Justice thought we had lost. And the headlines were just as grim. "Voting Rights Law Draws Skepticism from Justices," wrote *The New York Times.* "Supreme Court Likely to Strike Down the Voting Rights Act's Section 5," wrote *The Daily Beast.* "Voting Rights Act Under Fire," wrote *Politico*, true to form, characterizing the future of the most important law of the twentieth century in much the same way you would describe a football coach in the hot seat.

They weren't wrong.

Earlier that day, at the highest court in the land, with John Lewis in the audience, Chief Justice John Roberts had been hostile to our very able solicitor general, Don Verrilli. On behalf of the Department of Justice, Verrilli was defending Section 5 of the Voting Rights Act from a challenge to the law by Shelby County, Alabama, one of the jurisdictions subject to preclearance under Section 5 due to their history of discrimination. And the chief justice simply wasn't picking up what we were putting down.

Over and over, Roberts kept arguing that America had fundamentally changed—reciting the dubious argument that it was now easier for African Americans to vote in Mississippi than in Massachusetts, a claim whose fallaciousness was exposed in *The New York Times* by none other than budding data journalist Nate Silver. Justice Antonin Scalia, for his part, had dismissed the Voting Rights Act as a "racial entitlement." And this came on the heels of a 2009 case, *Northwest Austin Municipal Utility District No. One (NAMUNDO) v. Holder*, in which eight justices, including Anthony Kennedy, who we knew would be the swing vote in *Shelby*, had argued that the Voting Rights Act "raises serious constitutional concerns" and "differentiates between the states in ways that may no longer be justified." So I couldn't fault my colleagues in the Department of Justice for feeling worried.

But I wasn't really buying it just yet. Yes, Justice Roberts had been adversarial in the courtroom, but during his confirmation before Congress, he had said that "the existing Voting Rights Act, the constitutionality has been upheld, and I don't have any issue with that." Yes, America had made progress, but we had proven the necessity of Section 5 in the 2012 election—as court after court ruled we were justified in stopping bills that suppressed the vote. (Plus: When a jurisdiction did, in fact, demonstrate that it was no longer discriminatory, we would free it from oversight, something the Department of Justice did whenever warranted.) And yes, five justices on the Supreme Court might have believed the Voting Rights Act was no longer as important as it once was, but would they really strike down a bill that had been signed by a very conservative Republican president after Congress—by a vote of 390–33 in the House and 98–0 in the Senate—had extended it for another quarter of a century?

This issue came up in the courtroom. In response to Shelby County's lawyer, Bert Rein, arguing that the problems the Voting Rights Act had been passed to address had been solved, Justice Elena Kagan asked him: "Who gets to make that judgment really? Is it you, is it the court, or is it Congress?"

"The court," Rein answered.

"Well, that's a big new power you are giving us," Kagan quipped, "the power to decide whether racial discrimination has been solved. I did not think that fell within our bailiwick."

Rein didn't have a retort—because, fundamentally, he had a bad case. That's why Shelby County had lost in both the district court and the appeals court, which ruled that Section 5 remained a "congruent and proportional remedy to the twenty-first-century problem of voting discrimination in covered jurisdictions." And it's why challenges to the Voting Rights Act had failed the previous nine times they were brought before the Supreme Court. Because the law was constitutional, and America had not changed enough for its protections to be deemed superfluous. Plain and simple.

A few weeks after the arguments, I delivered this message in Selma, Alabama, where I had traveled to honor the forty-eighth anniversary of the march. "Let me be clear," I began, "although our nation has indeed changed, although the South is far different now, and although progress has indeed been made, we are not yet at the point where the most vital part of the Voting Rights Act can be deemed unnecessary.

"The struggle for voting rights for all Americans," I went on, "must continue," before finishing off on a hopeful note, declining to acknowledge that the Supreme Court might be on the precipice of causing irreparable harm: "In the moment of remembrance before us, as we reflect on our past and consider how far we've come in the days since Bloody Sunday, I cannot help but feel optimistic about the country and the world that, together, we will imagine; plan for; and surely help create."

Later that day, I marched across the bridge, hand in hand with John Lewis, singing "We Shall Overcome."

A dream I never even knew I had—never even dared to imagine—had been realized, as I stood on the sacred ground where the skull of the man next to me had been cracked forty-eight years earlier, while I watched, horrified, one thousand miles and a world away, on my black-and-white television, hoping that one day, I could be part of the fight. But was it a dream? Or a nightmare? Looking back, I think it was both. That John

Lewis was back on this bridge, nearly half a century later, struggling for the same basic right was a tragedy. But the fact that I was by his side in my role as attorney general of the United States was a reason to believe in the possibility of progress.

It's a lesson I will treasure forever—a lesson I looked back on for resilience when, two months later, the Supreme Court of the United States, declaring that "things have changed dramatically" since the civil rights movement, struck down the heart of the Voting Rights Act.

"I'm shocked, dismayed, disappointed," Congressman Lewis said when he learned about the decision. "These men never stood in unmovable lines. They were never denied the right to participate in the democratic process. They were never beaten, jailed, run off their farms, or fired from their jobs. No one they knew died simply trying to register to vote."

I, too, was dismayed—and angry, angrier than I had been on any day as attorney general. Immediately, I decided to invite civil rights leaders to the Department of Justice. And I delivered a statement of my own. "Like many others across the country, I am deeply disappointed with the court's decision in this matter," I said, calling it a "serious setback for voting rights" that had "the potential to negatively impact millions of Americans across the country."

I went on to emphasize the fact that even Chief Justice Roberts had admitted in his decision that "voting discrimination still exists." And I promised that "protecting the fundamental right to vote for all Americans [would] remain one of the Justice Department's highest priorities."

There was an issue, though: Many of the tools we had to protect that right had been taken from us. Within minutes of the Supreme Court's decision, then-Texas attorney general Greg

Abbott tweeted: "Eric Holder can no longer deny #VoterID in #Texas after today's #SCOTUS decision." The most painful part was that he was right. Only days later, Texas passed an even stricter version of the bill we had refused to preclear—the bill a court had ruled would "unquestionably [deny] or [abridge] the right to vote." States across the country followed suit with antidemocratic bills of their own. And while we continued fighting back in every way we could, without the statutory authority to use Section 5, we found little success, and suppressive law after suppressive law went into effect.

We were working harder than we ever had before—harnessing whatever leverage we could find to protect the voting rights of Americans—but we didn't have much leeway. And we were taking fire from all directions.

There was the shuttering of polling places—20 percent more of which took place in jurisdictions that had previously been subject to preclearance—leading to longer lines on Election Day. There was the purging of voter rolls, which quintupled across the country, disproportionately in states that were no longer under federal supervision. And there was the legislative assault on the right to vote, which led to everything from reductions in early voting to bans on same-day registration to photo ID laws that disenfranchised millions of Americans, especially those who happened to have Black or brown skin, happened to have less money in their bank accounts, and happened to vote for Democrats. It's no wonder the 2014 midterms saw the lowest turnout since before the Voting Rights Act was signed into law, leaving Republicans with control of the Senate, which they disgracefully used to block President Obama from filling the Supreme Court vacancy that emerged after Justice Scalia's death.

As I mentioned in the introduction, in her *Shelby* dissent,

Justice Ruth Bader Ginsburg wrote that "throwing out pre-clearance when it has worked and is continuing to work to stop discriminatory changes is like throwing away your umbrella in a rainstorm because you are not getting wet." By the end of President Obama's second term, America was already drenched, flooded by a wave of suppression unlike any we had seen since the era of Jim Crow.

And while we didn't know it at the time, a tempest was on the horizon, promising to wash away what was left of American democracy—unless we stopped it.

6

DEMOCRACY IN DESCENT

The Trump Years

You can say a lot of things about Donald Trump, but you can't say he didn't warn us.

In 2016, on the debate stage, Fox News anchor Chris Wallace asked a simple question of the Republican nominee: If you lose, will you concede?

Trump declined to provide an answer. "I will look at it at the time," he said, before adding: "I will keep you in suspense."

Refusing to accept the results of the election would have separated Trump from all the presidential candidates who had been defeated before him—from Thomas Jefferson and John Adams to John McCain and Mitt Romney—and Wallace, an institutionalist whose father had interviewed commanders in chief dating back to President Kennedy, wanted to give Trump a second chance to fall in line with that precedent.

"There is a tradition in this country—in fact, one of the prides of this country is the peaceful transition of power," Wallace explained. "Are you saying you're not prepared now to commit to that principle?"

Trump smirked, before repeating the same answer he'd offered seconds earlier: "I'll keep you in suspense, okay?"

The outcry was immediate—and the following day, at a rally in the swing state of Ohio, Trump seemed to have been pressured into backtracking: "I would like to promise and pledge to all of my voters and supporters, and to all of the people of the United States, that I will totally accept the results of this great and historic presidential election."

Better late than never, right?

He paused for dramatic effect.

And then he delivered the punchline: ". . . if I win."

The crowd roared. Trump laughed. A wolf in wolf's clothing, ready to blow the whole damn house down.

On Election Night 2016, defying the predictions of polls and the premonitions of pundits, Donald Trump did end up winning, but he refused to accept the results anyway. Because while he had come out on top in the Electoral College, the official tally said he had received about three million fewer votes than his opponent, a hit to the ego he could not countenance.

"I won the popular vote if you deduct the millions of people who voted illegally," he insisted. He went on to tell congressional leaders that he believed up to five million Americans had broken the law to cast ballots. The evidence? His friend Bernhard Langer, an over-the-hill golfer, saw people at the polls who "did not look as if they should be allowed to vote," as though you can identify who is on the rolls by their facial features. (Langer, for his part, is not a United States citizen, so if anyone could have committed voter fraud at the polling place that day, it was the German.)

Trump went on to argue—bafflingly—that every single one of the alleged illegal votes cast in the 2016 election went to Democrats. Every single one! "None of them come to me," he said. "They would all be for the other side." Of course, he had literally no backing for these claims. But Trump was no longer just a reality television star with a Twitter account, firing off hot takes about how the Emmys were rigged against him without being able to do anything about it.

Now this man was president of the United States. His desk was the Resolute Desk. His office was the Oval Office. His house was the White House. Donald Trump had managed to become the most powerful man in the world, and he was dead set on using the authority that had been vested in him to disenfranchise the Americans who had cost him the popular vote—even if he had to destroy democracy in the process.

When Dr. Martin Luther King, Jr., was assassinated, three hundred thousand Americans, from every corner of the country, paid their respects at his funeral—but only one was chosen to lead the mule wagon that carried his body: Albert Turner.

This is where Turner stood for so much of his life: by Dr. King's side, yes, but also at the collision of peril and promise. Like the Sankofa bird, which flies forward while looking back, he was always aware of the injustice behind him, but resolute in his commitment to keep on marching. He marched in Selma when Jimmie Lee Jackson was murdered. He marched on the Edmund Pettus Bridge when gas was sprayed and batons were swung. He marched from block to block, in town after town, registering citizens after the Voting Rights Act was signed into law—convincing Black Americans in Alabama that they had a place in our democracy.

He understood why so many of his fellow Alabamians were skeptical when he knocked on their doors. After all, even as a college graduate, Turner himself had been denied the franchise by a literacy test—so if anyone had reason to doubt whether Alabama would ever welcome Black Americans into politics, it was him. But he didn't believe that the answer to his state's legacy of oppression was resignation. He believed it was organization. So Turner devoted his life to persuading Black men and women in Alabama to make their voices heard at the ballot box; and because of his leadership, the state finally began electing candidates who looked like the people they were supposed to serve.

In the eyes of many Alabamians, this made Turner a hero, one of the founders of our nation's movement for voting rights. But in 1985, the U.S. attorney for the Southern District of Alabama didn't see it the same way. No, Jefferson Beauregard Sessions III believed Turner was a criminal—and spent extensive taxpayer dollars on an investigation whose goal was to convict this giant of the civil rights movement of voter fraud. How else, Sessions seemed to wonder, could this man have brought so many Black Americans to the polls?

Thankfully, the witch hunt failed, Turner was exonerated, and the man who led the investigation into him was denied a federal judgeship because of his history with race—a history that reportedly included calling the Voting Rights Act "an intrusive piece of legislation." But in the end, Jeff Sessions was not blacklisted for what he had done. Instead, he ascended, elected to the United States Senate by the people of Alabama and appointed attorney general by President Donald Trump.

That's right: Jeff Sessions, the same guy who tried to send civil rights leader Albert Turner to jail, was the person the forty-fifth president of the United States decided should be in charge of enforcing the Voting Rights Act.

America waited 219 years before allowing an African American to serve as attorney general. It took only eight more for that seat to once again be filled by a man with, well, let's just say a complicated view on race.

Given his history, perhaps it's no surprise that Attorney General Sessions didn't feel an obligation to respect the legacy I had left behind. From his first day in office, Sessions made it his mission to reverse as much of what we did as he could, day after day, policy after policy, case after case, bringing our country back to a darker (or, I suppose, whiter) era. That was especially true when it came to voting rights, because, in the mind of Jeff Sessions, suppression wasn't something to be condemned. It was something to be condoned.

That's why, within his first few months in office, he ordered the Justice Department to switch sides on voting rights litigation across the country. In Texas, where the Department of Justice had spent years fighting a law that made it harder to vote, Sessions decided to file a brief supporting that law. In Ohio, where 1.2 million voters had been purged from the rolls for infrequently showing up to the polls, Sessions dropped the objections we had filed. He even loosened our stance on gerrymandering—backing off efforts to stop the adoption of a map we had proven to be racially discriminatory.

In all these cases, Sessions was aided by the fact that Republicans had stolen a seat on the Supreme Court—refusing to hold hearings on President Obama's nominee, Merrick Garland, and then confirming President Trump's, Neil Gorsuch, in a matter of months. This theft left conservatives with an illegitimate 5–4 majority, which sided, over and over again, with suppressors, purgers, and gerrymanderers.

One of the most controversial of these decisions surrounded *Rucho v. Common Case*, a case in which Justice Roberts wrote that "partisan gerrymandering claims present political questions beyond the reach of the federal courts," essentially abdicating responsibility for policing the redistricting process. In response, Justice Kagan wrote a searing dissent: "In the face of grievous harm to democratic governance and flagrant infringements on individuals' rights—in the face of escalating partisan manipulation whose compatibility with this nation's values and law no one defends—the majority declines to provide any remedy.

"For the first time in this nation's history," she continued, "the majority declares that it can do nothing about an acknowledged constitutional violation."

She was livid, as were Justices Ginsburg, Breyer, and Sotomayor, all of whom signed the dissent with "deep sadness." And I was, too. Because I know how to read between the lines of Supreme Court rulings, and the consequences of this one were clear: Attorney General Sessions, President Trump, and Republican state legislatures across the country would have virtual carte blanche to continue gutting our democracy.

The biggest threat to our country over the course of President Trump's four years in office, as legal writer Benjamin Wittes first observed, was his administration's malevolence—and the biggest saving grace was its incompetence. This is why he never succeeded in kicking 30 million Americans off their healthcare plans, no matter how many times he tried. It's why he never pulled off building the wall, even with control of Congress. And it's why he never quite managed to suppress the vote to the extent he wanted to, despite a Supreme Court that had made it possible for him to do exactly that.

His malevolence, for instance, led him to launch the Voter Fraud Commission with the purpose of investigating the conspiracies he had manufactured, without any factual basis, as an excuse for losing the popular vote. With the resources of the federal government—and dozens of staffers devoted to the cause—the commission could have been weaponized to drive down voter turnout. Thankfully, incompetence led its leaders to violate the Constitution, over and over again, in such blatant ways—including asking all fifty states for information on the voting history of their residents—that President Trump was left with no choice but to dissolve the commission only months after it was created amid an avalanche of lawsuits. And when the commission shut down, it did so without producing a single shred of evidence supporting the idea of widespread voter fraud.

The Trump administration's malevolence is also what led them to try to add a citizenship question to the U.S. Census, with the hope that doing so would stop immigrants from filling it out, leaving their neighborhoods underresourced and underrepresented. But incompetence once again saved the day, as cabinet officials left behind a paper trail detailing the racist intent of what they were doing. (The question, leaked documents revealed, was included because it would be "advantageous to Republicans and non-Hispanic whites," despite the administration's perjurious claim that its purpose was to enable the federal government to better enforce the Voting Rights Act.)

Again and again, our country was rescued by the fact that, as *The New Republic*'s Alex Shephard noted, President Trump and his apparatchiks repeatedly had the wrong answer to the sage question posed by *The Wire*'s Stringer Bell: "Is you taking notes on a criminal fucking conspiracy?"

But while for much of his presidency, Trump's incompetence tended to mitigate the impact of his malevolence, he nonetheless managed to seriously wound our democracy. "So what if he was bad at it?" wrote *The Atlantic*'s Adam Serwer, one of our preeminent essayists, in an article comparing the damage Trump had done to our country to getting shot in the leg. "Even nonfatal gunshot wounds do terrible things to the human body," he explained. "They can twist flesh and muscle as if they were dough; shatter bones to dust; leave victims unable to walk without assistance; keep survivors from closing their fingers into a fist. They can poison the blood, drown the lungs, and—even when the body escapes being disfigured—leave the brain scarred by trauma."

So it was with Donald Trump. Sure, some of his most blatant attempts to subvert democracy had failed, but on the eve of the 2020 election, America's institutions had been severely wounded—damaged by a president who had spent four years abusing his power: sowing distrust in the press; fomenting divisions between parties; profiting from the presidency; and treating the Justice Department like his personal law firm, shutting down cases he didn't like and opening ones we didn't need.

What's worse, many of the checks we had on the presidency didn't work. The Supreme Court signed off on the key pillars of Trump's agenda. His attorneys general covered up investigations into his misconduct. The Senate refused to hold him accountable even after he committed the paradigmatic high crime: coercing a foreign power to help him win in an election.

Ultimately, it became clear that the only check left on his power was the people—and if we were going to defeat him, we would need to turn out in droves, despite all the suppressive laws that had passed in the absence of a functioning Voting Rights Act, and despite a global pandemic that threatened to make voting a comorbidity, in no small part because the sitting president sabotaged our country's response to it.

There was also the knowledge in the back of everyone's minds—knowledge they knew to be true but didn't want to believe; knowledge *I* knew to be true but didn't want to believe—that while defeating Trump would be hard, convincing him to leave would be even harder.

* * *

You can't fault Chris Wallace for trying.

Four years had passed since their back-and-forth at the presidential debate, and in 2020, Wallace once again had a chance to interview President Trump—so he asked the question he always asked, hoping, hopelessly, to receive a different answer: Will you accept the results of the election?

Trump's reply? "I'm not going to just say yes. I'm not going to say no."

Later in the summer, at the Republican National Convention, the president declared: "The only way they can take this election away from us is if this is a rigged election." And in the months that followed, while polls showed him down big, he began laying the groundwork for protesting the results—stoking fears about the widespread use of mail-in ballots, tweeting that they were "INACCURATE & FRAUDULENT"; spreading false rumors about "people that aren't citizens" voting; at one point, even tweeting that we should "Delay the Election," which isn't exactly the kind of thing you hear every day from the president in a democracy.

So when, at two-thirty A.M. on Election Night, President Trump claimed victory—boasting "we did win this election," even though, by that point, it was becoming clear he was losing—nobody should have been surprised. But what happened next, even if it wasn't unexpected, was unprecedented: The president of the United States wielded the power of his office in an effort to overturn the will of the people.

He started in the courts—filing sixty-three lawsuits that challenged the results of the election. In the days that followed, he lost sixty-two of them, a record that made the Bad News Bears look like the '27 Yankees. (The one case he did win could have affected only a handful of votes in Pennsylvania, where Joe Biden had come out on top by eighty thousand.) Even the Supreme Court, which by now had six conservatives on the bench—including two new Trump appointees, Brett Kavanaugh and Amy Coney Barrett, who had replaced the late Ruth Bader Ginsburg on the bench after Americans had already started voting (in a historic act of hypocrisy on the part of Senate Republicans that I will unpack in chapter 11, "Saving the Court")—refused to hear President Trump's arguments, prompting him to tweet: "It is a legal disgrace, an embarrassment to the USA!!!"

Realizing he would not be saved by the courts, Trump decided to take an extrajudicial approach to challenging the results of the election—an approach that relied on the antiquated and arbitrary process America uses to certify its elections, a process that dates back to our nation's founding.

As you know by now, our founders weren't the biggest fans of direct democracy. So at the Constitutional Convention, they decided that instead of sending whatever candidate received the most votes to the White House, they would leave presidential elections up to a body called the Electoral College. Every state, they decided, would send exactly as many delegates to the college as they had representatives and senators in Congress—and, at first, delegates had full discretion over which candidate they would support.

Over the following centuries, this system evolved (as I will detail in chapter 10, "Saving the Presidency"), and by 2020, the Electoral College had become a formality: Each delegate would support whichever candidate had won the most votes in their state—or, in the case of Maine and Nebraska, in their district—as determined by the officially certified results. Then it was up to Congress to formalistically tally up the verdict of the Electoral College and declare a winner.

Even Al Gore, who had won the popular vote and lost the decisive state in the Electoral College by fewer than six hundred votes, did not try to interfere with this process outside the legal system. But President Trump was going to do everything he could to stay in power—and he realized that while the customs surrounding the Electoral College had changed over the past centuries, most of the laws had not, meaning it was still possible, at least in theory, for obdurate certifiers, faithless electors, or rogue representatives to overturn the will of the people. And President Trump stopped at nothing in his attempts to make sure they would.

Brad Raffensperger wasn't only a Republican. Georgia's secretary of state was a Trump supporter. A man of MAGA. And he was "proud" of it. Now, because he was in charge of running the state's elections—and didn't want to pierce the veil of impartiality—he declined to make a public endorsement in 2020, but he had vocally stood by Trump in 2016, and he had been rooting hard for the Republican candidate to win another four years in the White House.

But when it came time to tally up the votes, there was a problem: Raffensperger saw himself first and foremost as an engineer who lived by the motto that "numbers don't lie." And the data couldn't have been clearer: Joe Biden had won the presidential election in the state of Georgia.

This, naturally, was not what President Trump wanted to hear—so after seeing Secretary of State Raffensperger announce the election results on television, the commander in chief decided to ring him up. "I didn't lose the state, Brad," he fumed, before diving into a cacophony of conspiracy theories outlining why he believed he had really won.

"Mr. President," Raffensperger insisted, "the data you have is wrong," responding to Trump's claim that there had been hundreds of thousands of fraudulent votes. But the president refused to be dissuaded. And by the end of the call, he had dubbed the secretary of state a "criminal," before making him an offer so blatantly over the line that if Chris Moltisanti had proposed it, Tony Soprano would have said: "Are you sure about this, Christopher?"

"I just want to find 11,780 votes," President Trump told the secretary of state, a number that would have closed the 11,779 vote gap that separated him from Biden. "So what are we going to do here, folks?" he continued. "I only need 11,000 votes. Fellas, I need 11,000 votes. Give me a break."

Of course, in a democracy, you don't find votes. You count them. And the numbers didn't add up for President Trump. But that didn't stop him from trying to pressure everyone he could into flipping the election his way.

It wasn't only Raffensperger. In Georgia, Trump had already tried and failed to strong-arm the governor, notorious vote suppressor Brian Kemp, into changing the results. He had also called Frances Watson, the state's chief elections investigator, and attempted to goad her into coming to "the right answer" in her inquiry. Meanwhile, the U.S. attorney from Atlanta, Byung Pak, faced so much pressure to back up President Trump's allegations of voter fraud in Georgia that he decided to resign before he could be fired. Across the state, election officials received so many threats to their safety that Gabriel Sterling, Georgia's voting systems implementation manager and himself a Republican, begged the president to lower the temperature. "Mr. President, you have not condemned these actions or this language," he pleaded. "Stop inspiring people to commit potential acts of violence. Someone is going to get hurt, someone is going to get shot, someone is going to get killed. And it's not right."

Trump's attempts to intimidate election officials went well beyond the Peach State. In Michigan, he hounded Republicans on the certification board, telling them to question the results of the election—an effort that might have succeeded but for the bravery of Aaron Van Langevelde, an ardent Republican, who certified the tally because he believed it was his duty to our democracy. "Time will tell that those who spread misinformation and tried to overturn the election were wrong," Van Langevelde declared, "and they should be held responsible for the chaos and confusion they have caused."

This didn't stop President Trump. In fact, two days later, he flew Republicans from the Michigan state legislature to the District of Columbia—hoping he could convince them to join his effort. Alas, "We have not yet been made aware of any information that would change the outcome of the election in Michigan," they wrote, "and, as legislative leaders, we will follow the law and follow the normal process regarding Michigan's electors, just as we have said throughout this election."

Over the following weeks, President Trump hit the phones with the verve of Gordon Gekko trying to corner the market on Teldar Paper. He was even seemingly caught calling Arizona governor Doug Ducey while the governor was being interviewed on television as the state's election results were being certified. And behind the scenes, he was orchestrating the ouster of Jeff Sessions's successor, a truly disgraceful attorney general named William Barr, one of the president's most loyal allies, because the AG had the audacity to say he hadn't seen "fraud on a scale that could have affected a different outcome in the election."

By the end of the year, it had become clear that President Trump could not stop the certification of the election in the states—and as a result, he couldn't block the Electoral College from awarding a majority of delegates to Joe Biden. This meant he had only one move left: interfering with the counting of the electoral votes in Congress, which was scheduled to take place on the sixth of January, 2021.

The stars and bars of the Confederacy waving, for the first time, on the floor of Congress. A noose and gallows, erected outside, swaying back and forth with the wind. A police officer, beaten over the head with a Betsy Ross flag, one of 140 injured that day, while rebels in Viking horns and "Camp Auschwitz" sweatshirts desecrated the Citadel of Democracy—encouraged by the president of the United States to "walk down to the Capitol" and "fight like hell."

Gabriel Sterling was right: President Trump's rhetoric did end up killing people—five, in fact, not to mention at least four police officers at the scene who took their lives in the months that followed.

In its aftermath, many have tried to erase the danger of the insurrection from our memory—framing the events of January 6 as the ending of President Trump's effort to overturn the election.

And I can understand why that's a tempting narrative to embrace. After all, it's true that by the end of the night, once police officers had swept the Capitol for bombs a final time, Congress had reassembled, counted up the votes, and declared that Joe Biden would be the next president of the United States. "To those who wreaked havoc in our Capitol today, you did not win," declared a triumphant Mike Pence, whom the insurrectionists had threatened to hang because he hadn't been willing to overrule the Electoral College and install President Trump for another four years. (President Trump, unsurprisingly, sided with the insurrectionists. Ten minutes after the vice president had been evacuated from the Capitol with his life under threat, @realDonaldTrump laid into him: "Mike Pence didn't have the courage to do what should have been done to protect our Country and our Constitution.")

Over the weeks that followed, leaders in the GOP initially condemned President Trump in stronger terms than they ever had before—which, of course, isn't saying all that much. "Count me out," Senator Lindsey Graham declared. "Enough is enough." Mitch McConnell admitted that President Trump had committed a "disgraceful dereliction of duty." In total, ten Republican congressmen and seven Republican senators, though not Graham or McConnell themselves, voted to convict President Trump of inciting the events of January 6, a bipartisan impeachment the likes of which our country had never seen.

This is one way the history books could tell the story of January 6—as a moment when politicians put partisanship aside to defend our democracy; as a moment when our institutions overcame an insurrection.

But the real story of that day isn't how our country came together to make sure this coup attempt failed. It's how close it came to succeeding—and how quickly, in states across the country, Republicans began working to make sure that, next time, it could.

The first reason Donald Trump's insurrection failed was simple: The election wasn't all that close. Joe Biden had defeated the incumbent 306–232 in electoral votes, which happened to be the same margin by which President Trump had beaten Hillary Clinton in what he then called a "massive landslide victory."

And, notably, unlike Trump, Biden didn't lose the popular vote; in fact, he won it by a whopping 7 million.

One of the reasons President Biden performed so well was that 2020 saw record turnout, as the pandemic forced states across the country to make it easier to vote—expanding access to mail-in ballots, setting up drive-through polling places, and increasing the number of early voting days. For anyone who believed in democracy, it had been one of the most promising developments in a year full of pain, proof that when you eliminate barriers to voting, Americans will make their voices heard. But for Republicans, aware that their agenda did not align with the interests of a majority of Americans—and that the country wouldn't become any more favorable to their ideas in the years ahead—it was a nightmare.

After all, as I mentioned in the note at the beginning of the book, this Trumpified Republican Party just isn't all that into democracy—regardless of its impact on their electoral prospects—because their priority isn't exercising the will of the people; it's accruing the power to implement their agenda *whether or not* it's aligned with the will of the people.

And so within days of President Biden's inauguration, in states across the country, Republican legislatures began rolling back the progress we'd made on turnout under the guise of protecting future elections from voter fraud—in the process, lending credibility to the "Big Lie" that President Trump had used to justify his attempted coup.

In fact, according to the Brennan Center, by June 2021, legislatures had introduced more than 380 bills that would have restricted access to the polls—dozens of which became laws across swing states like Florida, Georgia, and Nevada, as well as conservative strongholds like Idaho, Wyoming, and Kentucky. Many of these bills were designed to make it harder to vote by mail. Others made it more difficult to vote in person. One bill, in Georgia, criminalized offering food or water to voters waiting in line to cast their ballots, a seemingly random form of suppression that starts to make more sense when you remember how much longer lines are in predominantly Black neighborhoods across Georgia than they are in predominantly white ones.

By October 2021, thirty-three of these laws were enacted across nineteen states. And it's hard to imagine many of them being struck down by the courts—not only because of the ruling in *Shelby County,* which continued to limit the Justice Department's ability to fight voter suppression, but also because in the 2021 case *Brnovich v. Democratic National Committee,* the Supreme Court's conservative majority gutted the Voting Rights Act even further.

In his majority ruling, Justice Samuel Alito demonstrated a radical understanding of voting rights. Unlike in past decisions, where the court had consistently expressed a belief that barriers to the ballot should be looked at as suspect, Justice Alito's opinion attempted to normalize them. Walking outside your house in order to vote is already an obstacle, he argued, so why should we punish state legislatures for making it even harder to cast a ballot? It's a decision that will ultimately leave voting rights almost exclusively in the hands of the lower courts—and at this point, if they decline to strike down suppressive bills, I doubt the Supreme Court will overrule them.

The good news is, it remains to be seen whether these laws will achieve their desired ends—because studies have found that Republican attempts to strip people of the franchise can sometimes inspire Democrats to turn out in greater numbers. This isn't to say the bills won't flip some elections in favor of Republicans. They very well could, especially because reducing turnout at the margins by even a fraction of a percent can change the results of close races. Nonetheless, this isn't a reason to despair. It's a reason to organize, as Albert Turner would have.

Of course, Republicans understand these dynamics, too, which is why they have not been satisfied with simply trying to suppress the vote. They have also gerrymandered districts, so it's functionally impossible for them to lose, no matter how many people turn out. And since 2020, they have also been working methodically to make it harder for the Democratic Party to win the next presidential election, even if its candidate does manage to bring home more votes than their opponent.

This initiative has two components—and the first is simple: stripping everyone who stood up to Donald Trump in 2020 of their power. Remember Aaron Van Langevelde, who certified the results of the election in Michigan, despite President Trump's pressure campaign? He lost his seat on the board. Liz Cheney, who voted to impeach President Trump after the insurrection, also had her leadership positions taken away. Brad Raffensperger was targeted, too, faced with a primary campaign from a candidate backed by President Trump himself.

(Many of the other Republicans who criticized Trump in the aftermath of January 6, meanwhile, have repented by backing off their claims. Kevin McCarthy, the GOP leader in the House, who initially admitted that Trump "bears responsibility" for the attack on the Capitol, ended up spearheading the effort to punish Cheney. Mitch McConnell has now pledged to "absolutely" support Trump if he is the Republican nominee in 2024. Lindsey Graham, for his part, returned to regularly going down to Mar-a-Lago to golf with Trump.)

The upshot is clear: The reason President Trump's coup failed wasn't that Republicans were willing to stand up to him. It was that in most states, votes were still counted and certified by people who put their patriotism above their party—or weren't political to begin with. Which brings me to the second aspect of the Republican attack on democracy in the aftermath of the 2020 election: making sure that in the future, they will be the ones running elections.

As a report from the nonpartisan nonprofit organization Protect Democracy found, states across the country have introduced bills that would provide partisan, gerrymandered legislatures with more authority over how presidential elections are conducted, allowing them to micromanage who is on the voter rolls, how ballots are counted, and, in some cases, whether the results get certified.

It's unclear how many of these bills will become law, though in Georgia, one of them has already passed, transferring many of the responsibilities that were once in the hands of the secretary of state (read: Brad Raffensperger) to the Republican state legislature (read: die-hard Trumpers). But the fact that these bills are even being introduced is a terrifying prospect in itself. Because it's proof that the idea of questioning the results of a democratic election is no longer fringe. It's in the new Republican mainstream. And even with these bills still in limbo, conspiracy theorists who believed President Trump's allegations about the 2020 election have risen to power across the country, winning positions as local voting judges and inspectors in Pennsylvania and seats on canvassing boards in Michigan. As President Trump's chief strategist in the White House, Steve Bannon, declared on an episode of his podcast, "We're taking over all the elections."

And whether Trump ends up being on the ballot again in 2024 or not, it's difficult to picture the next Republican candidate for president rejecting help from these elements of the party willing to do anything to make sure they come out on top, whether or not they win the most votes.

* * *

We could always get lucky.

In 2024, Republicans could decide to do the right thing and certify the results of the election regardless of which candidate comes out on top.

But should we bet our democracy on it?

If a Democrat is winning—especially if there is a tighter margin than there was in 2020—Republicans may once again spread the lie that the election has been decided by widespread voter fraud. Perhaps this time, Republicans will control the certification process in swing states, while also maintaining control of Congress, which has the final say on whether a presidential election is ratified; and perhaps they will use that power to overturn the will of the people.

That would be the kind of wound from which a nation never recovers.

Which leaves us with an existential question: How do we save our democracy before it's too late?

Part III

A MORE PERFECT FUTURE

7

MAKING IT EASIER TO VOTE

There were only five months until one of the most important elections in history—and Harris County didn't have anyone to run its elections.

The county clerk had resigned, without leaving a plan behind, and no one wanted the job, which was a problem for Chris Hollins, because he was called on to help identify a replacement. "I was coming up kind of empty," he remembers, "and at some point, I was like: Maybe this is me."

By any objective measure, this was a bad idea. And when Chris told his mentors he was considering it, they asked him a simple question: "Are you crazy?"

The job, they explained, was a political land mine, telling him "it would be the beginning and end of your political career." It would also be a stain on his résumé, which would have been a shame, because Chris Hollins had built quite the CV. The son of an African American father who had spent more than three decades as a Houston police officer and a white mother who had fostered more than twenty kids during his childhood, Chris had gone on to receive an honors degree from Morehouse College—and then got degrees from Yale Law School and Harvard Business School . . . at the same time. He had work experience at McKinsey & Company, Goldman Sachs, and the White House. And as though that weren't enough, he had also been serving as vice chair for finance of the Texas Democratic Party while working on opening a small business, a sports bar called Stacked Pickle. In a game where credentials are currency, Chris Hollins owned Boardwalk and Park Place.

And then, after spending the first thirty-four years of his life navigating some of America's most hallowed halls, he was going to run elections in Harris County? Filling a vacancy whose previous occupants had been infamous—or, when they did their jobs well, anonymous? All those degrees, and Chris Hollins thought *this* made sense?

Not exactly. But he also didn't have much of a choice. There was an election to run, and since no one else with the chops for it had the desire to run it, Chris decided he was the guy for the job—in no small part, he says, because of how much he loved his country. "Being able to get out of the neighborhood I grew up in," he explains, "led me to believe more in what America could be or aspired to be.

"And for as long as I can remember," he continued, "I have been of the mind-set that free and fair elections are a central part of what makes the American project special."

So on June 1, 2020, with one month until runoffs in Texas and five months until the general election, Chris took over as clerk of the biggest county in the Lone Star State—the third largest in the country. It wasn't a fancy title—and during years without elections, the position entails clerical work and record keeping—but in 2020, it came with a Texas-size responsibility: administering a presidential race in the middle of a pandemic that could have made voting a death sentence.

When Chris took the job, he had two goals: making sure people didn't die on his watch—and making sure democracy didn't die. The former wasn't as easy as it sounds. On his first day, Chris found out the county hadn't even secured personal protective equipment for its election workers, let alone hand sanitizer for voters. In fact, no legitimate COVID-19 protocols of any kind had been put in place. So Chris got to work trying to keep everyone safe—calling grocery stores to see how much Purell they went through in a day for a frame of reference, finding wholesalers who could produce enough masks at a reasonable price, and fighting for an increased budget to pay for all of it.

The second goal, keeping democracy alive, was even harder. This was Texas, the state of the white primary—a state where the laws of the Jim Crow era and the lynchings that protected those laws had blocked African Americans from voting for more than a century. It was also the state where Republicans had begun trying to suppress the vote since the turn of the century and had only increased the pace of that effort after *Shelby County v. Holder.*

But Chris was convinced it was the county clerk's job to make it easier, not harder, to vote. So despite the forces working against him, despite the inertia of incompetence and the stain of suppression, that's what he set out to do. Placing ballot drop-off locations and drive-through polling sites across the county—so voting would be more safe and less difficult, especially for folks with disabilities. Expanding early-voting hours—so Texans could cast their ballots no matter what time they got off their shift or when they got their kids to sleep. Opening new polling locations—so commutes would be shorter and lines would be shorter, too. Sending letters to seniors informing them that they could vote by mail—so they wouldn't have to risk their health to make their voices heard. Paying election workers $17 an hour, which was more than double the state's minimum wage—so they could put food on the table and keep a roof over their heads.

At the time, the twenty-three-point plan Chris implemented was covered in the media as radical, and in some ways, that was true. After all, no one had ever done anything quite like it, especially in Texas. But if you look past the political context, what Chris did—hand in hand with leaders like Harris County commissioners Rodney Ellis and Adrian Garcia and then twenty-nine-year-old county judge Lina Hidalgo—wasn't revolutionary. It was bold common sense. And it was patriotic. Because if you believe in democracy, if you believe in a government of, by, and for the people, then making it easy to vote isn't a subversive thing for a county clerk to do. It's in his job description! And it's consistent with who we say we are.

Of course, this didn't insulate Chris from backlash. Practically as soon as he began implementing his agenda, Harris County started receiving threats from Texas's Republican secretary of state and governor. Chris was sent cease and desists. At one point, a state representative sued him and asked a judge to throw out 127,000 Harris County ballots because they had been cast at drive-through polling places. But none of this deterred Chris, or the election workers who put their lives on the line to implement his plan, or the voters determined to exercise their sacred civil right.

By the time Election Day came around, Harris County had already left its previous record for voter turnout in the dust—with 1.26 million ballots cast through early voting, more than double the previous record. And when the polls closed, more than six in every ten citizens in the county had made their voices heard. This included one couple, Chris remembers, both of whom were over seventy, who had never voted before: "They came out to vote this time because it was made simple for them.

"It was truly moving and inspiring," he explained, before listing off stories of other voters whose experiences "moved me to tears." The veteran who was suffering from PTSD and would have faced "debilitating anxiety" in a crowded polling place but was able to proudly vote at a drive-through location. The nurse who told Chris through "tears of her own" that she had been working back-to-back shifts for a month and was only able to vote because polling locations were open in the middle of the night. The caretaker who wouldn't have been able to cast her ballot in person because she was afraid of infecting her mother, who was fighting cancer—but rested easy after voting at a contactless site.

And it's important to note that all these new voters turning out didn't rig the election in favor of Democrats. In fact, Texas Republicans outperformed expectations up and down the ballot in 2020. These results don't dilute the importance of what Chris did. They underline it. Because they prove that when you make it easier to vote, you don't necessarily help one political party or another. You help America realize its promise—bringing us closer to becoming a true, real democracy, not just in theory, but in practice.

That's what Chris Hollins did for Harris County in 2020. And if we fight for voting rights, it's what we have a chance to do for our country in the years ahead.

This raises a question: What does it look like to make America a democracy? I believe the answer has two parts.

The first is fixing our elections. Because if the United States is going to be a representative democracy, then all our citizens need to be able to vote—and they shouldn't be stopped from doing so based on where they live, what they look like, how much money they have, who they're likely to vote for, or whether they can afford to wait in line.

The second is fixing our institutions. Because right now—with an unrepresentative Senate, an unnecessary and anti-democratic Electoral College, a gerrymandered House of Representatives and panoply of state legislatures, and a stolen Supreme Court—the ideal of every person having an equal say in our democracy, the idea of "one person, one vote," is far from a reality. And that would still hold true, even if we fixed the problems with our elections, even if we had 100 percent voter turnout. Because the reason our institutions are broken, the reason they overrepresent the interests of one segment of our population, is that this is how those who enslaved people who looked like me—and who guided the writing of the Constitution—designed them to work.

But here's the thing: The principal way to reform those institutions is by passing legislation, and the way to pass legislation is by winning elections, and the way those in favor of democracy are going to win elections is if those contests are a fair fight. So that's where I'm going to start, with the solutions to the problems plaguing our elections, which boil down to one key principle, the same principle that guided Chris Hollins: making it easier to vote.

Make It Easier to Register

In Germany, weeks before you turn eighteen years old, you receive a letter in the mail informing you that you will be registered to vote. In Argentina, they don't even need to notify you, because everyone already knows they're on the rolls. That's how it works in most functioning democracies: When you're old enough to cast a ballot, you can show up to the polls on Election Day and vote—without having to fill out any paperwork beforehand.

America, meanwhile, the birthplace of modern democracy, makes the process much more complicated. Instead of the government registering citizens, in the United States, you have to register yourself. In some states, you have to do it with pen and paper, by snail mail, regardless of whether you even have an address. In others, you aren't allowed to have family or friends help you, even if you have a disability. And for all these reasons, about one in four eligible voters has slipped through the cracks—left off the rolls and out of the democratic process. One in four.

This has real consequences: Even in 2020, a year with record turnout, more than eighty million eligible citizens didn't cast a ballot, and the number one reason they cited for their lack of participation was the fact that they had never registered in the first place.

There is a better way—and it starts with **automatic voter registration** (AVR).

Here's how it should work: Every American would be registered to vote as soon as they turn eighteen years old. Whenever they interact with the government—whenever they file their taxes or go to the DMV, apply for benefits or contact a government agency—their information would be updated, which would have the benefit of increasing the accuracy of our voter rolls. And only if they did something to lose their eligibility (say, commit a murder) would their registration be revoked.

To be clear: AVR would not force citizens to vote. If you want to stay home on Election Day watching reruns of *The Bachelor* or college football games, nothing is stopping you—

except your dignity and common sense. All AVR does is make sure that if you do want to vote, and you're eligible, you will be able to do so.

It's also worth noting that AVR doesn't require you to provide the government with any new information. Just the opposite: It allows the government to use the information you've *already* shared with them to get you on the voter rolls—not unlike how they sign you up for jury duty—so you don't need to fill out yet another form.

Now, AVR is only a first step. Sometimes, you're going to change addresses, without, for instance, updating your information on the rolls. For this reason, we also need to implement **same-day registration** (SDR)—so if you show up to the polls with proof that you live in the district, you can sign up right then and there. The states where SDR is already in place are the ones with the highest voter turnout in the country, and they've seen especially high turnout in communities of color. If the rest of the United States followed suit, according to a study from the Center for American Progress, we could see more than five million new voters at the polls, which is an astonishing number when you think about the fact that the last two presidential elections have come down to a few thousand votes in the decisive swing states.

Finally, as we continue building support for AVR and SDR, there are even simpler steps we can take right away to make it easier to register. One of these is **allowing sixteen- and seventeen-year-olds to preregister**—so on their eighteenth birthdays, they will immediately show up on the rolls—as is already the case in some form in twenty-five states. Another is **bringing the system online.** In Georgia, one of the states that has already done this, more than 350,000 voters have registered over the internet; and a study showed that they were 20 percent more likely to vote than those who had registered in other ways. That may not sound like all that many voters—but in 2020, Joe Biden edged out Donald Trump in Georgia by fewer than fifteen thousand votes. So online registration might very well have made the difference.

That's a demonstration of how even the minor steps we take to expand access to the ballot can have major consequences. And it's a reminder of why it's so important to fight for all policies that will make it easier to vote, no matter how incremental they may seem.

In 2018, millions of Floridians showed up to the polls and sent Ron DeSantis, one of the most conservative politicians in the country, to the governor's mansion. Like the presidential election in 2000, it was a close race, decided by less than 1 percent. But that same year, on the same ballot, the same electorate resoundingly voted in favor of a ballot initiative many had thought would only appeal to Democrats.

In a 65 percent to 35 percent landslide, Floridians decided to restore voting rights to the 1.7 million residents of the state who had formerly been incarcerated. The ACLU and Freedom Partners, an organization funded by the Koch brothers, both came out in support of the outcome. And Americans across the country, from all political persuasions, celebrated what seemed like the most widespread enfranchisement of voters in a generation.

But when Governor DeSantis took power, he refused to let this change go into effect. Instead of just allowing formerly incarcerated Floridians to register, he and the Republican legislature defied the people and implemented a policy mandating that they had to prove that they had paid off any fines or other court obligations they owed. But the state never built a database with information on who still owed money. So, as *The New York*

Times reported, sixteen months after the referendum passed, Florida "had failed to process any of the more than 85,000 voting registration applications submitted by former felons," since there was no way for them to prove they were no longer in debt to the state.

That includes people like Jamall Williams, who told *The Washington Post* that "they kept sending me from office to office to office to office." He had been excited to become a voter, he said, because his wife volunteered to register people in her free time. "That's how I met her," he explained. "She tried to register me to vote, and I wasn't able." At this point, he said, he wants to give up, because he has no idea if he has court debts and doesn't "want to go to jail" for registering if he does.

Florida isn't the only state where this is a problem. Across the country, 5.2 million citizens remain disenfranchised as a result of having committed a felony, even though they are no longer behind bars. And these Americans are more than four times more likely to be Black than they are to be white. It's an injustice folks from across the political spectrum know is wrong—and the federal government has it in its power to make it right by passing a law stating that if you have served your time and exit the criminal justice system, you are automatically registered to vote.

Enfranchising the formerly incarcerated is the right thing to do. The American people support it. And we've waited long enough to act.

Make It Easier to Cast Your Ballot

Of course, registering is only half the battle—because even if you're registered, you still have to figure out how to vote, which isn't always easy.

In five states, you can only cast a ballot on one day, which happens to be the first Tuesday of November, a day that was convenient for farm owners back when America was founded (because they could travel to their polling place after church on Sunday and be back in time to sell their produce at the market on Wednesday), but is, uh, less convenient for the tens of millions of Americans who have to work during the week, particularly those who also have kids at home. There is also the problem of lines at the polls, which are especially long in underfunded communities of color, and have been known to keep people waiting for hours in major elections.

This has left millions of Americans with a choice no one should have to face—between fulfilling their duties as citizens and fulfilling their duties as employees, between missing an election and missing a paycheck. But there is no reason this has to be the case. In fact, in forty-five states and the District of Columbia, it isn't. From Texas to Alaska, early voting has brought millions of Americans into our elections who wouldn't otherwise have been able to participate—and studies estimate that if it were implemented nationally, early voting would increase participation by as much as 4 percent in areas that offer it.

And think about who, exactly, that 4 percent would be. The mother working double shifts to provide for her family who couldn't find the time to vote on a Tuesday but could head to the polls after church on Sunday. The college student holding down two jobs to minimize student loans who can't squeeze waiting on the hours-long line but could find time between classes a few weeks before Election Day when the crowds tend to be smaller. The truck driver who knows he's going to have to make deliveries out of state on Election Day but could vote on his day off the week before. These Americans deserve a voice in our democracy.

Thankfully, most states in America have some form of early voting, but it's a patchwork system, starting as early as September in Minnesota and as late as seven days before polls close in Oklahoma. This should be standardized at the national level, with all voters having at least two weeks to vote, including weekends, so they have time to clear out a window in their calendar.

Some voting rights advocates have argued that there should be twenty days of early voting, which makes good enough sense. But honestly, I'm not sure I have a better guess at the optimal length than anyone else. We should run studies to figure out when there start to be diminishing returns. Here's what I do know: The right number of days during which citizens should be able to vote isn't "one," and making sure every American at the very least has two weeks to cast a ballot should be a no-brainer.

And here's something else I know: **You shouldn't have to travel a long distance to get to the polls.** The good news is that the days of people having to ride hundreds of miles on horseback to cast their ballots are over, but too many Americans still live too far from their polling locations. In fact, since *Shelby*, more than 1,688 voting sites have been shut down in former preclearance states alone—increasing wait times across the country, especially in Black and brown neighborhoods. In Georgia, for instance, where one in ten polling locations have closed since *Shelby*, during the 2020 election, if you went to vote after seven P.M. in a predominantly white Atlanta neighborhood, the average wait time was six minutes. In predominantly non-white neighborhoods? It was fifty-one, more than eight times longer. That's an utter disgrace. And the federal government should pass a law preventing this from happening, offering to fill funding gaps if local boards of elections demonstrate a legitimate need for capital to expand the capacity and number of their polling places.

Now, we should also make it easier to vote without having to travel at all—by establishing a **universal option to vote at home.** Historically, mail-in and absentee ballots have been disproportionately used by seniors, who tend to be more conservative, which means expanding these programs could benefit Republicans. But this Democrat says we should do it anyway, because doing so would make our elections better representative of the interests of the people.

What would that look like?

Rather than require voters to request a mail-in ballot, we would automatically send ballots to all voters. This would provide citizens with more time to research the candidates and issues on their ballots. It would make it easier to vote, too, since they wouldn't need to travel to a polling place and could instead leave their ballots in drop boxes or mailboxes. And if voters did want to show up in person, they would still have that choice—in fact, they would benefit from shorter lines, since so many people who ordinarily would have been waiting at polling locations would have already cast their ballots from home.

Colorado does this, and it's proven highly successful. By expanding access to voting by mail—and investing in 24/7 drop boxes like the ones Chris Hollins put up across Harris County—the Centennial State has significantly boosted participation in elections.

Of course, even if we did all this around the country, most voters would probably still want to cast their ballots on Election Day—whether because of tradition, camaraderie, or procrastination. So the last step we need to take to make it easy to vote is to enshrine **Election Day as a national holiday** so Americans can have time off from work to perform their civic duty. This would have the added benefit of bringing America back to the excitement of Election Days past when, as Jill Lepore writes, elections were treated as a "holiday, involving plenty of stumping, debating, and parading." Not only would making Election Day a celebration be more fun, studies have shown that creating a "more festive and social voting environment" would actually lead to greater turnout. So it wouldn't just be a good time. It would also be good policy.

I know all these proposals sound technical—and "More drop boxes!" isn't exactly a catchy slogan. But that's precisely the reason the system is so broken. For a long time, the only people paying attention to these issues were the ones trying to make it harder to vote. That needs to change. After all, while AVR, SDR, early voting, and mail-in ballots aren't sexy and don't make for a fun bumper sticker or a fierce water cooler debate, I promise that everything you care about—whether that's expanding access to healthcare, beating back climate change, reforming the criminal justice system, or stopping future attempts at suppression—comes down to us getting this right.

That's why Chris Hollins ignored his mentors to become a county clerk—he knew there was nothing more important he could be doing with his time than making our democracy, well, a democracy. And the same is true for the rest of us.

So let's get to work.

8

MAKING IT HARDER TO SUPPRESS THE VOTE

If I were a Republican in Texas after the 2020 election, I would have been feeling pretty good.

Democrats had been talking smack for years—and yet the Grand Old Party remained in control of both chambers of the state legislature. The governor was Republican, too, as were the lieutenant governor and attorney general. And this was in the aftermath of record voter turnout, powered by programs like the ones pioneered by Chris Hollins—so if ever there were a time for Republicans to sit back and bask in the glory of an election, this was it.

But in the era of Donald Trump—with the conspiracy theory of voter fraud spreading as uncontrollably as the pandemic to which his party seemed indifferent—Republicans didn't have any interest in accepting the results of elections, even when they won. Instead, wherever they could find power, they wielded their authority to make it harder to vote. And to that end, as soon as the legislative session began, Texas Republicans introduced a bill meticulously and methodically designed to disenfranchise Democrats across the state.

Remember the drive-through voting sites Chris Hollins erected in Harris County—so Texans who were elderly, immunocompromised, and disabled could exercise their right to vote without jeopardizing their health? The bill would ban them, just as it would ban 24/7 drop boxes so many parents had relied on to cast their ballots early in the morning before work or late at night after tucking their kids into bed. Voting by mail was made more difficult, too. And the bill also proposed reducing early voting hours, including on the Sunday before the election, when so many members of African American churches vote because pastors organize "souls to the polls" events immediately after service.

Perhaps most concerningly, it included a section titled "OVERTURNING ELECTIONS," which would have made it possible for any judge in Texas to stop the certification of results on the basis of alleged voter fraud.

This was a bill whose antidemocratic DNA was unambiguous—and it was exactly the kind of legislation a normal Department of Justice would have stopped from going into effect with an intact Voting Rights Act. But we were living in America after *Shelby*, which meant that if Texas's government passed the bill, there was very little chance of stopping it from becoming law. And on May 30, 2021, that seemed like it was going to happen.

But Democrats had an idea. In the Texas House of Representatives, even if a bill has support from the majority, it cannot pass unless two-thirds of members are present—and the legislative session was set to end at midnight. So if the Democratic representatives walked out of the building, they could block the passage of the bill, at least until the next session.

"I know the play," Trey Martinez Fischer, a representative from San Antonio, whispered to his colleague Gina Hinojosa. "We break quorum, fly to Washington, and tell Congress to pass the John Lewis Voting Rights Advancement Act," a piece of legislation that would have not only reinstated the protections of the 1965 bill but also expanded them.

Gina was down—and she decided to bring all her colleagues together to see if they would join her in taking this "leap of faith."

That is when Senfronia Thompson, a member who had been serving longer than Hinojosa had been alive, spoke up. The night before, after having to sit through a debate on the bill that lasted more than twenty-three hours, she hadn't slept much. But the eighty-two-year-old, known as the dean of the Texas House, wasn't out of energy. Not even close. And she had a story she wanted to tell.

Growing up in Texas during the era of white primaries and poll taxes, Senfronia was horrified by how hard it was for her grandmother to vote. "She would save pennies and nickels to buy a poll tax," she remembers, because for a woman who made only two dollars a week, "quarters were too much." And every Election Day, her grandmother would wake up at four-thirty A.M. to catch a bus to her polling place, miles and miles away from her home, carrying $1.25 in coins with her, a fee white Texans didn't have to pay because of grandfather clauses.

Senfronia had to pay a poll tax the first time she voted, too, and she was not going to let Texas go back to those days. "I was always taught by my grandparents that you fight for those things that you believe in," she explains, so that's what she's spent her life doing. It's the reason she participated in sit-ins during the civil rights movement, and it was the reason that, on that night in May, she told her colleagues they had an obligation to break quorum.

"We have fought for too long and too hard in this country to get away from having to count beans in a bag, having to count bubbles in a soap bar," she declared, "and I'll stay in this fight until I can't fight no more."

The room was in tears—and together, the Democrats in the Texas House of Representatives decided to go through with the plan—storming out of the building and running out the clock, the kind of spontaneous act of bravery too rarely seen in the craven, calculated political world we live in today.

Governor Abbott, as you might expect, didn't see it that way. He was pissed off. He threatened to strip the legislators of their pay—already a meager $7,200 a year—and decided to hold a special session of the legislature during which he would once again bring the voter suppression bill to the floor. But the genie was out of the bottle: The Democrats had realized they had power, and they intended to use it.

On the eve of the special session, they once again broke quorum—this time, flying to the District of Columbia and planning to stay indefinitely, at risk of arrest, hoping by their very presence and through their advocacy to persuade Congress of the urgency of enacting voting rights legislation. "I hugged my wife and daughters and let them know that I was leaving Texas to go fight for voting rights," Fischer remembers. "I had no idea how hard it was going to be, but the only thing that mattered was the fight for our democracy.

"We had jobs, we had family obligations that were sacrificed—missing my daughter's birthday comes to mind," he continues, "and we didn't know if our efforts would make a difference or not."

They did.

While the Democrats were gone, thousands of Texans marched in protest against voter suppression all across the state, organized by leaders like former presidential (and soon-to-be gubernatorial) candidate Beto O'Rourke. And forty-four days after they first landed in Washington, the representatives returned to Texas to find a bill that was still calamitous—but no longer featured some of its most dangerous elements. The attack on "souls to the polls" events, for instance, was removed, with Republicans claiming it had been a typo. "Call it a mistake," insisted representative Travis Clardy, who had helped author the bill. They also abandoned the "OVERTURNING ELECTIONS" section of the draft, which Clardy eventually admitted was a "horrendous policy" that would "never be healthy for the democracy."

These sections of the bill were not removed because the Republican caucus found goodness in its heart. They were removed because Democrats, for once, refused to take no for an answer. It was a testament to the power of fighting pessimism with optimism, complacency with courage—a testament to the idea that injustice is not inevitable, as long as you're willing to fight it.

Of course, there are limits to the influence of Democratic lawmakers in a state where Republicans have complete control of the government—so more than two months after it was broken, quorum was once again established, and on the night of August 26, after a twelve-hour debate on the floor, Texas Senate Bill 1 passed the House, clearing the way for it to become law.

It was a big day for Lone Star Republicans, who held strong in the face of unprecedented resistance, but Representative Thompson warned that their victory could end up being Pyrrhic. "If you think you're winning today," she threatened, "let me give you a prophetic statement: You will reap what you sow. And you know what? It won't be years or decades from now. It will be sooner than you think."

She may be right—and it's on all of us to make sure that she is—but there was no denying that Texas Republicans had managed to roll back much of the progress leaders like Chris Hollins had made in expanding access to the ballot, absent any justification for their antidemocratic efforts except for false claims of voter fraud. And without the Voting Rights Act in place, the Department of Justice didn't have much recourse to stop them.

In the years since *Shelby County* was decided, this pattern has repeated itself all across the country, over and over again, and as I describe in part II, the results have been devastating. A record number of polling places have been shut down. A record number of voters have been purged from the rolls. A record number of bills surgically designed to reduce turnout among Democrats, generally, and Black and brown voters specifically, have been passed.

And while we should all be inspired by the bravery of the Democratic legislators in Texas, we cannot accept living in a country where the only way to fight back against a suppressive bill is for legislators to flee their state—leaving their families, their constituents, and their paychecks behind—until America pays attention.

We need to bring the Voting Rights Act back from the dead.

And I know we can do it, because we've done it before.

More than three decades before *Shelby County*, the Supreme Court delivered a ruling that threatened the future of voting rights. The case was *City of Mobile v. Bolden*—and the opinion, written by Justice Potter Stewart in 1980, radically limited the enforceability of the Voting Rights Act.

"Action by a State that is racially neutral on its face violates the Fifteenth Amendment only if motivated by a discriminatory purpose," wrote Stewart, adding that "racially discriminatory motivation is a necessary ingredient of a Fifteenth Amendment violation." In other words, under the laws as they existed in 1980, the Supreme Court ruled that if the Department of Justice wanted to overturn a suppressive bill, it wasn't enough to identify a racially disparate impact—they would also have to find evidence of racially discriminatory intent.

This presented a proof problem to the Justice Department, because even back then, legislators were strategic enough to obfuscate their attacks on the franchise as being about something other than race—as they had been doing since the days of poll taxes and literacy tests. That is why Justice Thurgood Marshall delivered a searing dissent, arguing that the decision had made the Fifteenth Amendment's language "illusory in symbol and hollow in substance."

On the bright side, the Voting Rights Act was once again up for reauthorization, which, meant Congress had the opportunity to revise its contents—and change the standard back from intent to outcome, which, as Ari Berman writes about in *Give Us the Ballot,* is exactly what an amendment from Democratic senator Ted Kennedy and Republican senator Charles Mathias would have done. But at the time, it looked like a long shot.

Newly sworn-in president Ronald Reagan had expressed skepticism about the enduring necessity of providing oversight of the way some states ran their elections. Republicans, who were not as enthusiastic about the bill as Democrats were, had come into control of the Senate for the first time since *Brown v. Board of Education.* And the Department of Justice had decided to launch a full-court press in support of the *Mobile* decision—assigning one of its lawyers to write dozens of memos, totaling close to ten thousand words, pleading with the administration to take an "aggressive stance" toward blocking the amendment introduced by Kennedy and Mathias.

The memos were well written: cogent, logical, pointed. They had an authority to them, which would have been surprising considering their author's age—just twenty-six—but not his credentials. This was a man who had a résumé even Chris Hollins would have been impressed by, having graduated from Harvard College early, before becoming editor in chief of the *Harvard Law Review* and earning himself a clerkship at the Supreme Court.

But unlike Hollins, this Ivy League–educated prodigy didn't want to use his bona fides to make it easier to vote. He wanted to use them to make it harder. The problem was that at this moment in history, the wunderkind was only a lawyer at the Department of Justice; and as much as he wanted to gut the Voting Rights Act, ultimately, the decision wasn't up to him. It was up to the American people. And they made their voices heard.

Across the country, civil rights leaders organized protests and constituents lit up the phones of their representatives, and eventually, Congress agreed to not only reauthorize the bill but extend it for twenty-five years, longer than they ever had before—and included the Kennedy-Mathias amendment in the final draft, effectively reversing the damage that had been done by the *Mobile* ruling. At the signing of the bill, President Reagan declared, "This legislation proves our unbending commitment to voting rights," adding that "the right to vote is the crown jewel of American liberties, and we will not see its luster diminished."

It was a disappointing outcome for the Justice Department lawyer who had spent the prior months working so hard to stop it from happening—but it was an important milestone for our country, as access to the franchise was once again, though not eternally, protected.

You don't need me to tell you what happened to that twenty-six-year-old lawyer. Now he's in his sixties. He's the chief justice of the Supreme Court of the United States. And this time, he's winning—with the Voting Rights Act more wounded than it's been at any time since its passage, including in the months following *Mobile*.

But we can come together as a country and stand up to him once again.

That is what the John Lewis Voting Rights Advancement Act, the bill those Texas legislators flew to Washington to support, was all about: protecting the ballot for all Americans in the face of suppressive Republican legislatures and a Supreme Court that has accommodated them at almost every turn.

The purpose of the bill was simple: bringing back Sections 4 and 5 but doing so in a way that would pass muster at the highest court in the land. After all, in *Shelby*, Chief Justice Roberts didn't declare that preclearance in and of itself was unconstitutional; he simply ruled that the formula in Section 4 being used by the Department of Justice to decide which states would and wouldn't have oversight was antiquated, an artifact of the era of Jim Crow. I've always thought his characterization made no sense, in no small part because Congress had reviewed the evidence in great detail once again in 2006 and voted overwhelmingly to keep the formula in place. But Supreme Court decisions are binding, which is why, despite my feelings, I am glad the John Lewis Voting Rights Advancement Act was written to be constitutional even in a post-*Shelby* world.

Here's how this would work: Under a bill like the John Lewis Voting Rights Advancement Act, instead of the standard for preclearance being set based on actions taken by states over their entire history, it would be determined by their actions over the past twenty-five years. This way, former Confederate states wouldn't be the only ones covered. And the formula would be continuously updated with new data—so if states get sick of preclearance, all they would need to do to free themselves of it is demonstrate good behavior.

If a bill like this were enacted, it would be groundbreaking. For the first time since *Shelby*, the Department of Justice would once again be able to stop suppressive legislation from taking effect on a nationwide basis.

And in this chapter, I will lay out how we can navigate two of the most insidious policies—photo ID bills and voter purges—by combining the stick of a bill like the John Lewis Voting Rights Advancement Act with the carrot of automatic voter registration.

Voter ID, but Make It Free

My stance on photo ID bills is no secret. I've called the process of obtaining one of these forms of identification tantamount to a poll tax. And that's what I believe it is. After all, as I dove into in part II, tens of millions of Americans do not have the kind of government-issued identification required to vote in states across the country—and the cost of getting one of these IDs can be upward of $100.

You also don't need me to tell you which Americans are being targeted by these laws—if you're young, elderly, Black, brown, or low-income, you are far more likely not to possess the ID you need to cast a ballot than if you are middle-aged, white, or wealthy. This problem is compounded by the fact that Republicans have systematically shut down government offices in the neighborhoods where people of color live—or defunded them, making their already long lines even longer—all with the purpose of discouraging and reducing voter turnout.

What's most absurd about these bills is that they aim to solve a problem that practically does not exist—since, as we've established, an American is less likely to commit in-person voter fraud than to be struck by lightning. For all these reasons, in an ideal world, we might not have voter ID laws of any kind.

But look around: We don't live in an ideal world. We live in a world where for decades, Republicans have been proliferating this lie, and as Joseph Goebbels, chief propagandist for a certain German regime, has been repeatedly (and perhaps erroneously) quoted as saying, "If you tell a great lie and repeat it often enough, the people will eventually come to believe it." Which is exactly what has taken place: In the aftermath of the 2020 election, more than one in three Americans—and more than half of all Republicans—believed Joe Biden won "due to voter fraud." And an even greater number of Americans—four out of five—support the idea that you should have to show some form of identification to vote.

We could, of course, choose to ignore this fact—but in order to instill confidence in our voting systems, representatives should respond to the will of the people. And since a majority of Americans support requiring ID, it's hard to imagine a voting rights bill passing without Democrats making some concessions on this topic. So the question before us is how to implement voter ID laws without disenfranchising Americans in the process.

The answer has two components: First, under a bill like the John Lewis Voting Rights Advancement Act, we need the Department of Justice to target discriminatory photo ID bills that are, in fact, designed to suppress turnout in certain communities—like the one in Texas that allowed voters to prove their identities with gun licenses but not student IDs. There are no ifs, ands, or buts about it: Bills like these, ones that demand citizens show a *photo* ID to exercise the franchise, are discriminatory, and we need to stop them from going into effect.

At the same time, we need to make it easier for voters to prove their identities at the ballot box. Thankfully, this shouldn't be too hard—because while many Americans do not have a government-issued photo ID, they do have some proof of residence, whether that's a pay stub, a utility bill, or a lease. And we should pass a law mandating that states accept every credible one of these.

Of course, there will always be people who slip through the cracks, which is why as part of the automatic voter registration program I have proposed, the government would also send a voter ID to every single American free of charge, a copy of which they could pick up at the post office, DMV, or other designated government office in their neighborhood. Americans experiencing homelessness, meanwhile, could also acquire this voter ID from their local shelter.

Combining these measures, every single eligible voter would have a form of identification, which means voter ID bills would no longer qualify as poll taxes—and would, therefore, disenfranchise virtually no one.

Purging the Purgers

In the lead-up to the 2000 election, Florida purged around 58,000 residents from the voter rolls—at least 12,000 of whom should have been eligible to cast a ballot.

Al Gore lost the state—and, as a result, the presidency—by only 600 votes.

The upshot?

Had those citizens stayed on the rolls, Al Gore, not George Bush, very well could have been president of the United States.

That is the problem with purges—all too often, they wind up disenfranchising legitimate voters. And in elections as close as the ones our country has seen of late, they can prove to be the deciding factor.

That has become even more true in the aftermath of *Shelby County*. According to a Brennan Center report, in the first election cycle after the ruling, Texas erased 363,000 more voters from the rolls than during the prior cycle. And Georgia purged twice as many voters between 2012 and 2016 as it had over the previous four years. Nationwide, purges have surged by upward of 33 percent in recent years—and the Brennan Center estimates that if *Shelby* had gone the other way, in states previously subject to preclearance alone, around two million voters who have been removed from the rolls would still be on them.

Now, I want to be clear: Purging in and of itself isn't a problem—states have a right to make sure anyone who dies or moves out of state is no longer registered. But these numbers aren't explained by neutral, routine voter roll maintenance. Indeed, the number of voters purged has been increasing at a far higher rate than can be accounted for by the number of people who have passed away or changed their state of residence. And that's for two reasons.

First, states have begun enforcing use-it-or-lose-it policies that remove voters from the rolls for no reason other than failing to cast a ballot. This would be problematic on its own terms—since nowhere in the Constitution does it say that you have to exercise your right to vote in every election in order to keep it. And while I wish everyone would cast a ballot every chance they get, many people express their disenchantment with the system through silence, and that's their choice to make.

But these purges are made even worse by the fact that they are full of errors. Ohio, for instance, released a list of 235,000 voters it planned to purge under its use-it-or-lose-it policy, but when volunteers across the state audited the data, they identified at least 40,000 people who shouldn't have been on it. One woman on the list happened to be the director of the League of Women Voters of Ohio—and, as she told *The New York Times*, had voted in three elections the prior year.

"I don't think we have any idea," she said, "how many other individuals this has happened to."

The same story is playing out across the country. In Texas, for instance, Republicans implemented a policy of removing any registered voter whose name, date of birth, and last four Social Security number digits matched those of a dead person—which presented a problem for James Harris, an air force veteran who was blocked from casting a ballot because another guy named James Harris, from Arkansas, not Texas, had kicked the bucket more than a decade earlier.

It's impossible to know how many eligible voters have been removed from the rolls across the country—because audits like the one that took place in Ohio are so time-consuming, and because many states do not release the names of the people they have purged. But here's what's clear: Purges have done much more to stop legitimate voters from casting a ballot than they have done to stop nonexistent voter fraud. And under a bill like the John Lewis Voting Rights Advancement Act, we could once again hold states accountable for abusing this power.

But we shouldn't stop there. We should also create a better way to maintain voter rolls—and just as with voter ID laws, a big part of the solution should be automatic voter registration.

Under AVR, every voter's address would be stored securely in a centralized database, so if someone wanted to switch their registration to a new state, we would know to take them off the rolls in their old state. We could also automate the process of purging voters after they die by linking the AVR database with the database of fatalities maintained by the Bureau of Vital

Statistics. In both instances, we would contact voters before removing them from the rolls, just in case there is a flaw in the data set.

It's a simple solution, and one that would bring an end to the problematic purges that have proliferated in recent years—while helping the election officials who lead them achieve their stated goal of keeping the voter rolls accurate.

If this, not suppression, is indeed their intention, then there's no reason Republicans shouldn't get on board with AVR—and the registration of tens of millions of additional Americans.

These are only a couple of the many attacks on voting rights we could confront by passing a bill like the John Lewis Voting Rights Advancement Act—polling place closures and attacks on early voting also come to mind—and doing so would be an important step in reversing the damage our country has seen since the ruling in *Shelby County.* That is why Representatives Thompson, Hinojosa, Fischer, and the rest of the Texas legislators who came to Washington were so committed to getting it passed.

But the truth is, the most daunting threats to our democracy wouldn't be answered by a bill like this. Indeed, they're the reason this bill never became law in the first place. I'm talking, of course, about our institutions—our warped Senate, our gerrymandered House, our malapportioned Electoral College, and our politicized Supreme Court—which are the reasons America is a democracy in need of serious renovation.

How we confront these institutions and finally make our government reflective of the will of the people is the subject of the rest of this book.

9

SAVING CONGRESS

In January 2021, Democrats rode into power after a victorious performance in the 2020 elections—taking control of the presidency, the Senate, and the House of Representatives. They had received resounding support from the American people. And the first piece of legislation the new Congress introduced, HR-1, otherwise known as the For the People Act, couldn't have had a more urgent purpose: "To expand Americans' access to the ballot box."

The framework of this legislation included many of the ideas I've mentioned in this book, from automatic voter registration to expanded early voting. Designed to be coupled with the John Lewis Voting Rights Advancement Act, it was supported by practically every Democrat in Congress—and polls found that more than seven in ten Americans were on board with it. I was one of them. At a congressional hearing on the bills, I called them "the right remedy at the right time," arguing that if passed they would go down as "the greatest pieces of civil rights legislation since 1965."

At the National Constitution Center in Philadelphia, President Biden delivered an equally passionate address: "Guaranteeing the right to vote, ensuring every vote is counted," he declared, "has always been the most patriotic thing we can do."

But over the following months, it became clear that the bill (later renamed the Freedom to Vote Act)—a bill supported by a Democratic Congress, a Democratic president, and the American people—wouldn't become law.

In fact, there was never even an up-or-down vote on it. Ultimately, every single Republican senator, as well as two Democrats—Joe Manchin of West Virginia and Kyrsten Sinema of Arizona—decided they cared more about Senate procedure or winning the next election than about saving our democracy for the next generation.

But beyond any individual representative, the Freedom to Vote Act failed for a simple reason: Our Congress is fundamentally broken.

Saving the Senate

At the dawn of the 117th United States Congress, Democrats held more seats in the Senate than they had at any point in close to a decade—and yet compared to the share of the vote the party had received in the 2020 elections, they remained woefully underrepresented.

In total, Senate Democrats had control of fifty seats, just as the Republicans did, but they represented 41,549,808 more people than their GOP counterparts. That's because the Constitution provides the same number of Senate seats to every state, regardless of how many Americans live there, and Democrats tend to live in states that more people call home.

The numbers are striking: The half of the U.S. population that lives in its nine most populous states is represented by only twenty-nine senators—while the other half is represented by seventy-one. Right now, from the perspective of representation, one person in California actually only counts as one-fifth of a person, while someone in North Dakota counts as eight people, for no reason other than where they happen to live. (So much for the idea of one person, one vote.) That means an individual in North Dakota has 40 times more say in what happens in the Senate than someone in California. To put this in concrete terms: Picture a 200-on-5 basketball game. That's how much more representation North Dakotans have than Californians—and you don't need to be a basketball player to know it would be hard for five people to score against a team of two hundred, even if they all had jump shots as smooth as mine.

And here's what makes it worse: None of this is an accident. It's how our constitution was designed.

On the eve of Independence Day in 1787, months into the Constitutional Convention, our founders did what all procrastinators do: They decided they would answer one of their biggest questions—how to deal with representation—when they came back from break. The problem they faced was that small states were worried their interests would be overlooked by the federal government if representation were dictated by population, while big states were worried that the voices of their citizens would be silenced if seats in Congress were spread equally among all the states. Heading into July 4, every compromise on the table seemed Solomonic.

But during their day off, the founders brainstormed over the sound of fireworks, and when they returned to Philadelphia, they did so with a proposal in hand—a proposal that would go on to shape the future of American democracy. Its parameters were simple: One house of Congress, the House of Representatives, would apportion representation based on population. (Enslaved people, according to the proposal, would count as three-fifths of a person.) The other house, the Senate, meanwhile, would provide the same amount of representation to every state regardless of population.

When this proposal was introduced, it faced fierce backlash, including from James Madison, the primary author of the Constitution, who argued that agreeing to this compromise would mean "departing from justice in order to conciliate the smaller states and the minority of the people" at the expense of "justly gratifying the larger states and the majority of the people."

His logic was hard to refute—after all, without the principle of "one person, one vote," the government wouldn't really reflect the interests of the people—but the smaller states were threatening to walk away from the Constitution altogether if the bigger states didn't acquiesce. At first, Madison wanted to call them on their bluff, daring New Jersey to "stand on their own legs, and bid defiance to events" and Delaware to "brave the consequences of seeking her fortunes apart from the other States."

But when the proposal came up for a vote, it passed—by the narrowest margin possible. In the end, while many of the delegates to the convention had objections to this setup, they decided they'd rather have a constitution they didn't entirely support than no constitution at all, and they weren't willing to make the hard call and see if the smaller states were, in fact, bluffing.

This deal became known as the Great Compromise—and to its credit, it was responsible for the birth of American democracy.

It remains to be seen whether it will also contribute to its death.

At the time of our nation's founding, our framers knew the design of the Senate would benefit small states, but even its opponents, like Madison, had no idea just how extreme the disparities in representation would be—because in the eighteenth century, the differences in population among the states weren't nearly as large as they are today.

Back then, the largest state had less than thirteen times as many people as the smallest. Now that number is closer to seventy. And while Black Americans do have more of a voice today than we did back then—which, needless to say, is a low bar—people of color remain devastatingly underrepresented in the Senate because we tend to live in more populous states.

Indeed, David Leonhardt of *The New York Times* calculated that white Americans have about 25 percent more say in who ends up in the Senate than Black Americans do—in other words, even now, we don't quite count as four-fifths of a person, as far as Senate representation is concerned. And Latino and Asian Americans have even less.

Perhaps it's no surprise, then, that of the roughly two thousand senators elected since America's founding, only 33 have been Black, Latino, Asian American, or Native American. That's less than 1.5 percent. And this isn't only about who gets elected. It's also about the legislation that ends up passing. After all, in a Senate that looked like the country, do you really think a bill like the DREAM Act, which is backed by more than 70 percent of Americans, wouldn't have been passed into law?

It's also worth noting that America is exceptional in having a second chamber of Congress with such warped representation. According to a survey of democracies conducted by the Roosevelt Institute's Todd Tucker: "Roughly half of the world's countries, including highly economically successful nations, such as Denmark, Iceland, Israel, New Zealand, Norway, and Sweden, have only one chamber—elected generally on a one-person, one-vote basis. Others—including the UK, Canada, and

Germany—have unelected second chambers that are much weaker than the U.S. Senate and perform functions that in relative terms appear mostly advisory. Even those developed countries, such as Australia, that do have powerful second chambers are not marred by as much inequality."

Tucker goes on to note that one study found "only the second chambers of Brazil, Argentina, and Russia are less evenly represented than the United States," which I guess is better than if the opposite were true, but still shouldn't be much consolation.

What's worse: In America, all these problems are compounded by a procedure in the Senate that isn't even in our constitution but that has ground what was once known as the world's greatest deliberative body to a halt: the filibuster.

For most of American history, if you wanted to pass a bill through the Senate, you needed a simple majority of votes. These days, for the lion's share of legislation, you need a supermajority—and that's because of the relatively new use of a weapon known as the filibuster, which makes it possible for forty-one senators to block the agenda of the other fifty-nine.

Unlike the overrepresentation of small states in the Senate, which was consecrated by the Great Compromise, the filibuster wasn't even considered at the Constitutional Convention. In fact, most of our founders despised the idea of a supermajority threshold to pass legislation after seeing how poorly it worked in the era of the Articles of Confederation. And when representatives of slave states brought up the idea to Alexander Hamilton, he immediately shot it down.

"This is one of those refinements which, in practice, has an effect the reverse of what is expected from it in theory," Hamilton explained. "The necessity of unanimity in public bodies, or of something approaching towards it, has been founded upon a supposition that it would contribute to security. Its real operation is to embarrass the administration, to destroy the energy of government, and to substitute the pleasure, caprice, or artifices of an insignificant, turbulent or corrupt junto, to the regular deliberations and decisions of a respectable majority." This may sound polite, but it's Hamiltonian for "get out of here with that nonsense."

In Federalist No. 58, Madison shared a similar sentiment. If supermajorities were required to pass legislation, he argued, "In all cases where justice or the general good might require new laws to be passed, or active measures to be pursued, the fundamental principle of free government would be reversed. It would no longer be the majority that would rule; the power would be transferred to the minority."

This raises a question: How did we even end up with the filibuster if there was such consensus against it at the Constitutional Convention?

The answer is complicated—and it's detailed far more comprehensively in Adam Jentleson's brilliant book, *Kill Switch*, than it could be here. But, simply, the proliferation of the filibuster can be traced to a desire among senators to stop civil rights bills from becoming laws.

Now, there were a few filibusters early in American history—the most prominent of which was organized by John C. Calhoun, the Senate's most dogmatic defender of slavery—that didn't explicitly have to do with race. And from time to time over the following decades, a senator would hold the floor until they could stand no more in order to delay votes on legislation, as depicted by Jimmy Stewart in Frank Capra's *Mr. Smith Goes to Washington*. But it wasn't until after the Civil War that this procedure started to be used with regularity to block legislation. And even then, filibusters were deployed almost exclusively to preserve white supremacy. As Jentleson writes: "In the eighty-seven years between the end of Reconstruction and 1964, the only bills that were stopped by filibusters were civil rights bills. On the rare occasion a non–civil rights bill ran into a filibuster, it eventually passed."

What may be surprising is that across those eighty-seven years, most Americans were ready to support civil rights legislation—as early as 1937, Gallup found that 72 percent of Americans backed federal anti-lynching laws; and as early as 1941, more than six in ten backed anti–poll tax laws—and the majority of senators were on board with these bills, too. It was only because of the filibuster that they were blocked.

It's hard to even process the tragedy of this fact, of the carnage that could have been stopped—the bodies that wouldn't have ended up as strange fruit hanging from trees, the voters who wouldn't have been turned away from the polls—if these bills had been allowed to pass; if we had decided, half a century ago, that human lives were more important than a Senate procedure not even found in the Constitution.

Of course, after the longest filibusters in American history, we did finally manage to pass a civil rights act in 1957 and another one in 1964. But it wasn't until 2022, eighty-five years after the majority of Americans first supported it, that Congress passed an anti-lynching bill, and it did so only after a filibuster in 2020 by a loony and malevolent senator from Kentucky named Rand Paul, who thought we should have spent even more time debating its contents.

In fairness to Senator Paul, by the time he tried to block anti-lynching legislation, filibusters were no longer reserved for special-occasion civil rights bills. They were used to block legislation of all kinds. This was thanks to another senator from Kentucky, Mitch McConnell, who decided the best way to oppose President Obama was to filibuster his agenda into oblivion.

Which, by this point in American history, wasn't that hard. Gone were the days of Mr. Smith, when you had to stand for hours to filibuster. Now, as Jentleson explains, you don't even need to "set foot on the floor," let alone "explain the reasons for blocking the bill." Indeed, he writes, "the filibuster has become streamlined to the point that it can be launched by lifting a finger, as easily as opening an app." And in most cases, filibusters are no longer conducted by individual senators but by the entire minority party, so no one is held accountable for delaying the business of the Senate.

For all these reasons, today, filibusters aren't the exception. They have become the rule. And the consequences have been devastating.

As Ezra Klein explains in an article titled "The Definitive Case for Ending the Filibuster," "From 1917 to 1970, the Senate took 49 votes to break filibusters. Total. That is fewer than one each year." In contrast, since McConnell came to power in 2010, "It has taken, on average, more than 80 votes each year to end filibusters." Each year! That means, these days, there are close to twice as many filibusters every twelve months as there were during the fifty-three years between 1917 and 1970 . . . combined! And that doesn't even include all the bills Democratic senators never bothered bringing to the floor in the first place, knowing sixty votes was out of reach.

Do you ever feel like politicians spend all their time debating bills—and then never getting anything done? That's in large part because of the filibuster.

Now, even under Senator McConnell's reign in the Republican Party, there are a few ways to pass a bill with fifty-one votes. One bill per year, for instance, can be passed with a simple majority through a process called reconciliation—so long as its focus is on budgets. (This is how President Trump enacted his tax cuts and how President Biden is trying to pass his Build Back Better bill.) And judges, including Supreme Court justices, as well as cabinet members, can also be confirmed with fifty-one votes.

But generally speaking, if a bill is going to pass in the Senate, it's going to need sixty votes—a threshold that, as Hamilton predicted, has allowed our system of government to be hijacked by "an insignificant, turbulent, or corrupt junto."

If that sounds like an exaggeration, think about this: With the filibuster, forty-one senators from the least populous states, who could plausibly represent less than 15 percent of the total population, could stop a bill supported by the representatives of the other 85 percent.

That's not democracy.

It's tyranny of the minority.

And we need to bring an end to it.

So how do we fix the Senate?

Well, ideally, we would address disparities in representation—and allot more senators to states with more people.

The problem? There is no constitutional way to do this. In fact, Article V even has a clause that says: "No State, without its Consent, shall be deprived of its equal Suffrage in the Senate." For this reason, the idea of making the Senate more like the House is, unfortunately, out of the question.

We could, however, strip the Senate of many of its powers—as the United Kingdom did with its House of Lords. The issue is that this would require an amendment to the Constitution, which we could not ratify without the support of the very Republicans who benefit from the status quo.

As a result, we are left asking: How do we make the Senate better reflect the will of the people in its current form?

The first step, in my mind, is a simple one: providing representation to the taxpaying Americans who don't have any at all—specifically, those living in the District of Columbia and Puerto Rico.

Right now, there are more citizens in Washington, D.C., than in Vermont and Wyoming, and Puerto Rico has more citizens than twenty-one states. Yet neither has a single Senate seat. This would be an outrage in any country, but in America, a nation founded on the idea of "no taxation without representation," it is heresy. And we need to address it. Because Washingtonians and Puerto Ricans are as deserving of a voice in our government as any other Americans.

The best part? You don't even need an amendment to add states to the union. You just need to pass a bill. Which Democrats could do today, without needing a vote from a single Republican—just as they could have passed the Freedom to Vote Act—if only we embraced the second step we must take to save the Senate: eliminating the filibuster.

With apologies to the Democrats who are still on the fence, this isn't a hard call:

Door number one is preserving the filibuster.

Door number two is saving our democracy before it's too late.

Politics is full of difficult decisions. We should be grateful that this isn't one of them.

But if, for some reason, senators remain unwilling to budge on eliminating the filibuster entirely, at the very least, they should create a carve-out for bills that strengthen our democracy, a step President Biden has endorsed taking. After all, with reconciliation, Democratic senators have already agreed to an exception for budget reasons. Surely they can understand why voting rights are at least as important. As Senator Raphael Warnock of Georgia said in remarks from the floor, "The judgment of history is upon us. Future generations will ask, 'When the democracy was in a 911 state of emergency, what did you do to put the fire out? Did we rise to the moment or did we hide behind procedural rules?'" At this point, we have not risen to the moment, with senators like Manchin and Sinema continuing to value the filibuster more than voting rights—not to mention the Republicans actively attacking our democracy. But now is not the time to give up the fight. Because while their rhetoric might sound highfalutin, the case for a supermajority threshold doesn't stand up to scrutiny.

One of the most common cases filibuster defenders like Senators Manchin and Sinema make is that one day, Republicans will have control of the Senate—and we will want the ability to block their legislation.

This argument has two key weaknesses.

The first is practical: Even without the filibuster, America already has more checks and balances than almost any other democracy, so it's not as though a Republican Senate could ram through priorities on its own. Citing a study that compared the American political system to that of twenty-two other peer nations, Klein explains:

> The United States is alone among advanced democracies in how difficult it is to get anything done. Legislation can be blocked by the House, the Senate, or the president, all

of whom face different electorates, on different cycles. It can be overturned by the Supreme Court, where nine robed judges are protected by lifetime appointment. Constitutional amendments are uniquely difficult, and can be blocked by the states. To attain a governing majority across this many conflicting institutions requires parties to win multiple elections, over multiple election cycles, by appealing to multiple kinds of electorates. All that was true before the advent of the 60-vote supermajority requirement, and it will be true if that requirement is abolished.

This brings me to the second flaw in the argument against the filibuster—a moral one: If Democrats eliminate the filibuster; expand access to the franchise; provide statehood to Washington, D.C., and Puerto Rico; and *still* manage to lose control of the presidency and Congress to Republicans, then that is at least in part a reflection of the will of the people—and Republicans *should* be allowed to enact their agenda, without the added burden of needing a supermajority in the Senate.

Because that's how democracy works.

And if voters don't like what the party in power does, then they can show up to the polls, vote them out, and start passing legislation with a Senate majority of their own.

Saving the House

It's 2018—and I'm marching down Laurel Street, the avenue that divides North Carolina A&T, the largest of America's historically Black colleges and universities (HBCUs), into two congressional districts. Standing next to me is a student named Love Caesar, who is telling me about a classmate who had to change her voter registration because she moved from a dorm in the state's Sixth Congressional District to one in the Thirteenth.

Every day, she explains, her friend crosses back and forth between the two districts, traveling from her classroom to her library, her dorm room to her dining hall.

This doesn't make any sense—until you realize it was the result of a Republican gerrymander, designed to limit the power of Black voters in North Carolina. "The line was drawn with surgical precision," Caesar explains, to "dilute the vote."

She was exactly right: The map drawn by the North Carolina legislature was a prime example of "cracking," the process through which gerrymanderers water down the impact of any one community's vote by splitting its population between districts. In the case of A&T, this all but assured that Republicans would come out on top in both districts—by limiting the number of Black Americans registered to vote in either.

And A&T wasn't the only campus they divided. East Carolina University and UNC Asheville were split in half, too.

This is because North Carolina is one of the thirty-three states where maps are drawn by partisan legislatures instead of by independent commissions, which means the process ends up being run by hacks like Mark McDaniel, a North Carolina state senator who once admitted that he sees himself as being "in the business of rigging elections."

According to Caesar, the roughly decade-old division of her campus was creating "a lot of voter apathy" among students who knew about it, because they would say to themselves, "If my vote counts half, why should I vote at all?" And there were other students, she explains, who didn't even know this division had taken place. So she and a few of her classmates decided to try to raise awareness.

"The first thing we did was we got some chalk and walked around campus at night and wrote chalk messages on the ground," she remembers. These messages forced anyone who walked by to contemplate questions like "What is gerrymandering?" and "Do you know what district you live in?"

"There was a lot of shock," Caesar recalls, when her classmates realized there was an "intentional attack on their voting rights." But, she explains, "Once people *knew* something about it, they wanted to *do* something about it." Students all across A&T came together to form a movement opposing the gerrymander of their campus—a movement that inspired me to visit.

I was there in my capacity as founder of the National Democratic Redistricting Committee (NDRC), an organization fighting for fairer maps across the country, including in North Carolina, where we had filed a challenge to the A&T gerrymander. And the year after my visit, we won, with a court declaring the lines that had been drawn unconstitutional.

This meant that in 2020, for the first time in about a decade, A&T students voted together in one district, turning out in record numbers. That was a gratifying victory, credited in part to our case, yes, but also to committed students like Love Caesar, who made the world pay attention to what was happening in their community. And Caesar says she's only just getting started, because "we know we're going to have to fight just as hard to make sure that we keep going forward and don't take any more steps back."

Powered by grassroots organizers, NDRC has also succeeded in challenging maps in Virginia. We've helped reform the redistricting process in Colorado, Michigan, Montana, Ohio, and Utah. And we've supported the candidacies of politicians devoted to ending gerrymandering across the country—at all levels of government.

That's a big deal, and in 2021, we saw that work pay off during the redistricting process when some gerrymandering, much of which we are challenging in court, took place, but more maps were far more fair due to the reforms we backed.

The fact remains, though, that too many states still have gerrymandered districts. And as a result, the House of Representatives—the body of Congress even our founders hoped would represent people from all districts equally—doesn't uphold the principle of one person, one vote either.

As I describe in chapter 5, Republicans won a historic landslide victory in 2010, taking control of state legislatures across the country. And in 2011, they used that power to launch what professors from Princeton deemed to be the most egregious partisan gerrymandering of the past half century.

In 2012, after that gerrymandering, Democrats won 1.4 million more votes than Republicans in races for the U.S. House of Representatives, but Republicans engineered a thirty-three-seat majority. And according to a study by the Center for American Progress, gerrymandering brought Republicans an average of nineteen additional seats in the House over the following two election cycles. Even in 2018, when Democrats won a historic wave election, gerrymandering was estimated to have cost the party sixteen additional seats and seven additional state legislative chambers. And in 2020, Democrats held on to their majority in the House by only a few seats, even though they won the popular vote by about five million votes.

This has led to a crisis of representation—because the House of Representatives no longer reflects the will of the people. And just as important, it has led to a crisis of polarization.

Let me explain.

"Cracking" and "packing," the primary tactics of gerrymandering, both lead to blowout general elections—which means that instead of worrying about losing to the other party, incumbents are often more afraid of facing a challenge from a member of their own party, and as a result, they take on more and more extreme positions that are popular with their bases.

This is how state legislatures end up passing heartbeat bills, which ban abortion in the first trimester, even though the majority of residents, even in the most conservative states, are opposed to them. And it's how you end up with a Congress full of representatives willing to vote against policies like universal background checks, which are supported by nine in ten Americans, purely as a demonstration of partisan and gun-lobbied loyalty.

Thankfully, unlike the Senate, whose undemocratic nature is written into the Constitution, the House is relatively easy to fix—and the American people are on board with fixing it. In fact, a poll found that three out of every four voters support the idea of ending partisan redistricting, "even if it means their preferred political party would win fewer seats."

What would this look like?

First, we would ban partisan gerrymandering, as the voting bills in Congress proposed—not to mention racial gerrymandering, which has already been declared unconstitutional. As part of this effort, we would also need to establish a standard by which courts could determine if a map fails either of these tests.

One way to better ensure a fair redistricting process is by putting well-constructed independent redistricting commissions in charge, which is how it's already done in some states. These commissions are nonpartisan. They draw maps based on agreed-upon principles—optimizing for things like competitiveness and compactness rather than electoral domination.

And they are transparent, replacing backroom deals and secret handshakes with public hearings and town halls.

In some cases, these commissions have been overrun by partisan actors, as we saw in Virginia in 2021. But if they are designed well, as was the case in Michigan, they can lead to a much better process. And after our next census in 2030, we'd better encourage the rest of the country to get on board with this effort. Because no matter what political party you support or what policies you advocate, I promise all of us will be better off if voters once again pick their representatives instead of politicians picking their voters.

After all, in recent decades, Democratic and Republican politicians alike have won races as a result of gerrymandering. But through it all, the American people have been the losers, as politicians have governed like they only have to be responsive to the interests of the most partisan voters in their districts, not the country at large.

That has to change.

Because the House of Representatives and our state legislatures should represent all of us.

The legislative branch is one of America's most remarkable inventions, up there with the lightbulb, the telephone, and the chocolate chip cookie. It's the institution that from the beginning has prevented our democracy from becoming a monarchy—ensuring our government could one day be a reflection of the people. And over the course of American history, one of the most genius aspects of Congress has been its ability to evolve with the times as we continue to perfect our union.

Originally, for instance, senators weren't even elected by citizens. They were elected by state legislatures. For America to become a democracy, for Congress to hold legitimacy in the eyes of the people, that had to evolve. And so, it did.

This, I believe, is once again the question before us: Can the legislative branch transform with the times—and become reflective of the will of the people?

We'd better make sure the answer to that question is yes—because nothing less than our democracy is at stake.

10

SAVING THE PRESIDENCY

The 1800 presidential election was a showdown for the ages—the Ali vs. Frazier, Magic vs. Bird, Evert vs. Navratilova of its time. It was John Adams against Thomas Jefferson, mano a mano, Founding Father on Founding Father. Even better: It was a rematch, a vanilla "Thrilla in Manila," which meant everyone knew it would be close.

If an election with candidates this high profile were held today, voters would turn out in record numbers. But back then, no citizens had the power to decide presidential elections, except for the 138 (white, male) Americans chosen as delegates to the Electoral College. (That's it—138! There are dog catcher races with more voters than that!)

Now, it's worth clarifying that tens of thousands of Americans cast ballots anyway—but because of how our constitution was written, their votes didn't dictate whom the Electoral College ultimately supported.

Our founders rejected the idea of a popular vote for several reasons. For one, as I mentioned in the first chapter, they despised direct democracy, believing it would lead to elections decided by "men of factious tempers, of local prejudices, or of sinister designs." They were also afraid citizens wouldn't be able to learn enough about candidates to make an educated decision, since accurate information was much harder to come by back then than it is today—Fox News and Facebook notwithstanding. But the Electoral College was created for another reason, a reason we have chosen not to teach for centuries, but one that took preeminence over all others at the time:

Our founders wanted to protect the interests of slave states.

Well, not *all* our founders. James Wilson, a delegate to the Constitutional Convention from Pennsylvania, introduced the idea of holding a national election for the presidency, with the goal of ensuring the commander in chief's power comes from "the people at large." But another Founding Father, James Madison, immediately put Wilson in his place, explaining that his proposal would never fly with the slave states—because under such a system, they "could have no influence in the election." After all, a massive number of their residents—a third of their population—were being held in the condition of slavery, and thus were considered property, not people, let alone citizens. This meant that if elections were decided by popular vote, slave states would be outnumbered by free states every time.

Instead of embracing this outcome—and punishing these states for stripping hundreds of thousands of human beings of their humanity—our founders decided to protect them. That's how we ended up with the Great Compromise, and how, a few months later, as the Constitutional Convention was coming to a close, we ended up with the Electoral College, Madison's answer to Wilson's proposal.

Here's how it worked: Every state would nominate exactly as many delegates as they had representatives in the House and the Senate to the Electoral College, a body that would then meet once every four years to elect the next president. This meant that all the concessions big states made to small states in order to get them on board with the composition of Congress would apply to the presidency as well—allowing slaveholders to count everyone they held in bondage as three-fifths of a person for the purposes of representation in the Electoral College.

This, once again, provided slave states with disproportionate control over how our elections were decided—and in turn, as Yale Law professor Akhil Reed Amar has observed, "For 32 of the Constitution's first 36 years, a white slaveholding Virginian occupied the presidency."

Thomas Jefferson was no exception: In 1800, after all the ballots were counted, the slave owner had defeated John Adams, the abolitionist, by a vote of 73–65, a victory he could credit to delegates the slave states had earned through the three-fifths compromise.

And we should take a moment to process the significance of the fact that our framers ratified a constitution on such inane, fallacious grounds: At our founding, the U.S. Constitution permitted slave owners to oppress, maim, and murder human beings, separate them from their families and mutilate them for disobedience, and then vote on their behalf on Election Day, in support of candidates like Jefferson, who not only wanted to keep them in servitude but was a slave owner himself. It's a system as asinine as it was evil, as illogical as it was immoral.

And the election of 1800 was not the last time the Electoral College would serve the interests of states that supported slavery. Remember the election of 1876, which led Rutherford B. Hayes to pull America's soldiers out of the South—marking the end of Reconstruction and the beginning of Jim Crow? Well, President Hayes only made that concession because the results of the popular vote in key swing states were unclear, and he needed to make a deal with the former Confederate states in exchange for the support of their electors. They demanded he leave the South alone. And he acquiesced.

This led to almost a century of laws that stripped Black Americans of their rights and lynchings that stripped them of their lives. And yet while we have reformed the Electoral College in the years since—so delegates are now supposed to support whichever candidate wins more votes in their state (or, in the case of Maine and Nebraska, district), instead of having full discretion to back whomever they want—we have failed to get rid of it.

Indeed, but for the Electoral College, two of our last four presidents, George W. Bush and Donald J. Trump, would have lost the elections that made them commander in chief, both having received fewer votes than their opponents. That's in no small part because even today, a century and a half after the abolition of slavery and half a century after the passage of the Voting Rights Act, white voters, particularly conservative white voters, remain overrepresented in Congress—and, therefore, the Electoral College—and so, candidates who pander to them are at an advantage.

But let's be real: The Electoral College would be an idiotic, injudicious, risible institution even if it weren't racist.

We elect senators by popular vote. We elect representatives by popular vote. We elect governors by popular vote. Hell, we even elect class presidents by popular vote. Because that's how democracy works: You tally up the ballots—and whichever candidate's box is checked on more of them is the victor.

The idea that you could win the support of fewer Americans than your opponent *and still end up president of the United States* is patently preposterous. And we shouldn't treat this system like it has legitimacy just because it's been around for a long time.

The American people understand this, which is why 61 percent of them support abolishing the Electoral College.

So what are we waiting for?

Well, as I'm sure you can guess by now, the problem is that one of the two major parties in American politics is just fine with things staying the way they are—and its representatives have enough power in state legislatures (that they gerrymandered!) to block amendments to the U.S. Constitution from going into effect.

(An amendment to abolish the Electoral College came close to passing in the late 1960s, but ultimately fell short due to—you guessed it—a filibuster.)

There's another solution, though. It's called the **National Popular Vote Interstate Compact** (NPVIC). And you wouldn't need to amend the Constitution to implement it. In fact, states across the country have already begun signing up to do exactly that.

Under the NPVIC, instead of Electoral College delegates supporting whichever candidate receives the most votes *in their state* (the current system), delegates would be compelled to support whichever candidate receives the most votes *across the country*. This way, the Electoral College could never again overrule the will of the people, because its outcome would be a direct reflection of the national popular vote.

And you wouldn't need every state to sign on—all you would need is some combination of states with a combined total of 270 electoral delegates to agree to the NPVIC in order for it to render the Electoral College obsolete. Already, fifteen states and the District of Columbia have signed up to be a part of the compact. Together, they hold 195 electoral votes—so we are more than 70 percent of the way there. And figuring out how to get that final 30 percent on board should be a priority for people who believe in democracy everywhere.

Because while this compact may sound technical, it has the

power to be transformational. Just imagine how much different our country would look today if we'd had this system in place before the election in 2000—and Al Gore, not George W. Bush, had become president. There is no such thing as certainty when it comes to counterfactuals—but can you imagine how much better our past couple of decades would have been and how much brighter our future would look if we had elected a candidate who ran on reducing emissions before Greta Thunberg was even born? How many disasters, how many fires, how many floods could we have prevented? How many lives could we have saved? And I haven't even touched on foreign policy, which wasn't exactly George W. Bush's strong suit. (Can you spell Iraq War?)

It's dizzying to think about. And there's not much use in doing so. Because all counterfactuals are, ultimately, fiction. But while we can't change our history, we can learn from it. And that's why all of us, as citizens, need to make our own compact to support the NPVIC.

This will not only make our politicians better representatives of the people. It will also make our elections themselves better.

Under the current system, presidential candidates are incentivized to spend all their time in a few swing states—since their residents are the voters who decide the Electoral College. But with the NPVIC in place, they would have to campaign everywhere, for every vote, no matter how red or blue a state might be. Suddenly, Republicans would be compelled to spend their time in New York City and San Francisco. And Democrats would barnstorm towns across the south, listening to and learning from voters they have long written off.

In this way, the NPVIC would usher in a fundamental transformation in how candidates campaign; and even more important, it would change how presidents govern. They would no longer feel tempted to provide more favorable treatment to some states over others—after all, voters from all states would have the chance to hold them accountable.

And there's one more benefit of the NPVIC, one that has more relevance with every passing day: It would make it much harder for a losing presidential candidate to try to steal an election.

Every step of President Donald Trump's coup attempt—from his intimidation of state legislatures to the pressure campaign he launched on Mike Pence to his incitement of an insurrection at the Capitol—was predicated on the idea that he could change the result of the election by flipping the outcome in a few swing states. And he was right: It would have been much easier for him to "find" 44,000 votes across Georgia, Arizona, and Wisconsin, the states that decided the election, than it would have been to close the seven-million-vote gap he faced in the nationwide tally.

In other words: Only because of the Electoral College—because we don't simply count up all the votes across the country and declare a winner—did President Trump's putsch even stand a chance. And as I explained in chapter 6, in states around the country, Republicans have spent the years since the 2020 election trying to establish new ways to subvert our democracy by seizing control of election certification and consequently putting themselves in charge of who gets sent to the Electoral College.

This is a crisis, and—first things first—we need to be fighting, state by state, to make sure election administration remains in the hands of independent actors rather than partisan state legislatures. That way, Republicans can't direct a slate of electors to substitute its judgment for the will of the people.

But the truth is, as long as presidential elections are decided by individual states through the Electoral College, they will never be truly coup-proof. Which is why we need to eliminate it entirely, or remove its power with the NPVIC.

Ordinarily, this is the point in a chapter when I would present counterarguments, but on this issue, there really aren't any—at least not any valid ones.

The Electoral College has got to go.

Not just because of its bigoted past.

But because getting rid of it will help put us on a path to a truly democratic and representative future.

11

SAVING THE COURT

The NAACP Legal Defense and Educational Fund (LDF) is responsible for winning some of the most important cases in the history of the United States—but one of the most impressive testaments to the organization's strength is the fact that it survived the "Summer of Eric," back when I was one of its interns.

One day in June 1974, my boss assigned me a task even I knew I could not afford to mess up: filing a brief at the United States Supreme Court.

The next day, I hopped on a plane to Washington, landed at National Airport, grabbed a cab, and told the driver to take me to 1 First Street. Thinking back on it, he must have been seriously confused. What kind of twenty-three-year-old has business at the Supreme Court?

But he drove me there anyway—and I still remember what it felt like to see the building for the first time. My whole life, Washington had been in black-and-white, a city on a screen, where Dr. King had led marches; President Kennedy had delivered speeches; Thurgood Marshall, founder of the NAACP LDF, had argued cases. I was a New Yorker at heart, but when I climbed the steps of the Marble Palace, turned around, and looked at the Capitol, pillars straight out of the Pantheon all around me, I was in awe of this city.

After filing the brief, I jumped in a cab back to the airport and spent the entire flight combing through a pamphlet I had found in the building about the history of the Supreme Court. I was transfixed. In my first year at Columbia Law, I had read *Plessy v. Ferguson* and *Dred Scott v. Sandford,* so I didn't have the mistaken impression that the court was perfect, but I had also learned about *Brown v. Board of Education* and *Loving v. Virginia, Reynolds v. Sims* and *Miranda v. Arizona.* And even as an iconoclastic law student, I believed the Supreme Court was fundamentally a force for good.

I have had a reverence for the judicial branch ever since. It's why I became a judge. And when the Supreme Court started hearing cases that bore my name, I never lost sight of how cool that twenty-three-year-old intern would have thought that was; how mesmerized, how stunned, how proud he would have been. As attorney general, two of my best days were when President Obama's nominees to the court were confirmed; and I still remember how touched I was when I first entered the chamber to watch my colleagues at the United States Department of Justice argue consequential cases.

That is the kind of respect I have for the highest court in the land. And it is with that history in mind that I hope you read this chapter—in which I will argue that the mission of the Supreme Court has been compromised and that the institution is in need of reform.

Republicans might tell you it started with the smearing of Robert Bork, a Reagan nominee to the bench whose appointment was rejected by the Senate. Democrats might tell you it started with *Bush v. Gore.* Ultimately, it doesn't matter how the politicization of the Supreme Court began. What matters is figuring out how we are going to rebuild trust in this institution, an institution responsible for a task as sacred as any other in our democracy: protecting equal justice under the law.

For decades, the polarization of the Supreme Court has worried me—but reading the ruling in *Shelby County* was the moment that made me realize the court was facing a modern-day existential crisis. How, I kept asking myself, could five unelected judges, with lifetime appointments, gut a law that had been recently reauthorized by Congress in a historic bipartisan landslide, had been supported by every president since Johnson, and had, for nearly fifty years, secured the right to vote for millions of Americans?

There were plenty of past Supreme Court rulings that I didn't agree with—but at least with those, I believed the justices had come by their opinions honestly; that they had written them on the basis of their understanding of the Constitution.

With *Shelby*, I had a hard time convincing myself that this was still true. Because Congress had compiled such overwhelming evidence—thousands upon thousands of pages—that if the Voting Rights Act were overturned, access to the franchise would again come under attack. And in the end, that fact-finding was vindicated—not years down the line, but hours after Chief Justice Roberts announced his decision, when Texas moved forward with a suppressive bill that had previously been found to be unconstitutional.

That was when I realized I had to break a tradition that had been in place for generations.

From the day President Obama asked me to be attorney general, I had been looking forward to arguing a case at the Supreme Court, a tradition my predecessors from both political parties had embraced. And I was especially excited about the fact that I was all but guaranteed to win—since the attorney general is almost always sent to argue one of the relatively easy cases on the docket, leaving the big ones to the solicitor general.

But after *Shelby,* I came to the conclusion that I couldn't do it. I didn't want to pretend that this was a Supreme Court like any other; that the justices were good-faith actors; that a tradition should be followed. They had, without a legitimate basis, undermined our most fundamental right, a right that Americans of past generations, some of whom looked like me, had died to secure: the right to vote. And my protest—a silent protest I haven't told many people about until now—was that I wouldn't appear in that court as attorney general of the United States.

In the years since, the erosion of trust in the Supreme Court has accelerated—as the court's expanded conservative wing has not only continued attacking the right to vote but also delivered dubious decisions on everything from President Trump's Muslim ban, which they declared constitutional, to Obamacare's attempts to protect reproductive rights, which they declared unconstitutional, a harbinger of how they would begin to gut *Roe v. Wade* in the years ahead, despite overwhelming support for the right to choose among the American people.

Some of these minoritarian rulings were in no small part the result of the fact that, as I explained in part II, Republicans in the Senate, led by Mitch McConnell, had managed to steal a seat on the court. And if that word sounds harsh, think about this: They blocked President Obama's choice, Merrick Garland, who was selected in March 2016, because, they claimed, he was nominated too close to the presidential election—and then confirmed Amy Coney Barrett, President Trump's pick, even though she was nominated in September 2020, months later in the election cycle, when millions of people were already voting.

It's the kind of hypocrisy that makes the American people hate politics. And I don't blame them.

The good news is that it's not hard to reform the Supreme Court—in fact, it has been restructured over and over again throughout American history. And as with the National Popular Vote Interstate Compact, you wouldn't need a constitutional amendment to make it happen. You could do it through legislation.

But before diving into solutions, it's worth clarifying what, exactly, is at the heart of the trouble with the Supreme Court as it's currently constructed.

The most pressing problems with the court can all be traced to something that sounds like a good idea: life tenure.

While elected officials would have to compete to stay in office, our founders decided Supreme Court justices should be allowed to keep their jobs until they died or chose to retire. The theory was that this would preserve the independence of the justices—not only from the other branches of government, which founders like Alexander Hamilton feared would "overpower, awe, or influence" the judicial branch, but also from the public. Essentially, they wanted justices to be able to decide cases based on their reading of the Constitution, not out of a desire to curry favor or win reelection.

This all made sense—but there was one problem: The number of justices appointed by each president wound up being completely arbitrary. Franklin Delano Roosevelt, for instance, made eight nominations to the court, while Zachary Taylor, Andrew Johnson, and Jimmy Carter all made none.

At first, this wasn't that big a deal, because presidents had a hard time anticipating the ideologies of the justices they appointed—and so the court did not often swing too far to either side. That's why, from George Washington's presidency through Abraham Lincoln's, the Senate rarely exercised its confirmation authority to advise on and consent to Supreme Court nominees, generally signing off on them by voice vote.

Plus: People didn't live that long back when America was founded, which meant that on average, vacancies came about around twice as frequently as they do today. This made battles for Supreme Court seats less contentious and ensured the court wouldn't be dominated by any one ideology or group of justices for too long.

As you know, this has changed in recent years—for several reasons.

For one, because justices live longer, making vacancies rarer, the stakes of each one are extremely high. Congress has also become polarized, making practically every debate and decision before them adversarial. And the justices themselves have begun to take a partisan approach to stepping aside: Early in American history, the vast majority of them died in the job. But in the years since 1950, four out of five justices have chosen to retire and, in general, have timed their retirement to take place while a president whose ideology they supported was in office. This has, naturally, led to a cycle of even more perceived partisanship on the bench.

And as a result, both parties have treated every recent nomination, from Garland to Gorsuch to Kavanaugh to Barrett, as a war with the future of our country at stake. It's an untenable state, but thankfully, it's in our power to change it.

In an ideal world, I would expand the Court's size to counter the skullduggery of Republicans in stealing two Supreme Court seats. But whether or not we can make that happen, I would reform the way justices are nominated altogether.

What would that look like?

First, I would make sure that every president has the opportunity to appoint the same number of justices per term: two—one in the first year, one in the third. This would mean the balance of the court would reflect the will of the people, rather than being driven by acts of God and strategically timed retirements. I would also mandate that the Senate vote on these nominations within two months of them being announced, so senators are more likely to evaluate each potential justice on their own merit, knowing it will be much harder for them to leave a vacancy open until a new president takes office. (The Senate could, theoretically, reject each of a president's nominees every two months, but over time, that would carry tremendous political and game-theoretical costs.)

And second, I would establish eighteen-year terms, because life tenure no longer makes any sense. As none other than Chief Justice John Roberts once wrote:

> The Framers adopted life tenure at a time when people simply did not live as long as they do now. A judge insulated from the normal currents of life for twenty-five or thirty years was a rarity then, but is becoming commonplace today. Setting a term of, say, fifteen years would ensure that federal judges would not lose all touch with reality through decades of ivory tower existence. It would also provide a more regular and greater degree of turnover among the judges. Both developments would, in my view, be healthy ones.

No matter our disagreements, on this issue, he couldn't be more right. And the people of this country agree—with polls showing more than three in four Americans opposed to life tenure. That's because it's common sense that no one should be trusted in a position of such enormous authority for life, especially given how much longer people are living these days.

For context: The average tenure of a justice is estimated to double over the next century. This would, in turn, make vacancies even more rare—and the fights over them even higher stakes, further dooming the Supreme Court to a perpetual state of conflict.

Eighteen-year terms would still be long enough to insulate justices from the whims of any one political moment. And with appointments taking place every two years, this system would have the added benefit of enabling us to maintain a Supreme Court with nine seats in the long run, even if the number of justices expands in the short term, once everyone currently sitting on the bench has stepped down. (That is why, unlike the chief justice, I am in favor of eighteen-year terms rather than fifteen-year ones, which would result in an ever-changing court size.)

The policies would be a win for all parties involved—for senators who could once again advise on and consent to nominations with an eye toward what's good for America, not what's good for their party; for justices, who could focus on doing their jobs without having to think about when, where, and how they are going to step aside; and for the American people, whose faith in the highest court in the land could be restored.

I'll be honest: If I were a law school student today and I were asked to file a brief at the Supreme Court, I'm not sure I would have that same feeling in my heart that I did all those decades ago—and that's a shame. Because one of the things that makes America so special, one of the reasons I have been so honored to devote my life to serving this country, is our judicial system.

No, it's never been perfect, and I knew that, even as a twenty-three-year-old walking up those marble steps for the first time. But I never wavered in my belief that the nine people who sat on that bench went to work every day trying to make America a more just place than it was the day before.

What I would give to feel that way again.

CONCLUSION

As you read through the past few chapters, you may have nodded your head in agreement with the policies I outlined, but I bet you also thought to yourself that *none* of it is going to happen. I can't blame you. After all, in 2021, we had a Democratic Party–controlled government—and not a single protection of the franchise became law at the federal level.

The tragedy, of course, is that the very same institutions we so desperately need to fix—from an undemocratic Senate, where a majority isn't enough to pass voting rights legislation, to gerrymandered state legislatures that have relentlessly enacted laws that make it harder to vote, to a Supreme Court that refuses to strike down those laws and whose justices were mostly appointed by Republicans who became president after losing the popular vote—are the ones preventing us from getting anything done.

In this way, minority rule isn't just a threat we should be worried about facing down the road. It is already here. And we are living through the implementation of a kind of political apartheid, where Republicans are perpetually in control of what does and doesn't get to become law, even when they win fewer votes than Democrats at every level.

It's infuriating—and it's terrifying. Our country seems to have entered what *Kill Switch* author Adam Jentleson has called a "doom loop," where undemocratically elected lawmakers use their power to make America less democratic, which makes it easier for them to win elections, which makes it easier for them to attack democracy. And the thing about doom loops, the thing about cycles of any kind, is that they are hard to break, because they are self-perpetuating.

And that's the elephant in this book: Right now, our system of government doesn't look like it's going to get better. It looks like it's going to get worse. We are, in other words, in the middle of a crisis.

But we've been here before—in fact, for most of our history, America wasn't a true democracy at all. And yet suffragists in the generations before us never let that stop them from fighting for the right to vote, even though they faced much longer odds, and much harsher consequences, than we could imagine or will ever experience.

Think about Seth Luther, who was so outraged by the idea that only property owners should be allowed to vote that he helped write a constitution of his own—and put his life on the line to defend it. Or Alice Paul, being fed through a tube in prison because she refused to leave the steps of the White House until the Nineteenth Amendment became law. Or Frederick Douglass, a man born in captivity who didn't stop at the abolition of slavery—but went on to fight for the franchise, not only for Black Americans, but for women, too.

Think about Medgar Evers, shot in the driveway of his home, JIM CROW MUST GO T-shirts in hand, an act of untamable hope in the face of unimaginable cruelty.

And think about all those whose names we do not know—the bodies at the bottoms of rivers and hanging in trees, erased from history, that once carried the souls of suffragists.

As President Obama said at the 2020 Democratic National Convention, "If anyone had a right to believe that this democracy did not work, and could not work, it was those Americans. Our ancestors. They were on the receiving end of a democracy that had fallen short all their lives. They knew how far the daily reality of America strayed from the myth. And yet instead of giving up, they joined together and they said somehow, some way, we are going to make this work. We are going to bring those words, in our founding documents, to life."

These Americans—women, men, Black, white—who had much less reason for hope than any of us, who had never seen democracy in action, and in many cases had never seen anyone who looked like them cast a ballot, refused to give in to the paralysis of pessimism, and instead, just kept doing the work, because they knew it was right.

And across the country, that is the legacy the suffragists of today are building on. We see it in Chris Hollins and his army of election workers, who—with masks on their faces and hope in their hearts—went from block to block, in town after town, setting up drive-through voting sites, hoping they'd make it easier for working parents juggling two jobs; for grandparents worried about a virus; for folks with disabilities unable to wait in long lines to make their voices heard. We see it in Love Caesar and her classmates, who refused to be divided by a line drawn through the middle of their campus—and kept speaking up until the gerrymander was struck down. We see it in Senfronia Thompson and her colleagues in the Texas Legislature, who left their families and their paychecks behind to try to galvanize Congress and move our country forward.

These are some of the leaders of a modern-day civil rights movement—who hail from different backgrounds, races, and religions but are united by a common cause, a cause as important as any other: finally making America a democracy where every voice is heard and every vote is counted.

And we all have an obligation to be the foot soldiers in that fight.

Because unlike Luther, unlike Paul, and unlike Douglass, the vast majority of us are in possession of what John Lewis called "the most powerful nonviolent tool": the right to vote. And if, despite all the procedural and structural hurdles that have been placed in front of us, we manage to show up to the polls like never before, we have the numbers to vote out the politicians blocking progress—and replace them with leaders who are ready to bring about that more democratic America.

That means beating the Republicans who are attacking our democracy, yes, but it also means replacing the Democrats who are standing by and letting it happen—refusing to accept the existential national urgency of this issue.

Speaking now as a Democrat, capital D, I have to say that as a party, we need to become much more comfortable with doing what it takes to acquire power—and then using that power to fix the institutions we know are broken. Because if we don't, no one will, and our government will grow less and less reflective of the people while our institutions become harder and harder to change. (At a certain point, there simply becomes no way to out-organize a gerrymander.)

But I want to be clear: While Democrats are the only party that seems interested in expanding access to the franchise at the moment, the reason to pursue this cause isn't partisan. It's not about race, or about gender, or about region. It's about who we are as a country—and who we want to be. It's about whether America will, finally, become the democracy we say that we are. And I believe we will.

Now, anyone who tells you progress is inevitable is mistaken. Demography is not destiny. Moral arcs don't bend with certainty. History is not a Marvel movie—the good guys lose as often as they win. Since our nation's founding, the journey of American democracy has moved in every direction. We've gone forward and backward, won progress and seen it wiped away. Through it all, the right to vote has never been sacred.

But anyone who tells you progress can't be won is being just as ignorant. Because Americans bent that arc at a time when the resistance was much greater—when you could be lynched, buried alive, assassinated in front of your children for so much as trying to register to vote.

So do not give in to cynicism. Do not give in to fatalism. Do not give in to nihilism. We, more than any generation in history, are in control of our own destiny. We are the stewards of our democracy. And we have it in our power to shape where the journey goes next—as long as we put in the work.

As Cody Keenan, President Obama's longtime collaborator, who helped draft that keynote at the Democratic National Convention, said in a speech of his own: "Idealism is not the simplistic belief that things will get better. It's the belief that, with effort, things *can* get better. It's understanding the world as it is, and fighting for the world as it should be anyway. And there is joy to be found in that struggle."

There is joy to be found in that struggle.

It's the joy of improbable revolt against an empire—founding a country on an idea, one you understand but do not yet live by, that all of us are created equal. It's the joy of realizing that so much of our population isn't included in that promise and deciding to do something about it—standing up for the belief that you shouldn't need land, or need to be a man, or need to be white, to make your voice heard. It's the joy of binding the wounds of a house divided, of daring to have a dream and putting in the work, by any means necessary, of realizing it. It's the joy we all felt that day in Selma—the joy of knowing that as far as we'd come, we still had a debt to repay to all who had walked in the face of billy clubs and batons to make it possible for a Black president and a Black attorney general to follow in their footsteps on the Edmund Pettus Bridge, asking nothing of us in return but that we continue the march.

You know, when I was twelve, watching the civil rights movement unfold on television, I was in awe of the heroes who lit up the screen in black-and-white—even James Hood, with his questionable hat choice. But I also wondered whether, had I been born earlier, or had I been born in the South, I would have done the same. It's not a question I'll ever be able to answer.

But now we are faced with a more important question—not what would we have done to right the wrongs of the past, but what will we do to right the wrongs of today, with our democracy once again at risk of destruction. And I believe we have it in us to continue that march.

That means going door-to-door organizing our neighbors, registering them to vote, and bringing them to the polls on Election Day. It means calling our representatives and demanding they pass legislation that will protect the right that protects the rest. It means donating our time—and, if we have it, our money—to candidates and causes we believe in. It might even mean signing up to serve yourself—filling a county-supervisor or election-board seat, or registering as a poll worker and making sure the votes in your town are being counted fairly.

The question, though, isn't what we need to do. That isn't a mystery. The question is whether we'll actually do it, whether we'll fight for our democracy like our ancestors did, like our freedom depends on it. Because it still does.

Now, make no mistake: The path to progress is a winding road, full of roundabouts and cul-de-sacs. Some days, we'll be moving our feet as fast as we can, and it'll seem like we're going nowhere. Just imagine how Elizabeth Cady Stanton must have felt helping write the *History of Woman Suffrage* at the turn of the nineteenth century, with little to show at that point for her decades of activism. Or what must have been rushing through the minds of James Chaney, Andrew Goodman, and Michael Schwerner as they took their dying breaths, miles from home, executed during what was supposed to be a Freedom Summer. In the moment, everything these suffragists had done, everything they had sacrificed and everything they had fought for, would have felt futile.

But in a fight like this, progress isn't measured over seasons, or years, or decades. It's measured over generations. And what our ancestors did mattered. It's the reason we have the right to vote—and the reason we are in a position to defend it.

This is not to say there isn't urgency in this mission. Indeed, patience is not a virtue now. The only reason we've come this far is because of all who came before us, who did everything they could in their short time on earth to move us forward, even if they didn't live to see the democracy they helped build. And as a man with more yesterdays than tomorrows, I believe we have an obligation to do the same; to do as much as we can, in the limited time that we have, to protect the right to vote.

So do not despair over where we are today, as hard as that may be. Instead, set your sights on where we need to go and on figuring out how we are going to get there. It's the same destination Thomas Wilson Dorr was marching toward in Rhode Island, the same destination Ida B. Wells was marching toward in Washington, the same destination Albert Turner was marching toward in Alabama—a destination where the promises in the documents that shaped this country aren't empty words on paper but a lived reality for every single American.

That journey may be arduous, but we have no choice but to

embark on it. For we owe a debt to those who came before us and have a duty to those who will come after—to leave behind a country that may not be perfect, but is, at the very least, more perfect than the one we inherited.

May the journey to that destination be a faithful one. May it be a determined one. May it be a joyful one.

Because while we may not get there right away, as long as we refuse to stop marching, one foot after the other, together, we can save our democracy.

And we will.

ACKNOWLEDGMENTS

There are many reasons you shouldn't judge a book based on its cover—but in this case, it's because anything good about what we've produced is to the credit of way more than the two people whose names are listed.

First, we have to thank Chris Jackson, who came to Eric with the idea to write about voting rights in the first place. From helping conceptualize the structure of the book to providing inspired line edits and comments that made our writing sing and our arguments more sound, he has been an invaluable thought partner through every step of this process. There's a reason he's known as the best—and it's because there's no one better.

Then there's Gail Ross, who has been insisting to Eric that he should be an author since he left the attorney general's office. We are grateful for her passion from the beginning of this process, for introducing us to one another, and for continuing to provide such thoughtful feedback at every stage. Without Gail, this book doesn't exist.

There was another thought partner who worked with us from the beginning, and that's Mallika Machra, the research fellow at Fenway Strategies. She was a sounding board for Sam's (often ludicrous) ideas from the start—and chased down so many of the facts and figures that make this thing pop. Mallika is also a brilliant writer, with a bright future, so keep an eye out for a book with her name on it to hit the shelves.

Once we had a draft, she was joined by Elmo Tumbokon, who quickly and methodically helped her make sure everything in the book was properly cited. A legend. And then Andy Young came in and made sure all of it was accurate—or at least we hope! Andy is a world-class fact checker who worked quickly and with wit, and made what is normally the most painful part of the process (relatively) pain free.

We also want to thank everyone who read this book and provided feedback over the course of the process—from the folks at Fenway Strategies, especially Greg Bell, whose wisdom made each chapter richer in both style and substance, to Yascha Mounk, whose close readings are always invaluable, to Sharon Malone, who served as our final boss. Once she signed off and told Eric the book wasn't half bad, we knew we'd be all right.

But when they read our draft, it was just a Word document! Which brings us to our next acknowledgment: the entire team at OneWorld, which transformed what we produced into a bona fide book. Now that Word document is bound and will soon live on shelves in stores, in backpacks moving through subway stations, and by bedside tables in homes around the world. It's really mind-boggling to process the fact that people will actually read this thing, and that's because of the geniuses at One-World. Thank you to Sun Robinson-Smith, Mika Kasuga, Lulu Martinez, Andrea Pura, London King, Evan Camfield, Greg Mollica, Avideh Bashirrad, Sandra Sjursen, and Fritz Metsch. There's no team we'd rather have in our corner.

Eric would like to thank Sharon, again, as well as Buddy, Maya, and Brooke, who once again put up with me and gave me the time to dedicate to this effort. You all are my foundation, my inspiration, and my hope for the future.

Sam would also like to thank his parents, Amy and Brian,

and his sister, Anna, for always telling him he had talent—and an obligation to work hard to make the most of it. To whatever extent I have a moral compass, it's because of you guys, and making you proud is my only North Star.

Finally, we owe a deep debt of gratitude to the foot soldiers who have led the fight for voting rights since the founding of our nation—for bringing us this far and inspiring us to never stop marching.

NOTES

INTRODUCTION

3 **For most of:** "IMPORTANT FROM ALABAMA: The City of Selma—Its Great Military Importance to the Rebels—Its Manufactures of War Materials, Clothing, Salt, &c.—Description by a Resident of the Place," *New York Times,* April 5, 1864, nytimes.com/1864/04/05/archives/important-from-alabama-the-city-of-selmaits-great-military.html.

3 **We were two:** Peter Baker and Richard Fausset, "Obama, at Selma Memorial, Says, 'We Know the March Is Not Yet Over,'" *New York Times,* March 7, 2015, nytimes.com/2015/03/08/us/obama-in-selma-for-edmund-pettus-bridge-attack-anniversary.html.

3 **By seven-thirty A.M.:** Peter Holley and Juliet Eilperin, "Thousands Descend on Selma to Hear President Obama Mark the 50th Anniversary of 'Bloody Sunday,'" *Washington Post,* March 7, 2015, washingtonpost.com/news/post-nation/wp/2015/03/07/thousands-descend-upon-selma-to-listen-to-president-obama-mark-the-50th-anniversary-of-bloody-sunday/.

4 **And that was:** Aamer Madhani and David Jackson, "Obama, Bush, Civil Rights Icons Retrace Selma March," *USA Today,* March 8, 2015, usatoday.com/story/news/nation/2015/03/07/selma-50th-anniversary-bloody-sunday/24552475/.

4 **Congressman John Lewis:** Scott Horsley, "Obama in Selma: 'The Race Is Not Yet Won,'" NPR, March 8, 2015, npr.org/2015/03/08/391619519/obama-in-selma-the-race-is-not-yet-won.

6 **So when, on that day:** "Jimmie Lee Jackson," Southern Poverty Law Center, splcenter.org/jimmie-lee-jackson.

6 **In Marion, where:** C. G. Gomillion, "The Negro Voter in Alabama," *Journal of Negro Education* 26, no. 3 (Summer 1957): 281–82.

6 **Marion is where hundreds:** See especially Ari Berman, *Give Us the Ballot: The Modern Struggle for Voting Rights in America* (New York: Farrar, Straus and Giroux, 2015), 16–18.

7 **At sunset:** Sara Bullard, "Jimmie Lee Jackson," in *Free at Last: A History of the Civil Rights Movement and Those Who Died in the Struggle* (Montgomery, Ala.: Southern Poverty Law Center, 1989), 72.

7 **He even wrote:** Javonte Anderson, "'First Martyr of the Voting Rights Movement': How a Black Man's Death in 1965 Changed American History," *USA Today,* May 20, 2021.

7 **"They hauled me":** John Herbers and Anne Farris Rosen, *Deep South Dispatch: Memoir of a Civil Rights Journalist* (Jackson: University Press of Mississippi, 2018), 216.

8 **shot him from just feet away:** Ryan Jones, "Who Mourns for Jimmie Lee Jackson?," National Civil Rights Museum, February 12, 2015, civilrightsmuseum.org/news/posts/who-mourns-for-jimmie-lee-jackson.

8 **Wounded but not:** John Fleming, "The Death of Jimmie Lee Jackson," *Anniston Star,* March 6, 2005.

8 **A few days later, Jimmie:** Civil Rights Division Notice to Close File, May 3, 2021, File No. 144-3-1422, United States Department of Justice, justice.gov/crt/case-document/file/949466/download.

8 **And Dr. Martin Luther King, Jr.:** Martin Luther King, Jr., "Letter from a Selma, Alabama, Jail," 1964, as reprinted in David J. Garrow, *MLK: An American Legacy: Bearing the Cross, Protest at Selma, and the FBI and Martin Luther King, Jr.* (New York: Open Road Media, 2016), 142.

8 **"We are going":** Quoted in Roy Reed, "266 Apply to Vote as Selma Speeds Negro Registration," *New York Times,* March 1, 1965.

8 **At Jimmie's funeral:** Javonte Anderson, "'First Martyr of the Voting Rights Movement': How a Black Man's Death in 1965 Changed American History," *USA Today,* May 20, 2021, usatoday.com/in-depth/news/investigations/2021/05/20/george-floyd-jimmie-lee-jackson-murder-led-to-voting-rights-act/7153822002/.

8 **One idea they:** David Krajicek, "Long-Awaited Justice in Cop's Killing of Jimmie Lee Jackson, Whose Death Helped Spark Alabama Civil Rights Marches," New York *Daily News,* February 1, 2015, nydailynews.com/news/crime/long-awaited-justice-killing-jimmie-lee-jackson-article-1.2099217.

9 **On March 7:** Anderson, "First Martyr."

9 **"At times history":** Lyndon B. Johnson, "We Shall Overcome," March 15, 1965, an electronic publication of *Voices of Democracy: The U.S. Oratory Project,* dir. Shawn J. Perry-Giles (College Park, Md., 2005), voicesofdemocracy.umd.edu/johnson-we-shall-overcome-speech-text/.

9 **Watching LBJ's speech:** Robert Caro, "When LBJ Said, 'We Shall Overcome,'" *New York Times,* August 28, 2008, nytimes.com/2008/08/28/opinion/28iht-edcaro.1.15715378.html.

9 **President Johnson's administration:** Berman, *Give Us the Ballot,* 41–48.

10 **"He had to die":** Berman, *Give Us the Ballot,* 28.

10 **Indeed, I added:** Eric Holder, "Attorney General Holder Reaffirms Commitment to Voting Rights in Speech to Commemorate the 50th Anniversary of Bloody Sunday and the Selma-to-Montgomery Marches," United States Department of Justice, March 8, 2015, justice.gov/opa/speech/attorney-general-holder-reaffirms-commitment-voting-rights-speech-commemorate-50th.

10 **After Republicans won:** Hannah Klain, Kevin Morris, Max Feldman, and Rebecca Ayala, *Waiting to Vote: Racial Disparities in Election Day Experiences* (New York: Brennan Center for Justice, 2020).

10 **The motivation behind:** Carol Anderson, *One Person, No Vote: How Voter Suppression Is Destroying Our Democracy* (New York: Bloomsbury Publishing, 2019), 63.

11 **Across the country:** "The Effect of the Voting Rights Act," Introduction to Federal Voting Rights Laws (United States Department of Justice Civil Rights Division Voting Section), archive.epic.org/privacy/voting/register/intro_c.html; Berman, *Give Us the Ballot,* 37–43.

11 **To Chief Justice John Roberts:** *Shelby County v. Holder,* 570 U.S. 529 (2013).

11 **Of course, he had it:** *Shelby County v. Holder,* 570 U.S. 529, 32 (2013).

11 **On the very day:** "The Effects of Shelby County v. Holder," Brennan Center for Justice, brennancenter.org/our-work/policy-solutions/effects-shelby-county-v-holder.

11 **North Carolina followed:** *North Carolina State Conference of the NAACP v. Raymond,* 832 F.2nd (4th Circuit 2020).

12 **Since *Shelby*, state:** Kevin Morris, "Voter Purge Rates Remain High,

Analysis Finds," Brennan Center for Justice, accessed August 21, 2019, brennancenter.org/our-work/analysis-opinion/voter-purge-rates-remain-high-analysis-finds.

12 **Over the past decade:** See Klain et al., *Waiting to Vote.*

13 **"The American instinct":** Barack Obama, "Remarks by the President at the 50th Anniversary of the Selma to Montgomery Marches," The White House, March 7, 2015.

14 **As President Trump:** Sam Levine, "Trump Says Republicans Would 'Never' Be Elected Again if It Was Easier to Vote," *Guardian,* March 30, 2020, theguardian.com/us-news/2020/mar/30/trump-republican-party-voting-reform-coronavirus.

15 **From Michigan to:** Amy Gardner, Tom Hamburger, and Josh Dawsey, "Trump Allies Work to Place Supporters in Key Election Posts Across the Country, Spurring Fears About Future Vote Challenges," *Washington Post,* November 29, 2021, washingtonpost.com/politics/trump-allies-election-oversight/2021/11/28/3933b3ce-4227-11ec-9ea7-3eb2406a2e24_story.html.

15 **The numbers are:** John Gramlich, "How Trump Compares with Other Recent Presidents in Appointing Federal Judges," Pew Research Center, January 13, 2021, pewresearch.org/fact-tank/2021/01/13/how-trump-compares-with-other-recent-presidents-in-appointing-federal-judges/.

15 **The skew of:** Tom McCarthy and Alvin Chang, "'The Senate Is Broken': System Empowers White Conservatives, Threatening US Democracy," *Guardian,* March 12, 2021.

16 **All these are:** Sarah Repucci, "From Crisis to Reform: A Call to Strengthen America's Battered Democracy," Freedom House, 2021, freedomhouse.org/report/special-report/2021/crisis-reform-call-strengthen-americas-battered-democracy#footnote2_mf63alg.

19 **As I said in Selma:** Holder, "Attorney General Holder Reaffirms Commitment to Voting Rights."

NOTE: THE CASE FOR DEMOCRACY

21 **Republicans have begun:** Zack Beauchamp, "The Republican Revolt Against Democracy, Explained in 13 Charts," *Vox,* March 1, 2021, vox.com/policy-and-politics/22274429/republicans-anti-democracy-13-charts.

21 **This is in:** Christina Prignano and Travis Andersen, "Republican Senator Mike Lee Says 'Democracy Isn't the Objective' in Baffling Tweet," *Boston Globe,* October 8, 2020, bostonglobe.com/2020/10/08/nation/republican-senator-mike-lee-says-democracy-isnt-objective-baffling-tweet/.

22 **Fox News, meanwhile:** Zack Beauchamp, "It Happened There: How Democracy Died in Hungary," *Vox,* September 13, 2018, vox.com/policy-and-politics/2018/9/13/17823488/hungary-democracy-authoritarianism-trump.

22 **At one point:** Benjamin Novak and Michael Grynbaum, "Conservative Fellow Travelers: Tucker Carlson Drops In on Viktor Orban," *New York Times,* August 10, 2021, nytimes.com/2021/08/07/world/europe/tucker-carlson-hungary.html.

22 **Hungary later censored:** Erik Wemple, "Hungary Punked Tucker Carlson," *Washington Post,* August 14, 2021, washingtonpost.com/opinions/2021/08/14/hungary-punked-tucker-carlson/.

22 **They actually believe:** Kathy Frankovic, "Republicans Say It Should Be Harder to Vote in America, While Democrats Want to Make It Easier," YouGov, April 1, 2021, today.yougov.com/topics/politics/articles-reports/2021/04/01/republicans-say-it-should-be-harder-vote-poll; "Republicans and Democrats Move Further Apart in Views of Voting Access," Pew Research Center, April 22, 2021, pewresearch.org/politics/2021/04/22/republicans-and-democrats-move-further-apart-in-views-of-voting-access/.

23 **"public opinion, expressed by all":** United Kingdom, *Hansard Parliamentary Debates,* 3d ser., vol. 444 (1947).

23 **This is why:** Michael Massing, "Does Democracy Avert Famine?," *New York Times,* March 1, 2003, nytimes.com/2003/03/01/arts/does-democracy-avert-famine.html.

1. REBELLION: HOW WHITE MEN WON THE VOTE

31 **"The past is":** William Faulkner, *Requiem for a Nun* (New York: Knopf Doubleday Publishing Group, 2011), 73.

31 **There were exceptions:** The library of work on the history of voting rights in America is voluminous. See especially Alexander Keyssar, *The Right to Vote: The Contested History of Democracy in the United States,* rev. ed. (New York: Basic Books, 2009); Ari Berman,

Give Us the Ballot: The Modern Struggle for Voting Rights in America (New York: Farrar, Straus and Giroux, 2015); Carol Anderson, *One Person, No Vote: How Voter Suppression Is Destroying Our Democracy* (London: Bloomsbury, 2019); and Evette Dionne, *Lifting as We Climb: Black Women's Battle for the Ballot Box* (New York: Penguin, 2020).

32 **In New Hampshire:** Chilton Williamson, "The Age of Property Tests," in *American Suffrage: From Property to Democracy, 1760–1860* (Princeton, N.J.: Princeton University Press, 1960), 12.

32 **they needed to be well manicured:** Williamson, "The Age of Property Tests," 13.

32 **they were binding:** Chilton Williamson, "The Colonial Voter at the Polls," in *American Suffrage,* 49.

32 **unless you were Protestant:** Keyssar, *The Right to Vote,* 26–27.

33 **He was a:** See especially Erik Chaput, *The People's Martyr: Thomas Wilson Dorr and His 1842 Rhode Island Rebellion* (Lawrence, Kan.: University Press of Kansas, 2014).

33 **"gets up leisurely":** "New England Kitchen Lore," *Northern Junket* 12, no. 5 (March 1976): 45.

33 **"journeyman carpenter":** Seth Luther, "An Address on the Right of Free Suffrage," Providence, R.I., 1833, Providence College Digital Commons, digitalcommons.providence.edu/cgi/viewcontent.cgi?article=1000&context=dorr_pamphlets, 4.

33 **valued at upward of $134:** See Keyssar, *The Right to Vote,* 80–81; and Chaput, *The People's Martyr.*

33 **"strange that a self-evident truth":** Luther, "An Address on the Right of Free Suffrage," 5, 9.

33 **"May all Traitors":** Luther, "An Address on the Right of Free Suffrage," 4.

34 **Despite objections from:** Erik Chaput and Russell J. DeSimone, "Our Hidden History: Racism and Black Suffrage in the Dorr Rebellion," *USA Today,* November 21, 2020.

34 **In the months that followed:** See Chaput, *The People's Martyr,* 3–5; and Chaput, "'Let the People Remember!': Rhode Island's Dorr Rebellion and Bay State Politics, 1842–1843," *Historical Journal of Massachusetts* 39, no. 1–2 (2011).

34 **just 52 voted:** See Chaput, "'Let the People Remember!'"

34 **guilty of treason:** Chaput, "'Let the People Remember!'"

34 **Even President John Tyler:** Chaput, *The People's Martyr*, 90–91.

35 **"Peaceably if we can":** Luther, "An Address on the Right of Free Suffrage," 21.

35 **spurned by the rebels:** Chaput, *The People's Martyr*, 151.

35 **brutalized by the state:** Howard Zinn, *A People's History of the United States* (New York: HarperCollins, 2016), 215.

35 **riches-to-rags story:** Chaput, *The People's Martyr*, 204.

35 **an unmarked grave:** Carl Gersuny, "Seth Luther, Union Firebrand Who Railed Against Children Working in Mills," *Small State Big History* (Online Review of Rhode Island History), August 2, 2021, smallstatebighistory.com/seth-luther-union-firebrand-who-railed-against-children-working-in-mills/.

35 **But while the:** Erik J. Chaput and Russell J. DeSimone, "My Turn: How Rhode Island Expanded Black Rights," *Providence Journal*, September 16, 2017.

35 **its sixteenth governor:** Erik Chaput, "Proslavery and Antislavery Politics in Rhode Island's 1842 Dorr Rebellion," *New England Quarterly* 85, no. 4 (2012): 659.

36 **He went fishing:** Keyssar, *The Right to Vote*, 39.

36 **"We the People":** Meredith Hindley, "The Confessions of Gouverneur Morris: An Interview with Melanie Ralph Miller," *Humanities* 40, no. 2 (2019).

36 **"give the votes":** James Madison, *The Debates in the Federal Convention of 1787: Which Framed the Constitution of the United States of America*, ed. Gaillard Hunt and James Brown Scott (Clark, N.J.: The Lawbook Exchange, Ltd., 1999), 352.

37 **"exclude such persons":** Keyssar, *The Right to Vote*, 28–29.

37 **"If these persons had votes"**: William Blackstone, *Commentaries on the Laws of England, Volume 1: A Facsimile of the First Edition of 1765–1769* (Chicago: University of Chicago Press, 1979), 171.

37 **"Americans used to vote":** Jill Lepore, "Rock, Paper, Scissors: How We Used to Vote," *The New Yorker*, October 6, 2008, newyorker.com/magazine/2008/10/13/rock-paper-scissors.

37 **"Children do not vote":** "Madison Debates," Avalon Project at Yale Law School, avalon.law.yale.edu/18th_century/debates_807.asp.

37 **"the best guardians":** "Madison Debates."

38 **"Democracy," he exclaimed:** "Madison Debates."

38 **"vicious arts":** "The Federalist Papers: No. 10," Avalon Project at Yale Law School, avalon.law.yale.edu/18th_century/fed10.asp.

38 **"an immediate revolution":** "From John Adams to James Madison, 17 June 1817," Founders Online, National Archives, founders.archives.gov/documents/Adams/99-02-02-6772.

38 **"The same reasoning":** "From John Adams to James Sullivan, 26 May 1776," Founders Online, National Archives, founders.archives.gov/documents/Adams/06-04-02-0091.

39 **Edward Rutledge, from:** "Madison Debates."

39 **And George Mason:** "Madison Debates."

39 **At the convention:** "Madison Debates."

39 **"Today a man":** As cited in Alexander Keyssar, "The Project of Democracy," *Maine Policy Review* 11, no. 2 (2002): 93.

40 **Somehow, even with:** "Madison Debates."

40 **To put a number:** Lepore, "Rock, Paper, Scissors."

40 **As Chilton Williamson:** Williamson, *American Suffrage,* 57.

41 **Voter fraud may:** Williamson, *American Suffrage,* 49–51, 56–59.

41 **Then there was:** Williamson, *American Suffrage,* 43–44.

42 **As Lepore writes:** Lepore, "Rock, Paper, Scissors."

42 **Votes were easy:** Lepore, "Rock, Paper, Scissors."

42 **In 1792, Delaware:** Keyssar, *The Right to Vote,* 65–66.

42 **When Andrew Jackson:** Lepore, "Rock, Paper, Scissors."

42 **As Alexander Keyssar:** Keyssar, *The Right to Vote,* 49–54.

43 **After all, in:** Keyssar, *The Right to Vote,* 51.

43 **In Virginia, the landless:** Keyssar, *The Right to Vote,* 52.

43 **Of course, as:** Keyssar, *The Right to Vote,* 52–53.

43 **The Virginia delegation:** Keyssar, *The Right to Vote,* 51.

43 **What he meant:** Keyssar, *The Right to Vote,* 54.

44 **The second reason:** Keyssar, *The Right to Vote.*

44 **"Should we not":** Keyssar, *The Right to Vote.*

44 **Beginning in the:** Keyssar, *The Right to Vote,* 55.

44 **In North Carolina:** Keyssar, *The Right to Vote,* 56.

45 **Because people really:** Keyssar, *The Right to Vote,* 56–57.

45 **That's why, after:** Keyssar, *The Right to Vote,* 56.

45 **turnout nearly tripled:** Keyssar, *The Right to Vote,* 55.

45 **"there be something in the ownership of land":** Keyssar, *The Right to Vote,* 58.

46 **Because, as Frederick Douglass:** Frederick Douglass, *Two Speeches by Frederick Douglass: One on West India Emancipation and the Other on the Dred Scott Decision* (Rochester, N.Y.: C. P. Dewey, 1857), loc.gov/item/mfd.21039/.

2. A MOMENT IN THE SUN: HOW BLACK MEN WON THE VOTE—AND WHITE MEN STOLE IT

47 **On May 10:** "The Anti-Slavery Society; Exciting Debate and Final Action on Mr. Gurrison's Resolution of Dissolution," *New York Times,* May 11, 1865.

47 **Six days after:** Trevor Plante, "Ending the Bloodshed: The Last Surrenders of the Civil War," *Prologue,* Spring 2015, archives.gov/publications/prologue/2015/spring.

47 **With this progress:** "The Anti-Slavery Society," *New York Times.*

48 **"Rejoicing with joy":** "The Anti-Slavery Society," *New York Times.*

48 **He continued:** "Important Session of the Anti Slavery Society," *New York Times,* May 10, 1865, nytimes.com/1865/05/10/archives/the-anniversaries-important-session-of-the-antislavery-society.html.

48 **But his partner:** "The Anti-Slavery Society," *New York Times.*

48 **"Slavery is not abolished":** "The Anti-Slavery Society," *New York Times.*

48 **"this nation was in trouble":** Frederick Douglass, "What the Black Man Wants," 1865, an electronic publication of *Black Past,* March 15, 2012, blackpast.org/african-american-history/1865-frederick-douglass-what-black-man-wants/.

48 **"Shall we be citizens in war":** Douglass, "What the Black Man Wants."

48 "**Here where universal":** Douglass, "What the Black Man Wants."

49 **"No Reconstruction Without":** Wendell Phillips, *Commonwealth,* May 6, 2015; *N.A.S. Standard,* May 27, 1865.

49 **These Lost Cause propagandists:** Eric Foner, "South Carolina's Forgotten Black Political Revolution," *Slate,* January 31, 2018.

49 **In some cases:** Foner, "South Carolina's Forgotten Black Political Revolution."

49 **In D. W. Griffith's:** Eric Foner, "Rooted in Reconstruction: The First Wave of Black Congressmen," *The Nation,* October 15, 2008.

49 **It was nothing:** See W.E.B Du Bois, *Black Reconstruction in*

America: An Essay Toward a History of the Part Which Black Folk Played in the Attempt to Reconstruct Democracy in America, 1860–1880, ed. Henry Louis Gates, Jr. (New York: Oxford University Press, 2007).

50 **in just over a decade:** Foner, "South Carolina's Forgotten Black Political Revolution."

50 **And they used that power:** See especially Eric Foner, *Freedom's Lawmakers: A Directory of Black Officeholders During Reconstruction* (Baton Rouge, La.: Louisiana State University Press, 1996).

50 **As Du Bois wrote:** Du Bois, *Black Reconstruction in America,* 570.

50 **Within years, public school enrollment:** David Tyack and Robert Lowe, "The Constitutional Moment: Reconstruction and Black Education in the South," *American Journal of Education* 94, no. 2 (1986): 236–56, doi.org/10.1086/443844, 249.

51 **After all, before:** Alexander Keyssar, *The Right to Vote: The Contested History of Democracy in the United States*, rev. ed. (New York: Basic Books, 2009), 94.

51 **And across the country:** Steven F. Lawson, *Black Ballots: Voting Rights in the South, 1944–1969* (Lanham, Md.: Lexington Books, 1999), 2.

52 **in the eyes:** Andrew Johnson, *The Papers of Andrew Johnson,* vol. 9–10 (Knoxville: University of Tennessee Press, 1865–1866), 205.

52 **And unlike President Lincoln:** Abraham Lincoln, "Last Public Address," April 11, 1865.

52 **He wanted a:** Thomas Nast, Artist, *"This is a white man's government" "We regard the Reconstruction Acts so called of Congress as usurpations, and unconstitutional, revolutionary, and void"—Democratic Platform / / Th. Nast,* 1868, loc.gov/item/98513794/.

52 **When Black Americans in New Orleans:** Keyssar, *The Right to Vote,* 97.

52 **And over the:** Henry Louis Gates, Jr., *Stony the Road: Reconstruction, White Supremacy, and the Rise of Jim Crow* (New York: Penguin Books, 2020), 26.

52 **This included Union general William Tecumseh Sherman:** Keyssar, *The Right to Vote,* 95.

52 **And Republicans in Congress:** See especially Keyssar, *The Right to Vote,* 98–105.

52 **The problem, though:** Keyssar, *The Right to Vote,* 97.

53 **This is where the Reconstruction Act of 1867:** Keyssar, *The Right to Vote,* 98.

53 **Alabama, for instance:** Keyssar, *The Right to Vote,* 99.

53 **Over time, though:** "Reconstruction in America: Racial Violence after the Civil War, 1865–1876," Equal Justice Initiative, eji.org/report/reconstruction-in-america/.

53 **In South Carolina:** Foner, "South Carolina's Forgotten Black Political Revolution."

53 **The election of officials:** See especially Justin Behrend, *Reconstructing Democracy: Grassroots Black Politics in the Deep South after the Civil War* (Athens: University of Georgia Press, 2017), 176; and Eric Foner, *A Short History of Reconstruction* (New York: HarperCollins Publishers, 2015), 152–3.

54 **As a reporter:** Foner, *A Short History of Reconstruction,* 128.

54 **They embodied:** John Lewis, "Together, You Can Redeem the Soul of Our Nation," *New York Times,* July 30, 2020, nytimes.com/2020/07/30/opinion/john-lewis-civil-rights-america.html.

54 **Their goal, as:** Foner, *A Short History of Reconstruction,* 184.

54 **Black Americans who dared:** Foner, *A Short History of Reconstruction,* 184–85.

54 **to South Carolina:** Foner, "South Carolina's Forgotten Black Political Revolution."

55 **This is the democracy:** National Parks Service, "A Short Overview of the Reconstruction Era and Ulysses S. Grant's Presidency," U.S. Department of the Interior, n.d., nps.gov/articles/000/a-short-overview-of-the-reconstruction-era-and-ulysses-s-grant-s-presidency.htm.

55 **Against this backdrop:** See especially Foner, *A Short History of Reconstruction;* and Keyssar, *The Right to Vote.*

55 **It was written:** Keyssar, *The Right to Vote,* 101.

55 **There were more radical drafts:** Keyssar, *The Right to Vote.*

55 **Unfortunately, more representatives:** Keyssar, *The Right to Vote,* 109.

56 **Like Boutwell in the House:** Keyssar, *The Right to Vote,* 100–101.

56 **On the other side:** Keyssar, *The Right to Vote,* 102.

56 **He made a persuasive case:** Keyssar, *The Right to Vote,* 103.

56 **"The right of":** Keyssar, *The Right to Vote,* 105.

57 **For so-called Radical:** Eric Foner, *The Second Founding: How the Civil War and Reconstruction Remade the Constitution* (Canada: W. W. Norton, 2019), 104.

57 **Frederick Douglass declared:** Foner, *A Short History of Reconstruction,* 107.

57 **Wendell Phillips called the:** Keyssar, *The Right to Vote,* 82.

57 **William Lloyd Garrison:** Foner, *A Short History of Reconstruction,* 193.

57 **One of the biggest advocates:** Foner, "South Carolina's Forgotten Black Political Revolution."

57 **On the floor:** Foner, "South Carolina's Forgotten Black Political Revolution."

57 **His argument won out**: Foner, "South Carolina's Forgotten Black Political Revolution," 195.

57–58 **And for a moment:** Eric Foner, *Forever Free: The Story of Emancipation and Reconstruction* (2005), 129, as quoted in Aderson Bellegarde François, "To Make Freedom Happen: Shelby County v. Holder, the Supreme Court, and the Creation Myth of American Voting Rights," *Northern Illinois University Law Review* 34 (2014): 529, 543.

58 **Reconstruction was also:** *U.S. v. Cruikshank,* 92 U.S. 542 (1876).

58 **Perhaps it's no:** Keyssar, *The Right to Vote,* 111.

58 **From this moment forward:** Keyssar, *The Right to Vote,* 110.

59 **As Adelbert Ames:** Foner, *A Short History of Reconstruction,* 236.

59 **while he wasn't:** Douglas A. Blackmon, *Slavery by Another Name: The Re-Enslavement of Black Americans from the Civil War to World War II* (New York: Anchor Books, a division of Random House, Inc., 2009).

59 **Before taking office:** Barton Gellman, "The Election That Could Break America," *The Atlantic,* November 15, 2020, theatlantic.com/magazine/archive/2020/11/what-if-trump-refuses-concede/616424/.

59 **Within months, Georgia:** Evette Dionne, *Lifting as We Climb: Black Women's Battle for the Ballot Box* (New York: Penguin, 2020), 52.

60 **"We are in":** Keyssar, *The Right to Vote,* 111–12.

60 **Similar laws were:** Keyssar, *The Right to Vote,* 115.

60 **The goal, according:** Keyssar, *The Right to Vote,* 115–16.

60 **And in 1890:** Anderson, *One Person, No Vote,* 3–7.

61 **"This feigned legal":** Anderson, *One Person, No Vote,* 3.

61 **The numbers spoke:** Steven Mintz, "Winning the Vote: A History of Voting Rights," *History Now—Gilder Lehrman Institute of American History,* October 4, 2009, retrieved from gilderlehrman.org/history-resources/essays/winning-vote-history-voting-rights.

61 **In Louisiana, where:** Anderson, *One Person, No Vote*, 4.

3. RESISTANCE AND REALPOLITIK: HOW WOMEN WON THE VOTE

64 **"We stood appalled":** Lisa Tetrault, *The Myth of Seneca Falls: Memory and the Women's Suffrage Movement, 1848–1898* (Chapel Hill: University of North Carolina Press, 2017), 116.

65 **The story of women voting:** Gillian Brockell, "More Than a Century Before the 19th Amendment, Women Were Voting in New Jersey," *Washington Post,* August 4, 2020, washingtonpost.com/graphics/2020/local/history/new-jersey-women-vote-1776-suffrage/.

65 **But in Section IV:** "Constitution of New Jersey," Avalon Project at Yale Law School, avalon.law.yale.edu/18th_century/nj15.asp#1.

65 **In fact, historians:** "Discovering America's First Women Voters, 1800–1807," Museum of the American Revolution, amrevmuseum.org/virtualexhibits/when-women-lost-the-vote-a-revolutionary-story/pages/discovering-america-s-first-women-voters-1800-1807.

65 **There were African Americans:** "Constitution of New Jersey."

66 **As Sally Roesch Wagner:** See especially Sally Roesch Wagner, *The Women's Suffrage Movement* (New York: Penguin Books, 2019), xviii.

66 **After the signing:** Keyssar, *The Right to Vote,* 187.

66 **A few years:** Wagner, *The Women's Suffrage Movement,* 8.

66 **In fact, women:** Wagner, *The Women's Suffrage Movement,* 76.

66 **As Abigail Adams:** Wagner, *The Women's Suffrage Movement,* 282.

67 **In fact, even:** Wagner, *The Women's Suffrage Movement,* xxvi.

67 **This movement included:** See especially Nell Irvin Painter, *Sojourner Truth: A Life, a Symbol* (New York: W. W. Norton, 1996).

67 **Which is why:** Wagner, *The Women's Suffrage Movement,* 52–53.

67 **Abolitionism is also:** Wagner, *The Women's Suffrage Movement,* 57–60.

68 **That process started:** Wagner, *The Women's Suffrage Movement,* 58.

68 **It began with familiar words:** Elizabeth Cady Stanton, *History of Woman Suffrage*, vol. 1 (Rochester, N.Y.: Fowler and Wells, 1889), 70–71.

68 **"The history of mankind":** Wagner, *The Women's Suffrage Movement*, 76.

68 **Many of the:** Elizabeth Cady Stanton, "Declaration of Sentiments," *Report of the Woman's Rights Convention, Held at Seneca Falls, New York, July 19 and 20, 1848*, Rochester, N.Y.: *The North Star* office of Frederick Douglass, 1848.

69 **Sojourner Truth delivered:** Sojourner Truth, as quoted in Ellen Carol Dubois, "How Women's Suffrage Changed America Far Beyond the Ballot Box," *Wall Street Journal*, August 19, 2020, wsj.com/articles/how-womens-suffrage-changed-america-far-beyond-the-ballot-box-11596207771.

69 **"In every effort":** Dubois, "How Women's Suffrage Changed America Far Beyond the Ballot Box."

69 **Coming out of the convention:** Wagner, *The Women's Suffrage Movement*, 84.

69 **When a petition:** Wagner, *The Women's Suffrage Movement*, 103.

69 **In California, legislators:** Keyssar, *The Right to Vote*, 183.

70 **"One question at":** Keyssar, *The Right to Vote*, 171.

70 **As Susan B. Anthony:** Susan B. Anthony, as quoted in Sarah Jones, "The Complicated History of the Suffragette Movement," *New Republic*, November 8, 2016, newrepublic.com/article/138512/complicated-history-suffragette-movement.

70 **This is the context:** Martha S. Jones, *Vanguard: How Black Women Broke Barriers, Won the Vote, and Insisted on Equality for All* (New York: Basic Books, 2020), 95.

70 **"We are all":** Frances Ellen Watkins Harper, "We are All Bound Up Together," 1866, an electronic publication of *Black Past*, November 7, 2011, blackpast.org/african-american-history/speeches-african-american-history/1866-frances-ellen-watkins-harper-we-are-all-bound-together/.

71 **"Think of Patrick":** Wagner, *The Women's Suffrage Movement*, 194.

71 **Suffragist Anna Howard Shaw:** Wagner, *The Women's Suffrage Movement*, 404.

71 **Lucy Stone, a prominent feminist:** "Image 5 of Constitution of the

American Woman Suffrage Association and the History of Its Formation: With the Times and Places in Which the Association Has Held Meetings up to 1880," Library of Congress, loc.gov/resource/rbnawsa.n8291/?sp=5&st=text.

72 **One of the most:** Wagner, *The Women's Suffrage Movement,* 235.

72 **"It is the duty of women":** Wagner, *The Women's Suffrage Movement,* 108.

73 **In 1858, that:** Wagner, *The Women's Suffrage Movement,* 87.

73 **With Stone as:** Wagner, *The Women's Suffrage Movement,* 275.

73 **Unlike Elizabeth Cady Stanton and Susan B. Anthony:** Jessica Hynes, "The 1870s Tax Resistance of Julia and Abby Smith: From Natural Rights to Expediency in the Shadow of Separate Spheres," *Tennessee Journal of Race, Gender, & Social Justice* 2, no. 2 (2013).

73 **Abby believed this:** "The Smith Sisters, Their Cows, and Women's Rights in Glastonbury," Connecticut History: A CT Humanities Project, March 6, 2021, connecticuthistory.org/the-smith-sisters-their-cows-and-womens-rights-in-glastonbury/.

73 ***The Republican*, a local newspaper:** "The Smith Sisters."

74 **Susan A. King, one of the wealthiest women in America:** Wagner, *The Women's Suffrage Movement,* 285.

74 **As the authors of:** Wagner, *The Women's Suffrage Movement,* 249.

74 **"Gradually, then suddenly":** Ernest Hemingway, *The Sun Also Rises.*

75 **a quarter century after:** Wagner, *The Women's Suffrage Movement,* 247.

75 **For others, it meant:** See especially Ian Tyrell, *Woman's World/Woman's Empire: The Woman's Christian Temperance Union in International Perspective, 1880–1930* (Chapel Hill: University of North Carolina Press, 1991).

75 **For more radical suffragists:** Wagner, *The Women's Suffrage Movement,* 248.

75 **A lawyer who had:** Wagner, *The Women's Suffrage Movement,* 322.

75 **"If necessary":** Wagner, *The Women's Suffrage Movement.*

75 **That same revolutionary energy:** Wagner, *The Women's Suffrage Movement,* 307.

76 **it was voted:** Keyssar, *The Right to Vote,* 178.

76 **As Frederick Douglass:** Frederick Douglass, "Frederick Douglass

on Woman Suffrage," 1888, an electronic publication of *Black Past,* January 28, 2007, blackpast.org/african-american-history/speeches-african-american-history/1888-frederick-douglass-woman-suffrage/.

77 **There were more white women:** Elizabeth Cady Stanton et al., *History of Women's Suffrage,* vol. II (Rochester, N.Y.: Charles Mann, 1887), 929–30.

77 **"We call attention":** As quoted in JoEllen Lind, "Dominance and Democracy: The Legacy of Women's Suffrage for the Voting Right," *UCLA Women's Journal* 5, no. 1 (1994): 175.

77 **As part of this pivot:** Wagner, *The Women's Suffrage Movement,* 345.

78 **And in the years:** Wagner, *The Women's Suffrage Movement,* 342.

78 **Reflecting on this:** Wagner, *The Women's Suffrage Movement,* 360.

78 **She started raising money:** See especially Keyssar, *The Right to Vote,* 188.

78 **Next came California:** Jennifer Helton, "Woman Suffrage in the West," National Parks Service, U.S. Department of the Interior, n.d., nps.gov/articles/woman-suffrage-in-the-west.htm.

78 **The following year:** Keyssar, *The Right to Vote,* 195.

79 **The woman in charge:** "Alice Paul Talks," *Philadelphia Tribune,* Philadelphia, Pennsylvania, January 10, 1910. Manuscript/Mixed Material. loc.gov/item/rbcmiller003903/.

79 **It was set:** Alice Paul, "Conversation with Alice Paul: Woman Suffrage and the Equal Rights Amendment," July 10, 1977, an electronic publication of the *Suffragists Oral History Project* (Berkeley, Calif., 1976), oac.cdlib.org/view?docId=kt6f59n89c&doc.view=entire_text.

79 **The attendees included:** Sydney Trent, "The Black Sorority that Faced Racism in the Suffrage Movement but Refused to Walk Away," *Washington Post,* August 8, 2020, washingtonpost.com/graphics/2020/local/history/suffrage-racism-black-deltas-parade-washington/.

79 **"The participation of negroes":** Trent, "The Black Sorority."

80 **This was not a concession:** Cathleen D. Cahill, *Recasting the Vote: How Women of Color Transformed the Suffrage Movement* (Chapel Hill: University of North Carolina Press, 2020), 105.

80 **The rest of the women:** Trent, "The Black Sorority."

80 **By all accounts:** Wagner, *The Women's Suffrage Movement,* 432.

81 **For a while:** Terence McArdle, "'Night of Terror': The Suffragists Who Were Beaten and Tortured for Seeking the Vote," *Washington Post,* November 10, 2017.

81 **"They tied us down":** Wagner, *The Women's Suffrage Movement,* 448.

81 **The pain was:** Wagner, *The Women's Suffrage Movement,* 449.

81 **There were a few:** See especially Wagner, *The Women's Suffrage Movement,* 438; and Keyssar, *The Right to Vote,* 185.

82 **the organization was:** Susan Ware, *Why They Marched: Untold Stories of the Women Who Fought for the Right to Vote* (Cambridge, Mass.: Harvard University Press, 2019), 251–64.

82 **Before long, her tactics:** Ware, *Why They Marched,* 259.

82 **"When victory was":** Ware, *Why They Marched,* 448.

83 **Fortunately, the filibuster:** Ware, *Why They Marched,* 262.

83 **This meant the suffragists:** Elaine F. Weiss, *The Woman's Hour: The Great Fight to Win the Vote* (New York: Penguin Books, 2019), 277.

83 **"Nearly every day":** Wagner, *The Women's Suffrage Movement.*

83 **She was right:** See especially Weiss, *The Woman's Hour*.

83 **As Upton recalled:** Wagner, *The Women's Suffrage Movement,* 470.

84 **"They feared nothing":** Wagner, *The Women's Suffrage Movement,* 471.

84 **his mother had:** Weiss, *The Woman's Hour,* 305.

84 **He had sat through:** Weiss, *The Woman's Hour,* 288.

84 **And Burn knew:** Weiss, *The Woman's Hour,* 305.

84 **But as Elaine Weiss describes:** Weiss, *The Woman's Hour,* 306.

85 **And when the final count:** Weiss, *The Woman's Hour,* 307; and Wagner, *The Women's Suffrage Movement,* 72–78.

85 **"The right of citizens":** U.S. Const. amend. XIX, § 1, cl. 1.

85 **"The vote is the emblem":** Weiss, *The Woman's Hour,* 323.

4. REVOLUTION: HOW BLACK AMERICANS WON THE VOTE—AND MADE AMERICA A DEMOCRACY

88 **JIM CROW MUST GO:** "Medgar Evers," NAACP, May 11, 2021, naacp.org/find-resources/history-explained/civil-rights-leaders/medgar-evers.

88 **wife and children were waiting:** "Murder of Medgar Evers," Medgar Evers College, mec.cuny.edu/history/murder-of-medgar-evers/.

89 **He had met the same:** Debbie Elliott, "Integrating Ole Miss: A Transformative, Deadly Riot," *NPR Morning Edition,* October 1,

2012, npr.org/2012/10/01/161573289/integrating-ole-miss-a-transformative-deadly-riot.

90 **It was an emotional:** Theodore C. Sorensen, *Counselor: A Life at the Edge of History* (New York: Harper Perennial, 2009), 278–83.

90 **"One hundred years":** John Fitzgerald Kennedy, "Televised Address to the Nation on Civil Rights," June 11, 1963, an electronic publication of the John F. Kennedy Library (Piscataway, N.J.), jfklibrary.org/learn/about-jfk/historic-speeches/televised-address-to-the-nation-on-civil-rights.

91 **"It ought to":** Kennedy, "Televised Address to the Nation on Civil Rights."

91 **"We're interested in making":** Myrlie Evers-Williams and Manning Marable, *The Autobiography of Medgar Evers: A Hero's Life and Legacy Revealed Through His Writings, Letters and Speeches* (Washington: Perseus Books, 2006), 303.

91 **In 1946, hoping:** Gary May, *Bending Toward Justice: The Voting Rights Act and the Transformation of American Democracy* (Durham: Duke University Press, 2015), 165.

92 **In fact, as:** Ari Berman, "Jim Crow Killed Voting Rights for Generations. Now the GOP Is Repeating History," *Mother Jones,* June 2, 2021, motherjones.com/politics/2021/06/jim-crow-killed-voting-rights-for-generations-now-the-gop-is-repeating-history/.

92 **"By 1907 every":** Berman, "Jim Crow Killed Voting Rights for Generations."

92 **"The number of":** Berman, "Jim Crow Killed Voting Rights for Generations."

93 **And as historian C. Vann Woodward:** C. Vann Woodward, *The Strange Career of Jim Crow* (New York: Oxford University Press, 2006), 83–84.

93 **The "white primary":** *Grovey v. Townsend,* 295 U.S. 45 (1935).

94 **Medgar understood this:** Karen Grigsby Bates, "Trials & Transformation: Myrlie Evers' 30-Year Fight to Convict Medgar's Accused Killer," *Emerge* 2 (1994): 35.

94 **Just days after Emmett's arrival:** ArLuther Lee, "An American Tragedy—The Lynching of Emmett Till," *Atlanta Journal-Constitution,* October 19, 2020, ajc.com/news/weekend-read-an-american-tragedy-the-lynching-of-emmett-till/SSYUCF7CZRELXLS4UVEWJG5PDY/.

95 **"The world," she decided:** Juan Williams, *Eyes on the Prize: America's Civil Rights Years, 1954–1965* (Penguin Books, 2013), 44.

95 **So she held:** "The Trial of J. W. Milam and Roy Bryant," *PBS American Experience,* pbs.org/wgbh/americanexperience/features/emmett-trial-jw-milam-and-roy-bryant/.

95 **"Freedom has never":** Medgar Evers, as quoted in Minrose Gwin, *Remembering Medgar Evers: Writing the Long Civil Rights Movement* (Athens: University of Georgia Press, 2013), 100.

95 **"I opened the door":** "Murder of Medgar Evers," Medgar Evers College.

96 **The children screamed:** Karen Grigsby Bates, "Trials & Transformation," 35.

96 **For three decades, his killer:** Gina Holland, "Supreme Court Upholds Beckwith Conviction in Medgar Evers' Murder," Associated Press, December 22, 1997.

96 **That day was on the mind of Dr. Martin Luther King, Jr.:** Martin Luther King, Jr., "I Have a Dream," August 28, 1963, reprinted by Rebecca Roberts, NPR, January 18, 2010, npr.org/2010/01/18/122701268/i-have-a-dream-speech-in-its-entirety.

97 **It was on the mind of Lyndon B. Johnson:** Lyndon B. Johnson, "President Lyndon B. Johnson's Address to a Joint Session of Congress Regarding President John F. Kennedy's Assassination, Civil Rights Legislation, and Other Topics," November 27, 1963, Records of the U.S. House of Representatives, Record Group 233.

97 **"The Mississippi monolith":** Nikole Hannah-Jones, "Freedom Summer, 1964: Did It Really Change Mississippi?," *The Atlantic,* July 8, 2014, theatlantic.com/politics/archive/2014/07/the-ghosts-of-freedom-summer-in-greenwood-mississippi/374106/.

97 **This mindset inspired:** Matthew Wills, "How the Freedom Vote Mobilized Black Mississippians," *JSTOR Daily,* August 4, 2021, daily.jstor.org/how-the-freedom-vote-mobilized-black-mississippians.

97 **Over the course:** Camila Domonoske, "Officials Close Investigations into 1964 'Mississippi Burning' Killings," NPR, June 21, 2016, npr.org/sections/thetwo-way/2016/06/21/482914440/officials-close-investigation-into-1964-mississippi-burning-killings.

98 **Together, Andrew, Michael, and James:** Bruce Watson, *Freedom Summer: The Savage Season That Made Mississippi Burn and Made America a Democracy* (New York: Penguin Group, 2010), 239.

98 **For forty-four days:** Charles P. Pierce, "The Ku Klux Klan Murdered Them for Registering Citizens to Vote. That Was All," *Esquire,* June 21, 2021, esquire.com/news-politics/politics/a36792480/ku-klux-klan-murder-civil-rights-workers-mississippi/.

98 **Left to rest in an earthen dam:** Pierce, "The Ku Klux Klan."

98–99 **Goodman had been buried:** Julia Cass, "A Mississippi Freedom Summer Pilgrimage: An Atrocity We Must Never Forget," *HuffPost,* December 6, 2017, huffpost.com/entry/a-mississippi-freedom-sum_b_5622366.

99 **As Rita Schwerner:** Nikole Hannah-Jones, "A Brutal Loss, but an Enduring Conviction," *ProPublica,* July 22, 2014, propublica.org/article/a-brutal-loss-but-an-enduring-conviction.

99 **"Our most urgent":** Martin Luther King, Jr., "Give Us the Ballot," May 17, 1957, an electronic publication of the Martin Luther King, Jr. Papers Project at The Martin Luther King, Jr. Research and Education Institute (Palo Alto, Calif., 1985).

99 **In theory, President Johnson:** Louis Menand, "The Color of Law," *The New Yorker,* July 1, 2013, newyorker.com/magazine/2013/07/08/the-color-of-law.

100 **"I'm going to do":** Nick Kotz, *Judgment Days: Lyndon Baines Johnson, Martin Luther King Jr., and the Laws that Changed America* (Boston: Houghton Mifflin, 2005), 244.

100 **This was, after all:** See especially Anderson, *One Person, No Vote,* 19, 21, 649.

100 **Which was why:** Mark K. Updegrove, "What 'Selma' Gets Wrong," *Politico,* December 22, 2014, politico.com/magazine/story/2014/12/what-selma-gets-wrong-113743/.

100 **Within weeks:** Nick Kotz, *Judgment Days: Lyndon Baines Johnson, Martin Luther King Jr., and the Laws That Changed America* (Boston: Houghton Mifflin, 2005), 254.

100 **The problem, of course:** Brian Lyman, "Selma: 'The Last Revolution' of civil rights," *The Montgomery Advertiser,* March 1, 2015, montgomeryadvertiser.com/story/news/local/selma50/2015/03/01/selma-last-revolution-civil-rights/24213897/.

100 **"When the king":** King, "Letter from a Selma, Alabama, Jail."

101 **"I think that":** Malcolm X, as quoted in John Lewis and Michael D'Orso, *Walking with Wind: A Memoir of the Movement* (New York: Simon & Schuster, 2015), 324.

101 **It demonstrated:** Winston A. Grady-Willis, Challenging U.S. Apartheid: Atlanta and Black Struggles for Human Rights, 1960–1977 (Durham: Duke University Press, 2006), 75.

102 **Vivian Malone was there:** May, *Bending Toward Justice*, 27.

102 **In the years following:** See especially Berman, *Give Us the Ballot*, 45, 83.

102 **One of these:** Berman, *Give Us the Ballot*, 78.

103 **A civil rights hero:** John Fitzgerald Kennedy, "Televised Address to the Nation on Civil Rights."

5. BACKLASH TO A BLACK PRESIDENT: THE OBAMA YEARS

107 **To be honest:** Tom Wicker, "Johnson Bestows Pens Used on Bill," *New York Times*, July 3, 1964, timesmachine.nytimes.com/timesmachine/1964/07/03/97267720.pdf?pdf_redirect=true&ip=0.

107 **Within hours of:** Berman, *Give Us the Ballot*, 37–39.

107 **white Americans registered at record rates:** Dara Lind, "19 Maps and Charts That Explain Voting Rights in America," *Vox*, vox.com/2015/8/6/9107183/voting-rights-map-chart.

108 **The following year:** *South Carolina v. Katzenbach*, 383 U.S. 301 (1966).

108 **In 1971, the voting age:** Gemma R. Birnbaum, "'Old Enough to Fight, Old Enough to Vote': The WWII Roots of the 26th Amendment," The National WWII Museum, October 28, 2020, nationalww2museum.org/war/articles/voting-age-26th-amendment.

108 **In 1984, the Voting Accessibility for the Elderly and Handicapped Act:** The Voting Accessibility for the Elderly and Handicapped Act, U.S. Code 52 (1985), § 201.

108 **The next year:** Keyssar, *The Right to Vote*, 242.

108 **In the years since:** Hugh Davis Graham, "Richard Nixon and Civil Rights: Explaining an Enigma," *Presidential Studies Quarterly* 25, no. 1 (Winter 1996): 93–106; Pedro Noguera and Robert Cohen, "Remembering Reagan's Record on Civil Rights and the South African Freedom Struggle," *The Nation*, February 11, 2011, thenation.com/article/archive/remembering-reagans-record-civil-rights-and-south-african-freedom-struggle/.

108 **And as recently as 2006:** Raymond Hernandez, "After Challenges, House Approves Renewal of Voting Act," *New York Times*, July 14, 2006, nytimes.com/2006/07/14/washington/14rights.html.

109 **It wasn't even close:** U.S. Congress, House, *Fannie Lou Hammer, Rosa Parks, and Coretta Scott King Voting Rights Act Reauthorization and Amendments Act of 2006,* HR 9, 109th Cong., 1st sess., introduced in House May 2, 2006, congress.gov/bill/109th-congress/house-bill/9.

109 **According to a Brennan Center:** Brennan Center for Justice, "Debunking the Voter Fraud Myth" (New York: Brennan Center for Justice, 2017); Justin Levitt, "A Comprehensive Investigation of Voter Impersonation Finds 31 Credible Incidents out of One Billion Ballots Cast," *Washington Post,* August 6, 2014; NOAA US Department of Commerce, "How Dangerous Is Lightning?," National Weather Service (NOAA's National Weather Service, March 12, 2019), weather .gov/safety/lightning-odds.

109 **But even as Republican legislatures:** See especially Anderson, *One Person, No Vote,* 58–62.

109 **So when the:** Barack Obama, "Barack Obama's Remarks to the Democratic National Convention," *New York Times,* July 27, 2004, nytimes.com/2004/07/27/politics/campaign/barack-obamas-remarks -to-the-democratic-national.html.

110 **From the moment:** Glenn Kessler, "When Did Mitch McConnell Say He Wanted to Make Obama a One-Term President?," *Washington Post,* January 11, 2017, washingtonpost.com/news/fact-checker /wp/2017/01/11/when-did-mitch-mcconnell-say-he-wanted-to-make -obama-a-one-term-president/.

110 **Gone were the days:** Carla Herreria Russo, "The Real Story Behind John McCain's Famous Campaign Rally Moment," *HuffPost,* August 26, 2018, huffpost.com/entry/mccain-defends-obama-real -story_n_5b821dffe4b0348586o129c4.

110 **After two years:** Liz Halloran, "Obama Humbled By Election 'Shellacking,'" NPR, November 3, 2010.

111 **In the Senate, Republicans won:** Peter Roff, "Measuring the Size of Election 2010's Republican Sweep," *US News,* November 5, 2010, usnews.com/opinion/blogs/peter-roff/2010/11/05/measuring-the-size -of-election-2010s-republican-sweep.

111 **In the House:** Aaron Blake, "Which Election Was Worse for Democrats: 2010 or 2014? It's a Surprisingly Close Call," *Washington Post,* November 5, 2014.

111 **As Karl Rove:** David Daley, *Ratf**ked: The True Story Behind the*

Secret Plan to Steal America's Democracy (New York: Liveright Publishing Corporation, 2017), 4.

112 **The first was on our elections:** Klain, Morris, Feldman, and Ayala, *Waiting to Vote.*

112 **How else do you explain:** See Ari Berman, "The GOP War on Voting," *Rolling Stone,* August 30, 2011, rollingstone.com/politics/politics-news/the-gop-war-on-voting-242182/; German Lopez, "Voter Suppression in Alabama: What's True and What's Not," *Vox,* December 12, 2017, vox.com/policy-and-politics/2017/12/12/16767426/alabama-voter-suppression-senate-moore-jones.

112 **Or the laws in Ohio:** Berman, "The GOP War on Voting."

112 **As John Lewis, who was then a thirteenth-term congressman:** Eric Holder, "Attorney General Eric Holder Speaks at the Lyndon Baines Johnson Library & Museum," United States Department of Justice, December 13, 2011, justice.gov/opa/speech/attorney-general-eric-holder-speaks-lyndon-baines-johnson-library-museum.

113 **And I talked about:** Holder, "Attorney General Eric Holder Speaks at the Lyndon Baines Johnson Library & Museum."

113 **"For me, and for our nation's Department of Justice":** Holder, "Attorney General Eric Holder Speaks at the Lyndon Baines Johnson Library & Museum."

114 **The photo ID law in Texas:** Berman, *Give Us the Ballot,* 264.

114 **The day after:** Eric Holder, "Attorney General Eric Holder Speech at the NAACP Annual Convention," United States Department of Justice, July 10, 2012, justice.gov/opa/speech/attorney-general-eric-holder-speaks-naacp-annual-convention.

115 **"A poll tax in Alabama":** Berman, *Give Us the Ballot,* 266.

115 **"In our efforts":** Holder, "Attorney General Eric Holder Speech at the NAACP Annual Convention."

115 **In the end:** Berman, *Give Us the Ballot,* 266.

115 **In other words:** *State of Texas v. Eric H. Holder* (United States District Court for the District of Columbia August 30, 2012).

115 **on the eve of the 2012 election:** Berman, *Give Us the Ballot,* 266.

117 **The first time:** Daley, *Ratf**ked,* xvii.

117 **As Erick Trickey:** Erick Trickey, "Where Did the Term 'Gerrymander' Come From?," *Smithsonian,* July 20, 2017, smithsonianmag.com/history/where-did-term-gerrymander-come-180964118/.

117 **The map was:** Trickey, "Where Did the Term 'Gerrymander' Come From?"

117 **And thus the:** Trickey, "Where Did the Term 'Gerrymander' Come From?"

118 **The goal of this effort:** The RSLC redistricting majority project—REDMAP, redistrictingmajorityproject.com/?page_id=2.

118 **The story of how:** See especially Daley, *Ratf**ked,* xxv.

119 **It was an investment:** Daley, *Ratf**ked,* xix.

119 **As Vann Newkirk notes:** Vann R. Newkirk II, "How Redistricting Became a Technological Arms Race," *The Atlantic,* October 28, 2017, theatlantic.com/politics/archive/2017/10/gerrymandering-technology-redmap-2020/543888/.

119 **And we successfully:** *Texas v. United States,* F. Supp. 2d 133 (D.D.C. 2012).

120 **On the whole:** Daley, *Ratf**ked,* xxi.

120 **as Daley observes:** Daley, *Ratf**ked,* xxiii.

120 **In Michigan, Daley:** Daley, *Ratf**ked,* xxv.

121 **As soon as the opening arguments:** Adam Liptak, "Voting Rights Law Draws Skepticism From Justices," *New York Times,* February 27, 2013, nytimes.com/2013/02/28/us/politics/conservative-justices-voice-skepticism-on-voting-law.html; Adam Winkler, "Supreme Court Likely to Strike Down the Voting Rights Act's Section 5," *Daily Beast,* February 27, 2013, thedailybeast.com/supreme-court-likely-to-strike-down-the-voting-rights-acts-section-5; Josh Gerstein, "Voting Rights Act Under Fire," *Politico,* February 27, 2013, politico.com/story/2013/02/voting-rights-act-under-fire-at-supreme-court-088178.

121 **Over and over, Roberts kept:** Nate Silver, "In Supreme Court Debate on Voting Rights Act, a Dubious Use of Statistics," *FiveThirtyEight,* March 7, 2013, fivethirtyeight.com/features/in-supreme-court-debate-on-voting-rights-act-a-dubious-use-of-statistics/.

121 **And this came on the heels:** *Northwest Austin Municipal Utility District No. 1 v. Holder,* 557 U.S. __ (2009); *Shelby County v. Holder,* 570 U.S. 529 (2013).

122 **Yes, Justice Roberts had been adversarial:** Berman, *Give Us the Ballot,* 251.

122 **When a jurisdiction did:** Danielle Lang, "Five Decades of Section

5: How This Key Provision of the Voting Rights Act Protected Our Democracy," *Campaign Legal Center,* June 22, 2016, campaignlegal.org/update/five-decades-section-5-how-key-provision-voting-rights-act-protected-our-democracy.

122 **And yes, five justices:** Hernandez, "After Challenges, House Approves Renewal of Voting Act."

122 **In response to Shelby County's lawyer:** Berman, *Give Us the Ballot,* 274.

122 **That's why Shelby:** *Shelby County v. Holder,* 811 F. Supp. 2d 424 (D.D.C. 2011).

123 **And it's why:** "Shelby County v. Holder," Brennan Center for Justice, August 4, 2018, brennancenter.org/our-work/court-cases/shelby-county-v-holder.

123 **"Let me be clear":** Eric Holder, "Attorney General Eric Holder Speaks at the Edmund Pettus Bridge Crossing Jubilee," United States Department of Justice, March 3, 2013, justice.gov/opa/speech/attorney-general-eric-holder-speaks-theedmund-pettus-bridge-crossing-jubilee.

123 **"The struggle for":** Holder, "Attorney General Eric Holder Speaks at the Edmund Pettus Bridge Crossing Jubilee."

124 **It's a lesson:** *Shelby County v. Holder,* 570 U.S. 529 (2013).

124 **"I'm shocked, dismayed, disappointed":** Berman, *Give Us the Ballot,* 281.

124 **"Like many others":** Eric Holder, "Attorney General Eric Holder Delivers Remarks on the Supreme Court Decision in Shelby County v. Holder," United States Department of Justice, June 25, 2013.

124 **And I promised:** Holder, "Attorney General Eric Holder Delivers Remarks on the Supreme Court Decision in Shelby County v. Holder."

124 **There was an issue:** Berman, *Give Us the Ballot,* 280.

125 **Only days later:** *Texas v. Holder,* 888 F. Supp. 2d 113 (D.D.C. 2012).

125 **There was the shuttering of polling places:** Klain et al., *Waiting to Vote.*

125 **It's no wonder the 2014 midterms:** Jose A. DelReal, "Voter Turnout in 2014 Was the Lowest Since WWII," *Washington Post,* November 10, 2014, washingtonpost.com/news/post-politics/wp/2014/11/10/voter-turnout-in-2014-was-the-lowest-since-wwii/.

126 **"throwing out preclearance":** *Shelby County v. Holder,* 570 U.S. 529, 593 (2013).

6. DEMOCRACY IN DESCENT: THE TRUMP YEARS

127 **Trump declined to provide:** "Read the full transcript from the first presidential debate between Joe Biden and Donald Trump," *USA Today,* September 30, 2020, usatoday.com/story/news/politics/elections/2020/09/30/presidential-debate-read-full-transcript-first-debate/3587462001/.

127 **Refusing to accept the results:** Terry Gross, "Mike Wallace, Interviewer: 'You and Me,'" NPR, November 8, 2005, npr.org/templates/story/story.php?storyId=4992445.

128 **The outcry was immediate:** Sam Sanders, "Donald Trump Says He'll Accept the Results of the Election . . . if He Wins," *NPR,* October 20, 2016, npr.org/2016/10/20/498713509/donald-trump-says-hell-accept-the-results-of-the-election-if-he-wins.

128 **"I won the popular vote":** Cleve R. Wootson, Jr., "Donald Trump: 'I won the popular vote if you deduct the millions of people who voted illegally,'" *Washington Post,* November 27, 2016, washingtonpost.com/news/the-fix/wp/2016/11/27/donald-trump-i-won-the-popular-vote-if-you-deduct-the-millions-of-people-who-voted-illegally/.

128 **His friend Bernhard Langer:** Tim Hill, "Bernhard Langer: Trump Apologized to Me over Voter Fraud Story," *Guardian,* February 9, 2017, theguardian.com/sport/2017/feb/09/bernhard-langer-donald-trump-golf-voter-fraud.

128 **"None of them come to me":** Aaron Blacke, "Donald Trump Claims None of Those 3 to 5 Million Illegal Votes Were Cast for Him. Zero," *Washington Post,* January 26, 2017, washingtonpost.com/news/the-fix/wp/2017/01/25/donald-trump-claims-none-of-those-3-to-5-million-illegal-votes-were-cast-for-him-zero/.

129 **But Trump was no longer:** Christopher Rozen, "Donald Trump Emmy Tweets," *Entertainment Weekly,* October 20, 2016, ew.com/article/2016/10/20/donald-trump-emmys-tweets/.

129 **This is where Turner stood:** Emily Bazelon, "The Voter Fraud Case Jeff Sessions Lost and Can't Escape," *New York Times,* January 9, 2017, nytimes.com/2017/01/09/magazine/the-voter-fraud-case-jeff-sessions-lost-and-cant-escape.html.

129 **He marched in Selma:** Ari Berman, "Jeff Sessions Has Spent His Whole Career Opposing Voting Rights," *The Nation,* January 10, 2017, thenation.com/article/archive/jeff-sessions-has-spent-his-whole-career-opposing-voting-rights/.

129 **He understood why so many:** Bazelon, "The Voter Fraud Case Jeff Sessions Lost."

130 **Jefferson Beauregard Sessions III:** Bazelon, "The Voter Fraud Case Jeff Sessions Lost."

130 **Thankfully, the witch hunt:** Bazelon, "The Voter Fraud Case Jeff Sessions Lost."

131 **That's why, within his first few months in office:** Vann R. Newkirk II, "The End of Civil Rights," *The Atlantic,* June 18, 2018, theatlantic.com/politics/archive/2018/06/sessions/563006/.

131 **In Ohio:** Sari Horwitz, "Justice Dept. Sides with Ohio's Purge of Inactive Voters in Case Headed to Supreme Court," *Washington Post,* August 8, 2017, washingtonpost.com/world/national-security/justice-department-reverses-position-to-allow-ohio-to-purge-inactive-voters-from-rolls/2017/08/08/e93c5116-7c35-11e7-9d08-b79f191668ed_story.html.

131 **"partisan gerrymandering claims":** *Rucho v. Common Cause,* 588 U.S. __, 1 (2019)

131 **Justice Kagan wrote:** *Rucho v. Common Cause.*

132 **"For the first time":** *Rucho v. Common Cause.*

132 **over the course:** Benjamin Wittes, "Malevolence Tempered by Incompetence: Trump's Horrifying Executive Order on Refugees," *Lawfare,* January 28, 2017, lawfareblog.com/malevolence-tempered-incompetence-trumps-horrifying-executive-order-refugees-and-visas.

132 **His malevolence, for instance, led him:** Adam Serwer, "An Incompetent Authoritarian Is Still a Catastrophe," *The Atlantic,* January 20, 2021, theatlantic.com/ideas/archive/2021/01/wounds-trump-leaves-behind/617738/.

133 **The Trump Administration's malevolence:** Serwer, "An Incompetent Authoritarian Is Still a Catastrophe."

133 **Again and again:** Alex Shephard, "People Close to Donald Trump Do Not Seem to Have Seen *The Wire,*" *The New Republic,* September 21, 2017, newrepublic.com/article/144936/people-close-donald-trump-not-seem-seen-wire.

133 **"So what if he":** Serwer, "An Incompetent Authoritarian Is Still a Catastrophe."

134 **The Senate refused:** See especially Neal Katyal and Sam Koppelman, *Impeach: The Case Against Donald Trump* (Edinburgh: Canongate, 2019).

135 **"I'm not going to":** Chris Wallace, "Trump Says He Will 'Have to See' About Accepting Election," *Time,* July 19, 2020, time.com/5868739/trump-election-results-chris-wallace/.

135 **Later in the summer:** Morgan Chalfant, "Trump: 'The Only Way We're Going to Lose This Election Is if the Election Is Rigged,'" *The Hill,* August 17, 2020, thehill.com/homenews/administration/512424-trump-the-only-way-we-are-going-to-lose-this-election-is-if-the.

135 **And in the months:** Steve Inskeep, "Timeline: What Trump Told Supporters For Months Before They Attacked," *NPR,* February 8, 2021, npr.org/2021/02/08/965342252/timeline-what-trump-told-supporters-for-months-before-they-attacked.

135 **He started in the courts:** William Cummings, Joey Garrison, and Jim Sargent, "By the Numbers: President Donald Trump's Failed Efforts to Overturn the Election," *USA Today,* January 6, 2021, usatoday.com/in-depth/news/politics/elections/2021/01/06/trumps-failed-efforts-overturn-election-numbers/4130307001/.

136 **Even the Supreme Court:** Peters, "The Supreme Court Rejects Texas's Undemocratic Election Lawsuit," *Vox,* December 12, 2020.

137 **And he was "proud" of it:** Max Greenwood, "Georgia Elections Chief Says He Is a 'Proud Trump Supporter,' but 'the Numbers Don't Lie' After Recount," *The Hill,* November 20, 2020, thehill.com/homenews/campaign/526866-georgia-elections-chief-says-he-is-a-proud-trump-supporter-but-the-numbers.

137 **But when it came time:** Greenwood, "Georgia Elections Chief."

137 **"I didn't lose the state":** Amy Gardner and Paulina Firozi, "Here's the Full Transcript and Audio of the Call Between Trump and Raffensperger," *Washington Post,* January 5, 2021, docs.google.com/document/d/13HiToMaulQglg7Erm7orHuP3a1v1YbHHUi3N1YBNkOY/edit?pli=1.

138 **"Mr. President," Raffensperger insisted:** Gardner and Firozi, "Here's the Full Transcript."

138 **"I just want to find":** Gardner and Firozi, "Here's the Full Transcript."

138 **In Georgia, Trump had already:** Julia Jester, "'You'll Be Praised': Audio of Trump Call with Georgia Elections Investigator Offers New Details," *NBC News,* March 15, 2021, nbcnews.com/politics/elections/you-ll-be-praised-audio-trump-call-georgia-elections-investigator-n1261159.

138 **Meanwhile, the U.S. attorney from Atlanta:** Matt Zapotosky and Devlin Barrett, "U.S. Attorney in Atlanta Abruptly Resigns, and Trump Bypasses His Deputy in Picking Temporary Successor," *Washington Post,* January 5, 2021, washingtonpost.com/national-security/georgia-us-attorney-resigns/2021/01/05/5c7f9222-4f83-11eb-bda4-615aaefd0555_story.html.

138 **Across the state, election officials:** Stephen Fowler, "'Someone's Going to Get Killed': Ga. Official Blasts GOP Silence on Election Threats," *NPR,* December 1, 2020, npr.org/sections/biden-transition-updates/2020/12/01/940961602/someones-going-to-get-killed-ga-official-blasts-gop-silence-on-election-threats.

139 **"Time will tell that":** Paul Egan, "Republican Party Moves to Replace GOP Board Member Who Voted to Certify Michigan Election," *Detroit Free Press,* January 18, 2021, freep.com/story/news/politics/elections/2021/01/18/gop-does-not-reappoint-vanlangevelde-board-canvassers/4207223001/.

139 **"We have not yet":** Reuters Staff, "Michigan Republicans, After Meeting Trump, Say No Information to Change Election Outcome," *Reuters,* November 20, 2020, reuters.com/article/us-usa-trump-michigan/michigan-republicans-after-meeting-trump-say-no-information-to-change-election-outcome-idUSKBN2802CK.

139 **He was even seemingly caught:** Jonathan C. Cooper, "Arizona Governor Silences Trump's Call, Certifies Election," *Associated Press,* December 2, 2020, apnews.com/article/election-2020-donald-trump-arizona-elections-doug-ducey-e2b8b0de5b809efcc9b1ad5d279023f4.

139 **And behind the scenes:** Michael Balsamo, "Disputing Trump, Barr Says No Widespread Election Fraud," Associated Press, December 1, 2020, apnews.com/article/barr-no-widespread-election-fraud-b1f1488796c9a98c4b1a9061a6c7f49d.

140 **The stars and bars:** Clint Smith, "The Whole Story in a Single Photo," *The Atlantic,* January 8, 2021, theatlantic.com/ideas/archive/2021/01/confederates-in-the-capitol/617594/.

140 **A noose and gallows:** Paul D. Shinkman, "Prosecutors: Capitol Rioters Intended to 'Capture and Assassinate' Elected Officials," *U.S. News,* January 15, 2021, usnews.com/news/national-news/articles/2021-01-15/prosecutors-capitol-rioters-intended-to-capture-and-assassinate-elected-officials.

140 **140 injured:** Tom Jackman, "Police Union Says 140 Officers Injured in Capitol Riot," *Washington Post,* January 27, 2021, washingtonpost.com/local/public-safety/police-union-says-140-officers-injured-in-capitol-riot/2021/01/27/60743642-60e2-11eb-9430-e7c77b5b0297_story.html.

140 **Viking horns and "Camp Auschwitz" sweatshirts:** David K. Li and Shamar Walters, "Man in 'Camp Auschwitz' Shirt, Photographed at U.S. Riot, Arrested in Virginia," NBC News, January 13, 2021, nbcnews.com/news/us-news/man-camp-auschwitz-shirt-photographed-u-s-capitol-riot-arrested-n1254070.

140 **"walk down to the Capitol" and "fight like hell":** Brian Naylor, "Read Trump's Jan. 6 Speech, a Key Part of the Impeachment Trial," NPR, February 10, 2021, npr.org/2021/02/10/966396848/read-trumps-jan-6-speech-a-key-part-of-impeachment-trial.

140 **Gabriel Sterling was right:** Molly Ball, "What Mike Fanone Couldn't Forget," *Time,* August 5, 2021, time.com/6087577/michael-fanone-january-6-interview/.

140 **"To those who wreaked havoc:":** Ashley Parker, Carol D. Leonnig, Paul Kane, and Emma Brown, "How the Rioters Who Stormed the Capitol Came Dangerously Close to Pence," *Washington Post,* January 15, 2021, washingtonpost.com/politics/pence-rioters-capitol-attack/2021/01/15/ab62e434-567c-11eb-a08b-f1381ef3d207_story.html.

141 **Ten minutes after the vice president:** Josh Haltiwanger, "Trump Attacks Pence for Not Having the 'Courage' to Overturn the Election as President's Supporters Storm the Capitol," *Business Insider,* January 6, 2021, businessinsider.com/trump-attacks-pence-for-not-having-courage-to-overturn-election-2021-1.

141 **"Count me out":** Josh Dawsey, "Lindsey Graham Said 'Count Me Out' After the Capitol Riot. But He's All In with Trump Again," *Washington Post,* February 20, 2021, washingtonpost.com/politics/lindsey-graham-donald-trump/2021/02/20/178afc0a-72ca-11eb-a4eb-44012a612cf9_story.html.

141 **"disgraceful dereliction of duty":** Sahil Kapur, "After Acquitting Trump, McConnell Slams Him for a 'Disgraceful Dereliction of Duty,'" *NBC News,* February 13, 2021, nbcnews.com/politics/donald-trump/after-acquitting-trump-mcconnell-slams-him-disgraceful-dereliction-duty-n1257900.

141 **In total, ten Republican congressmen:** Aaron Blake, "Trump's Second Impeachment Is the Most Bipartisan One in History," *Washington Post,* January 13, 2021, washingtonpost.com/politics/2021/01/13/trumps-second-impeachment-is-most-bipartisan-one-history/.

141 **Joe Biden had defeated:** Arnie Seipel, "FACT CHECK: Trump Falsely Claims a 'Massive Landslide Victory,'" NPR, December 11, 2016, npr.org/2016/12/11/505182622/fact-check-trump-claims-a-massive-landslide-victory-but-history-differs.

142 **notably, unlike Trump:** Kate Sullivan and Jennifer Agiesta, "Biden's Popular Vote Margin over Trump Tops 7 Million," CNN, December 4, 2020.

142 **In fact, according to the Brennan Center:** Klain et al., *Waiting to Vote.*

143 **By October 2021:** Michael Waldman, Pastor Danielle Ayers, and Wendy R. Weiser, "Voting Laws Roundup: October 2021," Brennan Center for Justice, October 4, 2021, brennancenter.org/our-work/research-reports/voting-laws-roundup-october-2021.

143 **And it's hard to imagine:** *Brnovich v. Democratic National Committee,* 594 U.S. __ (2021).

143 **The good news:** David Litt, "The Strange Elegance of Joe Manchin's Voter-ID Deal," *The Atlantic,* June 18, 2021, theatlantic.com/ideas/archive/2021/06/democrats-joe-manchin-deal-voter-id/619247/.

144 **Remember Aaron Van Langevelde:** Beth LeBlanc and Craig Mauger, "Michigan Republicans Seek to Replace GOP Canvasser Who Certified Election," *The Detroit News,* January 18, 2021, theatlantic.com/ideas/archive/2021/06/democrats-joe-manchin-deal-voter-id/619247/.

144 **Liz Cheney, who voted to impeach:** Daniel Strauss, "Liz Cheney Removed from House Leadership over Trump Criticism," *Guardian,* May 12, 2021, theguardian.com/us-news/2021/may/12/liz-cheney-house-leadership-republican-caucus-vote.

144 **Brad Raffensperger was targeted:** Russell Berman, "Trump's Revenge Begins in Georgia," *The Atlantic,* July 12, 2021, theatlantic

.com/politics/archive/2021/07/trumps-revenge-brad-raffensperger-georgia/619407/.

144 **Kevin McCarthy:** Andrew Solender, "McCarthy Walks Back Saying Trump 'Bears Responsibility' for Capitol Riot," *Forbes*, July 29, 2021, forbes.com/sites/andrewsolender/2021/07/29/mccarthy-walks-back-saying-trump-bears-responsibility-for-capitol-riot/?sh=47f6d6aa3c52.

144 **Mitch McConnell has now:** Andrew Solender, "McConnell Says He'll 'Absolutely' Support Trump if He's the GOP Nominee in 2024," *Forbes*, February 25, 2021, forbes.com/sites/andrewsolender/2021/02/25/mcconnell-says-hell-absolutely-support-trump-if-hes-the-gop-nominee-in-2024/?sh=7159dcd111e3.

144 **Lindsey Graham, for his part:** Glenn Thrush, Jo Becker, and Danny Hakim, "Tap Dancing with Trump: Lindsey Graham's Quest for Relevance," *New York Times*, August 14, 2021, nytimes.com/2021/08/14/us/politics/lindsey-graham-donald-trump.html.

145 **As a report from the nonpartisan:** Protect Democracy, States United Democracy Center, and Law Forward, *A Democracy Crisis in the Making: How State Legislatures are Politicizing, Criminalizing, and Interfering with Election Administration* (Washington: Protect Democracy, 2021).

145 **And even with these bills:** Tim Alberta, "The Michigan Republican Who Stopped Trump," *Politico*, November 24, 2020, politico.com/newsletters/politico-nightly/2020/11/24/the-michigan-republican-who-stopped-trump-490984.

7. MAKING IT EASIER TO VOTE

149 **"I was coming":** Chris Hollins, in discussion with Sam Koppelman, July 2021.

149 **The job, they explained:** Hollins, in discussion with Koppelman.

150 **"Being able to":** Hollins, in discussion with Koppelman.

150 **"And for as . . ."** Hollins, in discussion with Koppelman.

151 **On his first:** Hollins, in discussion with Koppelman.

151 **This was Texas:** For a comprehensive history, see again Eric Foner, *The Second Founding: How the Civil War and Reconstruction Remade the Constitution* (Canada: W. W. Norton, 2019).

151 **It was also:** See especially Ari Berman, *Give Us the Ballot: The Modern Struggle for Voting Rights in America* (New York: Picador, Farrar, Straus and Giroux, 2016).

151 **Paying election workers:** Hollins, in discussion with Koppelman.

152 **At the time:** Hollins, in discussion with Koppelman.

152 **At one point:** Jolie McCullough, "Nearly 127K Harris County Drive-Thru Votes Appear Safe After Federal Judge Rejects GOP-Led Texas Lawsuit," *Texas Tribune,* November 2, 2020.

152 **By the time:** Emma Schkloven, "Meet County Clerk Chris Hollins, the Man Fighting for Your Right to Vote," *Houstonia,* November 3, 2020, houstoniamag.com/news-and-city-life/2020/11/meet-harris-county-clerk-chris-hollins.

152 **And when the polls:** Andrew Schneider, "In Texas, Efforts to Make Voting Harder Has Some Worried in Harris County," *Houston Public Media,* July 19, 2021.

152 **This included one couple:** Hollins, in discussion with Koppelman.

153 **"It was truly":** Hollins, in discussion with Koppelman.

153 **In fact, Texas Republicans:** Emma Platoff, "Democrats' Hopes of Flipping Texas Again Fall Short as Republicans Dominate the State's 2020 Elections," *Texas Tribune,* November 4, 2020.

154 **In Germany, weeks:** Jennifer S. Rosenberg and Margaret Chen, "Expanding Democracy: Voter Registration Around the World," Brennan Center for Justice, 2009.

155 **And for all:** Kevin Morris et al., "Automatic Voter Registration," Brennan Center for Justice, April 11, 2019, brennancenter.org/issues/ensure-every-american-can-vote/voting-reform/automatic-voter-registration.

155 **This has real:** "Domenico Montanaro, "Despite Record Turnout, 80 Million Americans Didn't Vote," NPR, December 15, 2020; Medill School of Journalism/Ipsos Poll, "Non-Voters in 2020 U.S. Election" (Washington, D.C., 2020).

156 **If the rest:** Danielle Root and Liz Kennedy, "Increasing Voter Participation in America: Policies to Drive Participation and Make Voting More Convenient," Center for American Progress, July 2018, 3.

156 **One of these:** Wendy Underhill, "Preregistration for Young Voters," National Conference of State Legislatures, June 28, 2021.

156 **In Georgia, one:** Underhill, "Preregistration for Young Voters."

157 **That may not:** Georgia Board of Elections, General Election—November 3, 2020—Recount (December 7, 2020), published by Georgia secretary of state Brad Raffensperger, results.enr.clarityelections.com/GA/107231/web.264614/#/summary.

157 **But that same year:** Tim Mak, "Over 1 Million Florida Felons Win Right to Vote with Amendment 4," NPR, November 7, 2018, npr.org/2018/11/07/665031366/over-a-million-florida-ex-felons-win-right-to-vote-with-amendment-4.

157 **The ACLU and Freedom Partners:** John Lantigua, "The Ability to Vote Is Not a Partisan Issue—Just Ask the Koch Brothers," ACLU Florida, October 12, 2018, aclufl.org/en/news/ability-vote-not-partisan-issue-just-ask-koch-brothers.

158 **sixteen months after the referendum:** Patricia Mazzei and Michael Wines, "How Republicans Undermined Ex-Felon Voting Rights in Florida," *New York Times,* September 17, 2020, nytimes.com/2020/09/17/us/florida-felons-voting.html.

158 **At this point:** Amy Gardner and Lori Rozsa, "In Florida, Felons Must Pay Court Debts Before They Can Vote. But with No System to Do So, Many Have Found It Impossible," *Washington Post,* May 13, 2020, washingtonpost.com/politics/in-florida-felons-must-pay-court-debts-before-they-can-vote-but-with-no-system-to-do-so-many-have-found-it-impossible/2020/05/13/08ed05be-906f-11ea-9e23-6914ee410a5f_story.html.

158 **Across the country:** Jean Chung, Nicole D. Porter, and Nazgol Ghandnoosh, "Voting Rights in the Era of Mass Incarceration: A Primer," The Sentencing Project, July 28, 2021, sentencingproject.org/publications/felony-disenfranchisement-a-primer/.

158 **And these Americans:** Chung et al., "Voting Rights in the Era of Mass Incarceration."

159 **In five states:** "Early Voting in-Person Voting," National Conference of State Legislatures, June 11, 2021, ncsl.org/research/elections-and-campaigns/early-voting-in-state-elections.aspx; Michael Ray, "How Does the Electoral College Work?," Encyclopedia Britannica, britannica.com/story/how-does-the-electoral-college-work.

159 **In fact, in:** "Early Voting in-Person Voting," National Conference of State Legislatures.

159 **From Texas to Alaska:** Root and Kennedy, "Increasing Voter Participation," 4.

160 **Thankfully, most states:** Root and Kennedy, "Increasing Voter Participation."

160 **In fact, since:** "Democracy Diverted: Polling Place Closures and the Right to Vote," Leadership Conference Education Fund, September 2019, civilrightsdocs.info/pdf/reports/Democracy-Diverted.pdf; Klain et al., *Waiting to Vote*.

160 **It was fifty-one:** Stephen Fowler, "Why Do Nonwhite Georgia Voters Have to Wait in Line for Hours? Too Few Polling Places," NPR, October 17, 2020, npr.org/2020/10/17/924527679/why-do-nonwhite-georgia-voters-have-to-wait-in-line-for-hours-too-few-polling-pl.

161 **Historically, mail-in:** "The Importance of Mail-in Ballots to Seniors," National Committee to Preserve Social Security and Medicare, March 25, 2021, ncpssm.org/documents/older-americans-policy-papers/the-importance-of-mail-in-ballots-to-seniors/.

161 **Colorado does this:** Fowler, "Why Do Nonwhite Georgia Voters Have to Wait in Line for Hours?"

162 **This would have:** Jill Lepore, "Rock, Paper, Scissors: How We Used to Vote," *The New Yorker*, October 6, 2008, newyorker.com/magazine/2008/10/13/rock-paper-scissors.

162 **Not only would:** Elizabeth M. Addonizio, Donald P. Green, and James M. Glaser, "Putting the Party Back into Politics: An Experiment Testing Whether Election Day Festivals Increase Voter Turnout," *PS: Political Science & Politics* 40: 721–27.

8. MAKING IT HARDER TO SUPPRESS THE VOTE

164 **If I were a Republican:** Texas Secretary of State, Presidential Election, November 3, 2020, sos.state.tx.us/elections/historical/presidential.shtml.

164 **The bill would:** Texas Legislature, *Relating to election integrity and security, including by preventing fraud in the conduct of elections in this state; increasing criminal penalties; creating criminal offenses; providing civil penalties,* SB 1, 87th Legislature, 1st Special Session, introduced in August 6, 2021, capitol.texas.gov/tlodocs/871/billtext/pdf/SB00001I.pdf.

164 **"I know the play":** Gina Hinojosa, Twitter post, August 25, 2021, 1:01 A.M., twitter.com/GinaForAustin/status/1430394947337916416?s=20.

165 **Gina was down:** Gina Hinojosa, Facebook post, June 11, 2021, pages.facebook.com/GinaForAustin/photos/a.271575946284758/3877390209036629/?type=3&source=48.

165 **But the eighty-two-year-old:** Senfronia Thompson, in discussion with Sam Koppelman, September 2021.

165 **"She would save":** Thompson, in discussion with Sam Koppelman.

165 **"I was always":** Thompson, in discussion with Sam Koppelman.

165 **"We have fought":** Senfronia Thompson, quoted by *The Recount*, Twitter post, July 13, 2021, 7:55 A.M., twitter.com/therecount/status/1414916344500326404?s=20.

166 **He was pissed:** Madison Hall and Grace Panetta, "The Texas Governor Said He Plans to Strip the Legislature's Pay After Democrats Staged a Walkout to Prevent Restrictive Voting Laws from Passing," *Business Insider,* May 31, 2021, businessinsider.com/texas-governor-strip-legislative-branch-of-pay-2021-5.

166 **"I hugged my":** Trey Martinez Fischer, Twitter post, August 25, 2021, 3:30 P.M., twitter.com/TMFtx/status/1430613547118104583.

166 **"We had jobs":** Trey Martinez Fischer, Twitter post, August 25, 2021, 3:30 P.M., twitter.com/TMFtx/status/1430613547118104583?s=20.

167 **"Call it a mistake":** "Texas Governor Vows Action After Democrats Walk Out Over Voting Bill," NPR, June 1, 2021.

167 **They also abandoned:** Judd Legum, "UPDATE: Something Extraordinary Is Happening in Texas," *Popular Information,* June 15, 2021, popular.info/p/update-something-extraordinary-is.

167 **Of course, there:** Texas Legislature, *Relating to election integrity and security,* SB 1, 87(1).

167 **"If you think":** Eric Bradner and Dianne Gallagher, "Texas House Approves GOP Voting Restrictions Bill After Months of Democratic Delays," CNN, August 27, 2021, cnn.com/2021/08/27/politics/texas-voting-bill/index.html.

168 **A record number:** Klain et al., *Waiting to Vote.*

168 **"Action by a State":** *City of Mobile v. Bolden,* 446 U.S. 55 (1980).

169 **That is why Justice Thurgood Marshall:** *City of Mobile v. Bolden.*

169 **On the bright side:** See especially Berman, *Give Us the Ballot.*

169 **And the Department of Justice:** John Roberts to the attorney general, "Talking Points for White House Meeting on Voting Rights Act," January 26, 1982, John G. Roberts, Jr., Misc., RG 60 Department of Justice, Box 30, National Archives at College Park.

170 **This was a man:** Emma Schkloven, "Meet County Clerk Chris Hollins, the Man Fighting for Your Right to Vote," *Houstonia,* November 3, 2020, houstoniamag.com/news-and-city-life/2020/11/meet-harris-county-clerk-chris-hollins.

170 **Across the country:** Berman, *Give Us the Ballot,* 155.

171 **Here's how this would work:** U.S. Congress, House, John R. Lewis Voting Rights Advancement Act of 2021, HR 4, 117th Cong., 1st sess., introduced in House August 17, 2021, congress.gov/bill/117th-congress/house-bill/4/text.

172 **tens of millions of Americans:** See especially Richard Sobel, "The High Cost of 'Free' Photo Voter Identification Cards," (Cambridge: Charles Hamilton Houston Institute for Race and Justice at Harvard Law School, 2014), 2.

172 **You also don't:** Brennan Center for Justice, *Citizens Without Proof: A Survey of Americans' Possession of Documentary Proof of Citizenship and Photo Identification,* 3; Zoltan Hajnal, Nazita Lajevardi, and Lindsay Nielson, "Voter Identification Laws and the Suppression of Minority Votes" (University of California San Diego, 2016), 16, pages.ucsd.edu/~zhajnal/page5/documents/voterIDhajnaletal.pdf.

172 **What's most absurd:** Klain et al., *Waiting to Vote.*

173 **"If you tell a great lie":** Quoted in Michael J. Klarman, "The Degradation of American Democracy—and the Court," *Harvard Law Review* 134, no. 1 (November 2020): 13.

173 **Which is exactly:** Chris Cillizza, "1 in 3 Americans Believe the 'Big Lie,'" CNN, June 21, 2021, cnn.com/2021/06/21/politics/biden-voter-fraud-big-lie-monmouth-poll/index.html.

173 **And an even greater number:** Monmouth University Poll, "National: Public Supports Both Early Voting and Requiring Photo ID to Vote," Monmouth University, 2021, monmouth.edu/polling-institute/documents/monmouthpoll_us_062121.pdf/.

174 **In the lead-up:** Ari Berman, "How the 2000 Election in Florida Led to a New Wave of Voter Disenfranchisement," *The Nation,* July 28, 2015.

174 **Al Gore lost:** Andrew Glass, "Bush Declared Electoral Victor over Gore, Dec 12, 2000," *Politico,* November 12, 2018.

175 **According to a Brennan Center report:** Kevin Morris et al., "Purges: A Growing Threat to the Right to Vote," Brennan Center for Justice, accessed July 20, 2018, brennancenter.org/our-work/research-reports/purges-growing-threat-right-vote.

175 **Indeed, the number:** Morris et al., "Purges."

175 **But these purges:** Casey, "Ohio Was Set to Purge 235,000 Voters."

175 **Ohio, for instance:** Nicholas Casey, "Ohio Was Set to Purge 235,000 Voters. It Was Wrong About 20%," *New York Times,* October 14, 2019, nytimes.com/2019/10/14/us/politics/ohio-voter-purge.html.

176 **In Texas, for:** Morris et al., "Purges."

9. SAVING CONGRESS

178 **And the first:** U.S. Congress, House, *For the People Act of 2021,* HR 1, 117th Cong., 1st sess., introduced in House January 4, 2021, congress.gov/bill/117th-congress/house-bill/1.

178 **Designed to be:** "67 Percent of Americans Support H.R.1 For the People Act," Data for Progress, January 22, 2021, dataforprogress .org/blog/2021/1/22/majority-support-hr1-democracy-reforms.

178 **At a congressional hearing:** Eric H. Holder, Jr., "Why We Need the For the People Act," *Medium,* March 24, 2021, ericholder.medium .com/why-we-need-the-for-the-people-act-8c79afa36aec.

178 **At the National Constitution Center:** "President Joe Biden's Speech on Voting Rights: TRANSCRIPT," ABC News, July 13, 2021, abcnews.go.com/Politics/president-joe-bidens-speech-voting-rights -transcript/story?id=78827023.

179 **In total, Senate Democrats:** Ian Millhiser, "America's Anti-Democratic Senate, by the Numbers," *Vox,* November 6, 2020.

179 **The half of:** See especially Millhiser, "America's Anti-Democratic Senate"; and "The Senate Is an Irredeemable Institution," Data for Progress, December 17, 2019.

180 **So much for:** "The Senate," Data for Progress, 5.

180 **On the eve:** Adam Jentleson, *Kill Switch: The Rise of the Modern Senate and the Crippling of American Democracy* (New York: Liveright Publishing Corporation, 2021), 25.

180 **The other house:** "The Major Debates at the Constitutional Convention," Constitutional Rights Foundation, 2009.

181 **When this proposal:** "Major Debates," Constitutional Rights Foundation.

181 **At first, Madison:** Jentleson, *Kill Switch,* 26.

182 **Back then, the:** Jonathan Chait, "The Senate Is America's Most Structurally Racist Institution," *New York Magazine,* August 10, 2020.

182 **Indeed, David Leonhardt:** David Leonhardt, "The Senate: Affirmative Action for White People," *New York Times,* October 14, 2014.

182 **Perhaps it's no:** See especially Daniel C. Bowen and Christopher J. Clark, "Revisiting Descriptive Representation in Congress: Assessing the Effect of Race on the Constituent–Legislator Relationship," *Political Research Quarterly* 67, no. 3 (2014): 695–707; and Jennifer R. Garcia and Katherine Tate, "Race, Ethnicity, and Politics: Controversies and New Directions," in *New Directions in American Politics,* ed. Raymond La Raja (New York: Routledge Press, 2013).

182 **After all, in:** Jens Manuel Krogstad, "Americans Broadly Support Legal Status for Immigrants Brought to the U.S. Illegally as Children," Pew Research Center, June 17, 2020, pewresearch.org/fact-tank/2020/06/17/americans-broadly-support-legal-status-for-immigrants-brought-to-the-u-s-illegally-as-children/.

182 **It's also worth:** Todd N. Tucker, *Fixing the Senate: Equitable and Full Representation for the 21st Century* (New York: Roosevelt Institute, 2019), 9.

183 **Tucker goes on:** Tucker, *Fixing the Senate.*

183 **"This is one":** "The Federalist Papers: No. 22," Avalon Project at Yale Law School, avalon.law.yale.edu/18th_century/fed22.asp.

184 **In Federalist No. 58:** "The Federalist Papers: No. 58," Avalon Project at Yale Law School, avalon.law.yale.edu/18th_century/fed58.asp.

184 **Now, there were a few:** See especially Jentleson, *Kill Switch.*

185 **As Jentleson writes:** Jentleson, *Kill Switch,* 70.

185 **What may be surprising:** Jentleson, *Kill Switch,* 3.

185 **they only did so after a filibuster:** David Smith, "Rand Paul Stalls Bill That Would Make Lynching a Federal Hate Crime," *Guardian,* June 11, 2020, theguardian.com/us-news/2020/jun/11/rand-paul-lynching-hate-crime-bill-limbo.

186 **Which, by this point:** Jentleson, *Kill Switch,* 7.

186 **As Ezra Klein:** Ezra Klein, "The Definitive Case for Ending the Filibuster," *Vox,* October 1, 2020, vox.com/21424582/filibuster-joe-biden-2020-senate-democrats-abolish-trump.

187 **But generally speaking:** "The Federalist Papers: No. 22," Avalon Project at Yale Law School, avalon.law.yale.edu/18th_century/fed22.asp.

187 **If that sounds:** "State Population Totals and Components of Change: 2010–2019," Census.gov (U.S. Census Bureau), accessed Novem-

ber 17, 2021, census.gov/data/tables/time-series/demo/popest/2010s-state-total.html#par_textimage_1574439295.

187 **There is no:** U.S. Const. art. V, § 1, cl. 1.

188 **Because Washingtonians and Puerto Ricans:** Klein, "The Definitive Case for Ending the Filibuster."

188 **But if, for:** Kyle Blaine and Veronica Stracqualursi, "Biden Says He Supports Filibuster Carve-out for Voting Rights," CNN, December 23, 2021, cnn.com/2021/12/23/politics/joe-biden-filibuster-voting-rights/index.html.

189 **As Senator Raphael Warnock of Georgia:** "Warnock Calls for Changes to Filibuster in Order to Preserve Voting Rights," December 14, 2021, twitter.com/PodSaveAmerica/status/1470892645631332368?s=20.

189 **The first is:** Klein, "The Definitive Case for Ending the Filibuster."

189 **Klein explains:** Klein, "The Definitive Case for Ending the Filibuster."

191 **"The line was":** Love Caesar, in discussion with Sam Koppelman, September 2021.

191 **This is because:** Hayden DuBlois, "In Defense of Gerrymandering," *Manchester Journal* (Vermont), March 24, 2015, manchesterjournal.com/archives/in-defense-of-gerrymandering/article_46191b03-d107-59d8-812f-c4443399112e.html.

191 **According to Caesar:** Caesar, in discussion with Sam Koppelman.

192 **"There was a":** Caesar, in discussion with Sam Koppelman.

192 **And the year:** *Rucho v. Common Cause,* 588 U.S. __ (2019).

192 **And Caesar says:** Caesar, in discussion with Sam Koppelman.

193 **And in 2011:** Eric Holder, "Why We Need the For the People Act," Medium, March 24, 2021, ericholder.medium.com/why-we-need-the-for-the-people-act-8c79afa36aec.

193 **In 2012, after:** David Daley, *Ratf**ked: The True Story Behind the Secret Plan to Steal America's Democracy* (New York: Liveright Publishing Corporation, 2017), 182.

193 **And according to:** Alex Tausanovitch, "The Impact of Partisan Gerrymandering," Center for American Progress, October 1, 2019, americanprogress.org/issues/democracy/news/2019/10/01/475166/impact-partisan-gerrymandering/; David A. Lieb, "GOP Won More Seats in 2018 than Suggested by Vote Share," Associated Press, March 21, 2019.

193 **And in 2020:** Sophie Andrews et al., "2020 House Tracker," *The Cook Political Report,* accessed June 2021, cookpolitical.com/2020-house-vote-tracker.

194 **And it's how:** Chris Abele, "90 Percent of Americans 'Support Universal Background Checks' for Gun Purchases," *Politifact,* October 2, 2017, politifact.com/factchecks/2017/oct/03/chris-abele/do-90-americans-support-background-checks-all-gun-/.

194 **In fact, a poll:** "America Goes to the Polls 2018: Voter Turnout and Election Policy in the 50 States," America Goes to the Polls, March 2019, nonprofitvote.org/wp-content/uploads/2021/05/america-goes-polls-2018.pdf, 28.

194 **independent redistricting commissions:** "Redistricting Commissions: Congressional Plans," National Conference of State Legislatures, July 12, 2021, ncsl.org/research/redistricting/redistricting-commissions-congressional-plans.aspx.

10. SAVING THE PRESIDENCY

197 **Now, it's worth:** Michael Gonchar and Nicole Daniels, "Is the Electoral College a Problem? Does It Need to Be Fixed?," *New York Times,* October 8, 2020, nytimes.com/2020/10/08/learning/is-the-electoral-college-a-problem-does-it-need-to-be-fixed.html.

197 **for several reasons:** James Madison, "Federalist No. 10," in *The Federalist Papers,* ed. Robert A. Rutland, Charles F. Hobson, William M. E. Rachal, and Frederika J. Teute (Chicago: University of Chicago Press, 1977), 263–70.

198 **James Wilson, a delegate:** Wilfred Codrington III, "The Electoral College's Racist Origins," *The Atlantic,* November 17, 2019, theatlantic.com/ideas/archive/2019/11/electoral-college-racist-origins/601918/.

198 **But another Founding Father:** Robert A. Rutland, Charles F. Hobson, William M. E. Rachal, and Frederika J. Teute, eds., *The Papers of James Madison,* vol. 10, 27 May 1787–3 March 1788 (Chicago: University of Chicago Press, 1977), 107–8.

199 **This, once again:** Akhil Reed Amar, "The Troubling Reason the Electoral College Exists," *Time,* November 8, 2016, time.com/4558510/electoral-college-history-slavery/.

199 **And the election of 1800:** Jeffrey Davis, "How Donald Trump

Could Steal the Election," *The Atlantic,* March 29, 2020, theatlantic.com/ideas/archive/2020/03/coronavirus-election/608989/.

200 **The American people:** Megan Brenan, "61% of Americans Support Abolishing the Electoral College," *Gallup,* September 24, 2020, news.gallup.com/poll/320744/americans-support-abolishing-electoral-college.aspx.

201 **An amendment to abolish:** Kurtis Lee, "In 1969, Democrats and Republicans United to Get Rid of the Electoral College. Here's What Happened," *Los Angeles Times,* December 19, 2016.

201 **Already, fifteen states:** Nicole Goodkind, "Colorado Joins 15 States in Favor of Popular Vote in Presidential Elections," *Fortune,* November 5, 2020, fortune.com/2020/11/05/colorado-national-popular-vote-compact-electoral-college/.

203 **And he was right:** Andy Sullivan and Michael Martina, "In Recorded Call, Trump Pressures Georgia Official to 'Find' Votes to Overturn Election," *Reuters,* January 3, 2021, reuters.com/article/us-usa-election-trump/in-recorded-call-trump-pressures-georgia-official-to-find-votes-to-overturn-election-idUSKBN2980MG.

11. SAVING THE COURT

207 **How, I kept asking:** Jose A. DelReal, "Voter Turnout in 2014 Was the Lowest Since WWII," *Washington Post,* November 10, 2014, washingtonpost.com/news/post-politics/wp/2014/11/10/voter-turnout-in-2014-was-the-lowest-since-wwii/.

208 **In the years since:** *Trump v. Hawaii,* 585 U.S. __ (2018); *Burwell v. Hobby Lobby,* 573 U.S. 682 (2014).

209 **And I don't:** Peter Baker and Maggie Haberman, "Trump Selects Amy Coney Barrett to Fill Ginsburg's Seat on the Supreme Court," *New York Times,* September 25, 2020.

209 **The theory was:** Alexander Hamilton, "The Federalist Papers: No. 78," Avalon Project, avalon.law.yale.edu/18th_century/fed78.asp.

209 **Franklin Delano Roosevelt, for instance:** "Supreme Court Nominations (1789–Present)," U.S. Senate, November 10, 2020, senate.gov/legislative/nominations/SupremeCourtNominations1789present.htm.

210 **That's why from:** Frederick A. O. Schwarz, "Saving the Supreme

Court," Brennan Center for Justice, September 13, 2019, brennan center.org/our-work/analysis-opinion/saving-supreme-court.

210 **People didn't live:** Schwarz, "Saving the Supreme Court."

210 **And the justices themselves:** Schwarz, "Saving the Supreme Court."

211 **And second, I:** Maggie Jo Buchanan, "The Need for Supreme Court Limits," *Center for American Progress,* August 3, 2020, ameri canprogress.org/issues/courts/reports/2020/08/03/488518/need-su preme-court-term-limits/.

211 **And the people:** Adam Rosenblatt, "Fix the Court: Agenda of Key Findings," Fix the Court, May 2020, fixthecourt.com/wp-content/up loads/2020/06/PSB-May-2020-key-findings-TL.pdf.

212 **The average tenure:** David Fishbaum, "The Supreme Court Has a Longevity Problem, Term Limits on Justices Won't Solve It," *Harvard Business Review,* June 13, 2018, hbr.org/2018/07/the-supreme -court-has-a-longevity-problem-but-term-limits-on-justices-wont -solve-it.

CONCLUSION

215 **The tragedy:** Andrew Prokop, "Joe Manchin Reelected in West Virginia: The Most Conservative Senate Democrat Survives," *Vox,* November 7, 2018, vox.com/2018/11/6/18049648/election-results -west-virginia-joe-manchin-wins.

215 **It's infuriating:** Adam Jentleson, "How to Stop the Minority-Rule Doom Loop," *The Atlantic,* April 12, 2021, theatlantic.com/ideas /archive/2021/04/how-stop-minority-rule-doom-loop/618536/.

216 **As President Obama:** "Transcript: Barack Obama's DNC Speech," CNN, August 20, 2020, cnn.com/2020/08/19/politics/barack-obama -speech-transcript/index.html.

218 **Because unlike Luther:** Sean Collins, "Rep. John Lewis's Voting Rights Legacy Is in Danger," *Vox,* June 18, 2020.

219 **As Cody Keenan:** Cody Keenan, Convocation Address for Weinberg College of Arts and Sciences at Northwestern University, June 23, 2018.

INDEX

Photo: Courtesy of Covington & Burling LLC

ERIC HOLDER is a civil rights leader and the chairman of the National Democratic Redistricting Committee. He served as the eighty-second Attorney General of the United States, the first African American to hold that office. During his six years in the Obama administration, he directed the Department of Justice's efforts on voting rights, marriage equality, the environment, and criminal justice reform. A graduate of Columbia Law School, he was appointed by President Ronald Reagan to serve as an associate judge of the Superior Court of the District of Columbia before being appointed United States attorney and deputy attorney general by President Bill Clinton. Now a senior counsel at Covington & Burling, he lives in Washington, D.C., with his wife, Dr. Sharon Malone. Together, they have three children.

To inquire about booking Eric Holder for a speaking engagement, please contact the Penguin Random House Speakers Bureau at speakers@penguinrandomhouse.com.

TWITTER: @ERICHOLDER

Photo: Mark Seliger

SAM KOPPELMAN is a *New York Times* bestselling author who served as director of surrogate speechwriting on the Biden-Harris presidential campaign. He is also a principal at Fenway Strategies, where he has spent half a decade telling the stories of people working to make the world a better place—and he's written under his own name for publications including *The New York Times, Time,* and *The Washington Post*. Koppelman holds a B.A. in government from Harvard College, where he was named a John Harvard Scholar and wrote columns like "Shut Down Harvard Football" that he insists were great for his social life.

TWITTER: @SAMMYKOPPELMAN

ABOUT THE TYPE

This book was set in Caledonia, a typeface designed in 1939 by W. A. Dwiggins (1880–1956) for the Mergenthaler Linotype Company. Its name is the ancient Roman term for Scotland, because the face was intended to have a Scottish-Roman flavor. Caledonia is considered to be a well-proportioned, businesslike face with little contrast between its thick and thin lines.